Launching Missional Communities

[a field guide]

By Mike Breen and Alex Absalom

Launching Missional Communities: A Field Guide

3DM,
PO Box 719,
Pawleys Island,
SC, 29585

www.weare3DM.com

First Printed 2010

Printed in the United States of America by Sheriar Press.

Cover Design: Libby Culmer
Interior Design: Libby Culmer

ISBN: 978-0-9824521-9-6

Sally, you have been my partner in mission for thirty years. Behind the scenes, you have often recognized the missional frontier before I did and pioneered the way. In many ways, you represent the brave and hardworking trailblazers who have planted, developed, and multiplied Missional Communities down through the years. This book honors you all.

-M.B.

Hannah, you are an amazing, godly Kingdom leader, from whom I have learned so much. I am so grateful to be able to share this adventure together – I love you! This book is also dedicated to our three growing Jesus adventurers, Joel, Samuel, and Isaac, and to all our friends and family who have encouraged and blessed us along the way. We are thankful for each one of you.

-A.A.

Acknowledgments

This work borrows heavily from the ideas and practices first discussed in the book that Bob Hopkins and Mike wrote in 2006 called Clusters. Since then, even more has been fleshed out, and with the worldwide growth in interest in Missional Communities, the need for a more detailed "how-to" guide has emerged. While Clusters remains an important text on the Missional Community movement that emerged in Sheffield at the turn of the twentieth century, we hope that this new publication will give you all you need to build and launch your own Missional Communities.

In addition to Bob and Mary Hopkins, we are deeply indebted to the hundreds of churches, pastors, and practitioners worldwide – many of whom are members of our 3D Learning Communities – who have contributed their stories and experience. First among these is the St. Thomas Church network in Sheffield, England. In addition, gratitude is due to all the members of The Order of Mission (TOM), a movement of missional leaders who are the "ninjas" of much that is written here.

Special thanks for help with the production of this book go to many people, including Doug and Elizabeth Paul, Steve and Helen Cockram, Laura Florio, Eric Taylor, Ken Primrose, Bob Rognlien, Jon Tyson, Kevin Penry, Jon Peacock, Gavin and Libby Culmer, and all those who contributed their stories and experiences.

Mike and Alex

Contents

3dm

OPENING THOUGHTS
THE MISSION AHEAD

NAME

No.

A brief introduction to Missional Communities: why they matter, where they came from, our experiences and how to use this field guide.

1.1 | INTRODUCTION

There seem to be moments.

Moments when God is clearly taking the church in a certain direction and saying something quite specific.

We sense and recognize these moments when people from different places in the world, with different backgrounds, different denominational affiliations, and different socio-economic statuses all seem to be sensing the *same thing independently of each other*. It's as if all of the barriers that would normally separate us are mysteriously broken down, and in one clarion moment, people who may not agree on a lot all share one thought, one big idea.

We seem to be in that kind of moment right now.

Whether you live in the United States or elsewhere, whether you read books or blogs, listen to podcasts, or simply talk with friends over dinner, people are starting to talk about a new, vibrant expression of church that is emerging in the hearts and minds of all these people at one time.

Missional Communities.

They are being called different things in different places, but the idea is the same: A group of people, about the size of an extended family, doing the mission of God together outside the regular confines of the church building.

I found myself in this moment a little more than three years ago. I had this sense that God was calling our community to start doing church in a more "missional" way, that it would involve some level of decentralization, with unpaid leaders leading groups larger than small groups to join God's mission in the world. I knew it would still be part of a greater whole, that there would be a dynamic interplay between these groups on the fringes and the resourcing, equipping center of a larger body. It would be an *organization* of agile, networked *organisms*.

I talked to other pastors in the United States, and they were reading the same statistics I was from Thomas Rainer:

> About 65% of the Builder Generation are in a church each week.
>
> With the Boomers, it's about 35%.
>
> You will find 15% of Gen X'ers gather to a church this Sunday.
>
> For Gen Y (Millennials), the oldest of whom turned 30 in 2010, it's only 4%.

And in the midst of this, we all seem to be getting the same sense from God about the way forward.

But there was one problem: What does this look like?

I did what any inquisitive person might do. I started picking up every book I could find and poured through them. I read every book and article I could get my hands on, listened to every interview or podcast I could find.

Quickly, something began to emerge: No one really knew what this looked like.

Many people were writing about the social theory and theology of movements and mission, but there were no clear practices for doing it.

Only a few people were writing practical books on the way forward, and even then it only seemed incrementally different from what had come before. It really wasn't any more "missional."

It seemed like there were a lot of thinkers who didn't practice and a lot of practitioners who didn't think.

During this time of vapid frustration, I met the authors of this book, people who have been wrestling with *Missional Communities* practically and theoretically for more than fifteen years. And perhaps it is the marriage of these two things (the practical and the theoretical) that has made their churches and now their global movement so wildly successful.

Recently, I had the opportunity to visit Sheffield, England, where the movement of Missional Communities began in the mid-1990s. St. Thomas' Church in Sheffield multiplied into two distinct churches a few years ago, and once a year, these two churches open their doors, and people flock from across the world to see what these churches have created (they call it *Pilgrimage*).

The highlight of the trip was probably the missional tour we took on the Thursday of that week. About forty of us hopped on a charter bus and spent three hours driving around the city of Sheffield. Every minute or two, they'd point to where a Missional Community was meeting and what they were doing.

"This MC is reaching into the Slovakian gypsy population. Dozens of people have come to know Jesus." A minute or two later . . .

"This MC started reaching out to Somalian refugees, and they have multiplied into three MCs." A minute or two later . . .

"This is where a lot of the university students go clubbing, so this MC meets at 3a.m. on Saturday mornings. Hundreds of people have come to know Jesus."

"This MC focuses on this wealthier neighborhood to your left."

"This MC has hooked up with one of the most dangerous gangs in Sheffield. The leader went to prison for murder, and we worked with him and he became a Christian, and then his family became Christians, and slowly the people in the gang are becoming Christians."

"This MC meets in the state park every Saturday morning and reaches out to people who love the park and the outdoors."

"This MC reaches out to parents with babies."

"This MC has seen a lot of Iranian Muslims come to know Jesus."

"This MC reaches out to teenagers and their parents."

On and on and on. We probably looked at dozens and dozens of MCs in that three-hour period. It was nothing short of extraordinary. The MCs spanned the entire city and were about the most diverse group of people you have ever seen. Some churches in the United States like to talk about ethnic diversity, but I've rarely seen them succeed at this, and when they do, they are usually made up of the same socio-economic group of people. These two churches had every race, color, age, religious upbringing, and socio-economic status you can possibly imagine.

St. Thomas Crookes is, by all accounts, the fastest-growing church in Europe, seeing more than 500% growth in less than five years.

St. Thomas Philadelphia is now one of the largest churches in Europe.

In partnership with the European Church Planting Network, this way of doing church has been streamlined and has contributed to the planting of 725 churches in just over three years. And we aren't talking about two guys in a bar and calling it church. These are the real deal. This has never been done before in European church history.

In a city where less than 3% of the people were in a church on a Sunday morning, a movement is afoot that is calling a city back to God and is spreading across the region and continent and into the United States. Today, hundreds of American churches are beginning to engage with these missional, mid-sized groups and seeing similar substance and growth.

The results, in Europe, in the United States, and around the world, have been staggering.

So many of these Missional Communities are doing things most have never seen in our lifetime or may have only read about in the Acts of the Apostles.

This field guide takes more than fifteen years of experimenting, successes, failures, and honing and puts the best practices into one, centralized resource. The vehicle of Missional Communities was pioneered and is seeing significant success in post-Christian Europe, but has also been further developed and fleshed out in the context of the United States.

Most church leaders I've talked to seem to be asking three simple questions:

1) What does the church of the future look like?

2) How do we reach people who don't know Jesus?

3) How do we make missional disciples?

This book is about these three questions.

Doug Paul
Directional Pastor | Eikon Community Church

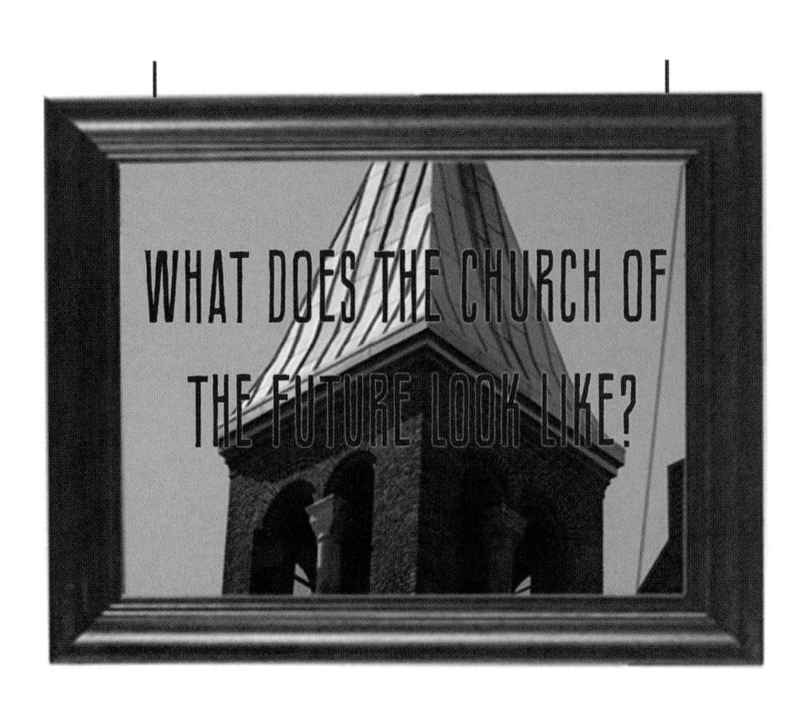

1.2 | AUTHORS

Mike Breen

Mike Breen has been an innovator in leading missional churches throughout Europe and the United States for more than twenty-five years. In his time at St. Thomas' Church in Sheffield in the UK, he created and pioneered Missional Communities, mid-sized groups of twenty to fifty people on mission together. The result, less than six years later, was the largest church in England, and ultimately, one of the largest and now fastest-growing churches in the whole of Europe. In 2006, Mike was approached by Leadership Network to lead an initiative into church planting. Through this partnership, more than 725 churches were planted in Europe in three years. Today, Mike lives in South Carolina, leading 3DM, a movement/organization that is helping hundreds of established churches and church planters move into this discipling and missional way of being the church. He is also the senior guardian of The Order of Mission, a collection of hundreds of missional leaders and entrepreneurs throughout the world.

Mike has been married to Sally for thirty years, and they have three grown children. Mike's passions include contemporary design and architecture, travel, movies, cycling, golf, fine wine, and food – though not necessarily in that order.

For more from Mike, go to
http://mikebreen.wordpress.com

Alex Absalom

Alex Absalom has served as a church leader for almost twenty years in the United Kingdom and the United States. Experimentation with mid-sized communities, friendship with Mike, and a subsequent role on the Senior Leadership Team of St. Thomas' Church gave Alex a deep immersion in the theology and practice of Missional Communities. Alex and his family moved to the United States a number of years ago specifically to help a local church develop Missional Communities and the associated structures for leadership development. On average, he has overseen the planting of fifteen MCs a year, all of which are defined by a clear mission vision and developed into an average group size of thirty. At this point, Alex has launched and overseen the development of more Missional Communities in the United States than anyone in North America. Having previously coached many European leaders and churches on MCs and transitioning churches, Alex has become increasingly sought after to coach and help leaders across the US as they develop Missional Community life.

Hannah and Alex have been married since 1994 and have three very energetic sons, with whom they do Labrador parenting (lots of love, food, and outdoor exercise). Alex loves playing sports and is a passionate fan of Liverpool Football Club and a connoisseur of tea!

For more from Alex, go to
www.alexabsalom.com

1.3 | WHERE DID MISSIONAL COMMUNITIES BEGIN?

The journey toward publishing this book has been long, covering several decades. For me (Mike), the journey began in 1984. I was a newly ordained Anglican minister working in Cambridge, England. Feeling the need to grapple with the ever-deepening issue of church decline, I was reading *I Believe in Church Growth* by Eddie Gibbs. I read that, wherever the church was growing throughout the world, the church appeared to be organized into three levels of church life, representing three different types of groups and three distinct experiences for the members.

These were described as cell, congregation, and celebration.

With no reason other than the prompting of the Holy Spirit, I asked God where I should concentrate my efforts in the coming years. To be honest, I was pretty much expecting him to direct me toward "cells" because that's where a lot of the thinking was at the time.

But quite surprisingly, he clearly said that I should concentrate on the "congregational level."

After listening and thinking further, I realized that my knowledge of congregational life was entirely dependent upon my experience as a twentieth-century Christian. Seeing this disparity, I became an avid reader on the subject of New Testament ecclesiology and contemporary models of congregational life.

By the time I was called a few years later to work in a poor inner-city London community with my wife Sally and our young family, I started to radically rethink what "church" could look like.

The first thing we did was to ensure that all our life together as a church was defined by the three dimensions of UP-IN-OUT (see the Definitions section which follows). The second was to experiment. In three or four years, I'm sure we tried pretty much everything. Looking back, I have to admit: I feel very sorry for those dear people in that little church who had to suffer my continual experimentation and quest for knowledge!

We discovered that the small groups (cells) that wanted to maintain a missional outlook were "small enough to care but not big enough to dare."

We decided to gather them together to form larger mid-sized groups so that the mission focus would be better supported and therefore more easily maintained. I can still remember the feeling of seeing members of the congregation gathering in what we called a "Pastoral Base" and going out to witness and serve – it was overwhelming. We were starting to see things happen we had never seen before.

Somehow we had stumbled onto something that felt entirely new.

Over the coming years in which I served in the US as a consultant to pastors and then as the senior pastor of St. Thomas' Church Sheffield, the idea crystallized into "Clusters" – now known as Missional Communities. Thinking back, it is remarkable to reflect upon the courageous and pioneering spirit of St. Thomas' that took a fairly simple idea and expanded it in down-to-earth missional outreach to every conceivable community and sub-culture in Sheffield. By the end of the 1990s and since then, Missional

Communities have moved from something just at St. Thomas', spreading across the north of England, to the whole country, then into Europe and the United States, South America, Africa, Asia, and Australia.

In total, MCs are now thriving on every continent (Antarctica being the obvious exception) and in thousands and thousands of churches.

MY NOTES

1.4 | DEFINITIONS

Missional Communities

A group of anything from twenty to more than fifty people who are united, through Christian community, around a common service and witness to a particular neighborhood or network of relationships. With a strong value on life together, the group has the expressed intention of seeing those the group impacts choose to start following Jesus, through this more flexible and locally incarnated expression of the church. The result often is that the group grows and ultimately multiplies into further Missional Communities. They are most often networked within a larger church community (often with many other Missional Communities). These mid-sized communities, led by laity, are "lightweight and low maintenance", and most often gather formally and informally numerous times a month in the groups' missional context.

Huddle

A group of four to twelve current or future missional leaders who gather to be discipled, encouraged, and held accountable. A Huddle differs from a small group in that the leader acts as the primary discipler of the members of the group and not as a facilitator. Huddles generally meet at least every other week, though some churches have Huddles that meet every week. Each Huddle meeting eventually leads to the two fundamental questions of Christian spirituality we see at the conclusion of the Sermon on the Mount:

1) What is God saying to me? (Build your house on the rock–Jesus' words)

2) How will I respond? (The fool is the one who doesn't put the words into practice)

UP-IN-OUT

As we read in the Gospels, Jesus had three great loves and thus three distinct dimensions to his life:

UP: deep and connected relationship to his Father and attentiveness to the leading of the Holy Spirit

IN: constant investment in the relationships with those around him (his disciples)

OUT: entering the brokenness of the world, looking for a response individually (people coming into relationship with Jesus) and systemically (systems of injustice being transformed)

This three dimensional pattern for living a balanced life is evident throughout Scripture and needs to be expressed in community life as well. Because of this, we believe all Missional Communities need a balanced expression of UP-IN-OUT in order to be healthy, growing communities.

People of Peace

As you seek to go out and reach the lost with the Good News of Jesus, he gives you a simple strategy for doing just that. He tells you to look for the person who welcomes you, serves you, and responds to you. This person likes you and, probably, you like him or her. A Person of Peace will in time prove to be a gatekeeper to a whole network, or neighborhood, of relationships. Therefore, once you recognize a Person of Peace, you stay and intentionally invest in that relationship to see where God will take it. (This is most clearly laid out in Luke 9 and 10.)

3DM

A movement of churches across the world that have put discipleship and mission at the center of everything they do. These churches most often do this with the vehicles of Missional Communities and Huddles. The organization of 3DM (3 Dimension Ministries) produces *Content* (such as this book) and provides *Coaching* and the opportunity to enter into a *Learning Community* with other transitioning churches and church plants.

MY NOTES

1.5 | MISSIONAL COMMUNITIES – THE HEADLINES

Further on, we will provide plenty of details, but here are the bare essentials.

A Missional Community:

- Is a group of between twenty and fifty people (at the most seventy)
- Can be either a new church plant or, more commonly, a sub-set of a larger gathered church
- Centers on Jesus, helping people become and then grow as his disciples
- Has a defining focus on reaching a particular neighborhood or network of relationships
- Takes place in community and often revolves around shared times of food and fun
- Has a healthy balance of UP, IN, and OUT
- Does not require that members be professing Christians to belong
- Is unashamed about following Christ, in values and in vision
- Conducts worship, prayer, and Scripture reading as core practices (since members are disciples of Jesus)
- Looks outwards through a mixture of service and verbal witness
- Has a common mission focus that is the key glue for the shared sense of togetherness
- Gathers informally throughout the week, not just at formal meetings
- Includes a high value on small groups for support, challenge, and closeness in members' life together
- Has leaders who receive ongoing help, coaching, and accountability
- Has leaders who do not do everything – they facilitate and release others to serve and lead

Missional Communities are known by all sorts of different names – clusters, house church, home church, mission-shaped community, mid-sized community (MSC), villages, call-out ministries, pastorates, neighborhood communities, Missional Community hubs, canvas groups – and more besides! For the sake of simplicity, throughout this book we use the term "Missional Community" (or MC for short), which is not necessarily our favorite name but is the most naturally descriptive for our purposes.

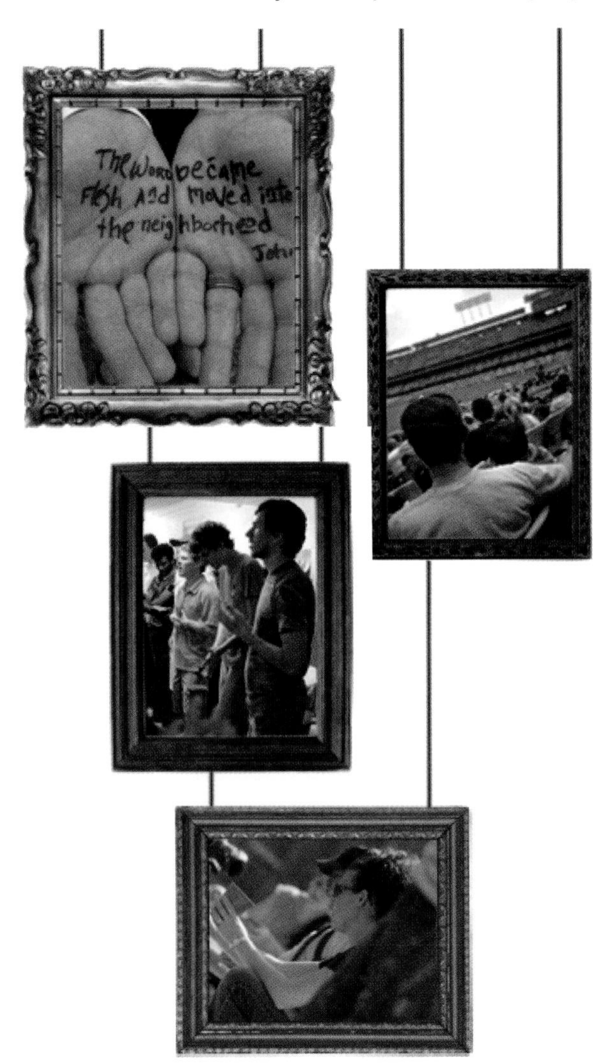

1.6 | HOW TO USE THIS FIELD GUIDE

We hope that you will read this handbook with pen in hand, jotting down notes and responses. We'll be praying that, as you reflect, the Lord will give you insight and revelation for your church and community. We certainly don't think that we have all the answers. But we hope that this material will be a helpful stimulus to you as you seek the Lord for what he wants to do through you in this time.

The following couple of chapters deal with the idea of Missional Communities. The chapters define our terms and then paint a picture of what MCs can look like. We cover important topics such as how MCs relate to the whole church and why community is so important. Then we have a Launch Guide for preparing and starting MCs, which covers the strategies and issues leaders should be thinking through. There's a step-by-step plan to launch MCs, as well as other helpful tools to ensure that you and your teams make the most of what you're learning and experiencing.

This is followed by a section on MC Life, a practical, nuts-and-bolts guide for running MCs, which should answer many of your practical questions about MCs – how you could run children's work, arrange finances and meetings, deal with pastoral issues, worship, etc. We have included a section of case studies of transitioning churches and church plants that are now using Missional Communities. We found these case studies to be supremely helpful in allowing leaders to see the trajectory of other churches as the leaders consider their own church and context with MCs.

Throughout the book, we have included real-life stories from people and churches who have been implementing Missional Communities in the United States. We wanted some examples to help put the theory into reality, to inspire you with real tales from the frontlines. Our hope and prayer are that you will be provoked to experience your own stories of Missional Community life in your place of calling. We would love to hear some of those accounts from you – at the end of the book, there's contact information for us.

We've also put all the footnotes at the end, with book references, and the website details for all the churches mentioned in this Guide.

Last, know that this Field Guide can take you only so far. We are excited by all of the information and years of work that have gone into this book, but it alone will not effectively implement MCs in your church. This Guide will serve as a great starting point and reference guide, but ultimately, every church that has started to use MCs and seen success has been in community with other churches doing the same thing. Other than seeking the guidance of the Holy Spirit, the number one thing we could recommend is taking this journey with other churches. Even if you never team up with 3DM and one of our Learning Communities, at the very least find a few other churches and be in community with them and take this journey together.

KEY CONCEPTS
THE LAY OF THE LAND

Here you'll find the theological, practical and sociological reasons Missional Communities work – in addition to the thoughts shaping them over the last 20 years.

2.1 | DEFINING MISSIONAL

Jesus and Mission

It's official: *Missional* is a Christian leader buzzword.

It's hard to pick up a book written for Christian leaders right now on which the word missional isn't slapped across the cover or permeating the book's contents. Some writers get it; some do not.

Simply put, mission is God's activity of love toward the world. He is a sending God, a going God, a God who incarnates himself in a specific time and context, so that every person may come to know and love him.

> **"To be a follower of Jesus means that you, too, are called to be a missionary."**

Each and every follower has this calling.

As has been quipped, God had only one Son, and he was a missionary. If that was what Jesus did, then we his followers are to do likewise. Going in mission is not an optional extra – an upgrade for the "mature disciple." Going in mission is fundamental to the journey of discipleship and from day one we should view ourselves as missionaries.

In the New Testament, we see a continual train of totally ill-prepared followers of Christ being sent out in mission. Jesus starts sending the disciples out as early as Matthew 10, at a stage when they hadn't even declared Jesus as Messiah, let alone Lord, and their response to his teaching was primarily marked by misunderstanding and shallow selfishness.[1]

In the book of Acts, Paul frequently wins a few people to Christ, starts a church, and then skips town. He leaves these baby disciples to fend for themselves, with only an occasional follow-up visit months, even years, later.[2] It feels like reckless abandon – and yet it is there in black and white.

Jesus showed us that going in mission is something we can start doing from our earliest days of starting to follow him. Bible study, training, and growth in maturity are vital, and often they can supercharge our mission efforts. In the same way, mission – like worship and fellowship – is an essential part of discipleship from the very start of our Christian journey.

Reggie McNeal puts it like this: "We must change our ideas of what it means to develop a disciple, shifting the emphasis from studying Jesus and all things spiritual in an environment protected from the world, to following Jesus into the world to join him in his redemptive mission."[3]

Jesus, in his mission, was attractional and missional, drawing huge crowds of followers eager to learn from him. The Western, and in particular the North American, church has tended to be very successful in this attractional model of doing and being church. Unfortunately, the missional component is often lacking or completely absent. Bringing in the missional emphasis often "feels" as though we are removing the attractional from our model, but this is not the case. Often the church has been most effective when missional and attractional have worked together.

Missio Dei

"Our mission has not life of its own: only in the hands of the sending God can it truly be called mission. Not least since the missionary initiative comes from God alone . . . mission is thereby seen as a movement from God to the world; the church is viewed as an instrument for that mission. There is church because there is mission, not vice versa. To participate in mission is to participate in the movement of God's love toward people, since God is a fountain of sending love."[4]

The Bible is packed full of examples of how our God is on a mission to restore fallen humanity to himself. Christopher Wright goes as far as to say, "Mission is what the Bible is all about; we could as meaningfully talk of the missional basis of the Bible as of the biblical basis of mission."[5] Theologians have long identified that our role is less to start mission than to recognize and in response join in with God's mission to the world (or Missio Dei, a Latin phrase that literally translates as "the sending of God").

In each of the four Gospels, Jesus makes it clear that his disciples are to go to the lost and that we are to make that the center of how we think, love, and live (Matthew 28:19-20; Mark 16:15-16; Luke 24:46-48; John 15:26-27). Reading Acts, we see that missional driver highlighted repeatedly (Acts 1:8; 13:2; 14:1, 21; 16:9, 13, 32, etc.). Paul, for instance, clearly saw reaching out in mission as the primary filter for all his decisions and actions (e.g., Philippians 3:12-14). As has been humorously put, when we become Christians, there are two things we can do on earth that we won't be able to do in heaven: sin and witness. The question for us is to decide which one we think Jesus left us here to do.

Responding to God's Mission

As we compare the reality of church life today with the nature of the Bible's witness, we can feel bewildered or frustrated about what we are to do in response. Obviously, there are many answers to that question, and in this book, we are going to talk about one possible route for you to consider taking. We recognize that there are many other possibilities and ways of doing things, for which we rejoice and give thanks to God for the wonderful creative diversity across his body.

An increasing number of church communities are doing authentic, bold, and effective mission, which any Christ follower should be delighted about. So if at any point we sound as if we are saying "ours is the only way" (or even the best way), that is not our intention, and we ask for your forgiveness in advance.

We are, however, hugely excited about the possibilities of Missional Communities, having lived hands-on with them for many years now. We have seen repeatedly how Missional Communities can transform churches and individual Christians into highly effective witnesses for Christ, without burning them out or requiring an alien abduction and a resultant complete character change along the way! We both are experienced practitioners with Missional Communities, which means that we have gone ahead and hopefully made many of your mistakes for you. So we don't apologize for our passion and energy in sharing with you something that we, along with many others, have found to have worked extremely well.

Becoming Missional

"The church exists to go into the cultures and nations of the earth and live sacrificially for the good of others."[6]

Mission is all about going. It is following the Lord of the Harvest into the fields, becoming the answer to his (and our own) prayers, "Send more workers into the fields" (Matthew 9:37-38).

Do we realize that we live on a mission field here in the United States?

"North America is often not seen as a mission field, or it is seen as a 'reached' field only in need of an evangelism strategy. We tend to think that true missional engagement is not necessary in our paganized, secularized, spiritualized North American culture."[7]

Eddie Gibbs and Ian Coffey talk about missionary engagement, which they define as occurring when "the church recognizes not only its distinctive identity in the gospel but also its calling within a specific culture."[8] They write that the church must be rooted in God's plan to heal and restore creation, only being able to do so when the church accepts Christ's commission to go in mission.

We are all rapidly coming to the conclusion that attendance at Sunday services alone won't produce disciples, however good the programs on offer. With enormous experience in church planting, Neil Cole writes that the church has to rediscover what it means to go with the Gospel – to "where life happens and where culture is formed – restaurants, bars, coffeehouses, parks, locker rooms and neighborhoods."[9]

We are not to simply accept and "baptize" the culture to which we go, but rather to understand, affirm where we can, offer a better way where we can't, and demonstrate that to become a Christian someone does not have to leave his or her original culture, language, and ethnic identity behind.

Stetzer and Putnam[10] summarize the current shift toward missional thinking as follows:

- From programs to processes
- From demographics to discernment
- From models to missions
- From attractional to incarnational
- From uniformity to diversity
- From professional to passionate
- From seating to sending
- From decisions to disciples
- From additional to exponential
- From monuments to movements

Reggie McNeal describes this process[11] in terms of three shifts, in thinking and behavior:

- From internal to external in terms of ministry focus
- From program development to people development in terms of core activity
- From church-based to Kingdom-based in terms of leadership agenda

Of course, just because someone calls what he or she does "missional" does not mean it is! Alan Hirsch rightly states that "the word 'missional' over the years has tended to become very fluid as it was quickly co-opted by those wishing to find new and trendy tags for what they themselves were doing, be they missional or not. It is often used as a substitute for seeker-sensitive, cell-group church, or other church growth concepts, thus obscuring its original meaning."[12]

Witness and Service

Going occurs in two related yet distinct forms, service and witness. In Luke 9 and 10, Jesus sends out the disciples with the instruction to do two things:

heal the sick and cast out demons, and proclaim the Kingdom. One represents service; the other represents witness.

As we first looked at in the Definitions section with UP-IN-OUT, we see Jesus entering the brokenness of the world and asking for a response (OUT) in two distinct ways:

- He wants people who don't know him yet to come to know him (to experience the healing and restoration of that relationship), and
- He also wants to see systems of injustice brought to an end. As NT Wright says, Jesus came "to put the world to rights."[12a]

There is witness. There is service.

Very often, the best way to engage with a community is by living out the presence and values of the Kingdom. We identify where there is a need that we can meet and do so. This builds our credibility with those we are reaching and allows the Holy Spirit to soften our hearts as we humble ourselves in that way. It has been said that people don't care how much we know until they know how much we care, so finding ways to serve is the Kingdom way to reach that breakthrough point.

Our service does not have to be an amazing venture that the grateful locals are still going to be talking about decades later. But as we go with a servant's heart, the Lord will bring people and opportunities across our paths in order to train and direct us. Our eyes will be opened to see a more strategic and longer-term pattern of service in that context. As we follow that guidance, this will then build momentum, bear fruit, and genuinely begin to change that mission context in tangible ways.

We tend to think of service primarily as an event, rather than seeing service through the lens of process. Once we see the process aspect as primary, we release much of the pressure off ourselves to produce the best event ever, focusing more on serving the real needs of those we are trying to reach, however unspectacular that may feel to us.

As an aside, Robert Lupton has produced a hugely insightful review of effective compassion ministries. Lupton has more than thirty-five years' experience in inner-city Atlanta and brings much pragmatic wisdom to this whole arena. For instance, under the heading, *10 Questions Ministries want to ask volunteers/donors but seldom do*, he piercingly asks, "Will your volunteering cost us more than it is worth? Is this about you having a meaningful experience or about serving the poor? Will you attempt to control me with your money?"[13]

Particularly for evangelicals, service is something we are just starting to re-engage with.

But then there is old faithful: witness.

But perhaps, as Dallas Willard says, "Familiarity has bred unfamiliarity."[14] We are so familiar with the concept of evangelism that it has become unfamiliar.

We know seeing people come to know Jesus is important, *yet we rarely see people come to know Jesus.*

We have a crucial responsibility to specifically bear witness for Christ, and we do this by not buying into the secular/sacred divide. We naturally show what it means to be a follower of Jesus, not in a forced artificial way but rather as life takes its course. In doing so, we begin to disciple the lost and show them practically the difference that knowing Christ makes. This leads to openness to spiritual things, since we are sharing our authentic lives rather than trying to sell something.

We (Alex and my wife Hannah) have shared so much "real life" with our neighbors that we now gather a group of families monthly and are discipling them in the things of God – including some surprisingly in-depth Bible study. Our neighbors are totally appreciative because it feels authentic and real to who we are, while they feel loved and valued by us for who they are.

Being naturally supernatural means being sensitive to what God is doing in someone's life, rather than forcing our agenda on that person. YWAM's Laurence Singlehurst writes of the difference between sowing and reaping, noting that the latter usually occurs only after many have invested in the former. He argues that moving someone from a -7 to a -6 in his or her view of God[15] is no less important than when someone goes from -1 to 0 and accepts Christ as Savior. Missional Communities create an amazing context for ongoing sowing strategies.

How Is the Twenty-first-century Church Doing Mission?

In recent years, much ink has been spilled on how the church should be looking less inwards and more outwards, moving from in-drag to out-reach, thereby changing our message from "come to us and look like us" to "we're coming to you and showing you Christ where you are." While all this debate has been going on, many Christians have simply gone off and started experimenting with other ways to be church in the twenty-first century. For some, this is clearly driven by a genuine desire to reach the lost, by planting authentic Christian communities in contexts where there is no

> **"The twentieth century saw the emergence of a Churchless Mission and a Missionless Church."**
>
> Eddie Gibbs[16]

effective indigenous witness for Christ. These groups are led by humble, godly, and accountable men and women, who are seeing many won for Christ and neighborhoods affected for the Kingdom.

At the same time, we need to be honest and say that there have been train wrecks along the way. Some high-profile attempts to rework church for the next generation have ended in huge pastoral messes. Some new groups have sprung up solely in reaction to perceived wrongs in their previous church, so at times these groups can feel more like a teenage rebellion against accountability rather than a true Kingdom witness.

In the midst of this, a movement was happening. And very few saw it.

A German missiologist, having done much research, believes that there are between 6 million and 12 million Americans in what he calls house churches.[17] Although his definition is not identical to what we call Missional Communities (for instance, we are talking about groups of between twenty and fifty (up to seventy) people, whereas he is including much smaller groups) and we feel far more is gained through this missional identity, it is interesting to see how he identifies eight streams of what he calls house churches.[18] He categorizes and comments on them as follows:

(i) Regular house churches with groups of Christians that meet in homes. These occur both as single groups and also as organized networks, some of which have websites and are resourced by leadership teams.

(ii) Off-the-grid house churches with "Out of Church Christians," that intentionally do not want to be known, listed, or on anybody's radar.

iii) Business groups, either within a company or those connecting people in the business world.

(iv) More and more traditional churches are changing their home groups or even transitioning everyone into house churches.

(v) Inside the Roman Catholic culture, a surprisingly large amount of "small churches" are intentionally set up to cut out the middle layer of clergy and directly connect the people with Jesus and the Bible. In many cases, these groups are supported by bishops and cardinals.

(vi) Many historical churches, like the Anglican Church, are developing "small Missional Communities."

(vii) Insider movements within other religions. There are a staggering amount of under-the-radar house churches emerging within religious mega-blocks like the Buddhists, Hindus, Muslims, New Agers and even within certain cults. But they choose to stay within their religious culture for effectiveness and to build bridges to God. One example is a former Hindu priest, fully painted up and in his saffron dress, who now very effectively plants Christian house churches amongst Brahmins in India.

(viii) Media-birthed house churches, initiated by television, radio or online community facilitators.

The growing movement is toward mid-sized gatherings, advancing the Kingdom in ways most of us have not seen in our lifetimes. Many people are being reached through these lighter-weight, more flexible structures, which are finding amazingly creative ways to incarnate the Gospel message into their host culture.

2.2 | DEFINING COMMUNITY

God has hard-wired a truth deep within us: it is not good for us to be alone (Genesis 2:18). We are designed not only to live in community but also to be at our most fruitful there. It should come as no great surprise to discover that we will usually be most effective missionally when we go with others. Put simply, we go as a community, inviting people into community.

The balance to the zeal of the missionary endeavor, with its inevitable lows and disappointments, is that we come from of a place of belonging, of encouragement, and of accountability.

Fragmented Community

Our default mode as Western Christians can be to see mission as a solo activity ("me and my witness in my workplace/neighborhood/golf club"). But the under-girding of the Bible is covenant relationships, when "two became one." While we do have a personal witness, the evidence of the New Testament is that everything happened in teams. Jesus sent his disciples out in teams – he even sent two disciples to fetch a donkey (Luke 19:29-30). The Acts of the Apostles show teamwork within almost every missionary venture,[19] while we only have to read the greetings in the letters to see how highly Paul valued his team members.[20]

In the Old Testament, there was a tremendously strong belief in covenant community. This began with Israel's relations with God and then extended to each person in the community. The understanding of God's calling was rarely individual and primarily seen as for the whole people group. The people of Israel were chosen and set apart together to be a blessing to all nations, starting with Abraham's call in Genesis 12:2-3.[21] Sin was also viewed through a community lens, for the impact resonated around the whole nation (e.g., the holiness laws in Leviticus 26, whereby the whole nation reaped the rewards for obedience or punishments for disobedience, or Achan's sin in Joshua 7 by plundering from Jericho).

We all know in theory that people are hungry for authentic community. Robert Putnam wrote about this in *Bowling Alone*,[22] in which, using statistics and time diaries, he plotted indicators of civic engagement from its peak in the early 1960s through its decline thereafter. He showed the resulting loss of social capital, a term he used to describe the emotional and practical benefits of personal relationships. He warned that unless we find ways to reconnect with one another, we will experience a deepening impoverish-ment in our lives and communities.

Data from the University of Chicago's National Opinion Research Center has shown that people with five or more close friends (not including family) are 50% more likely to describe themselves as "very happy."[23] As John Piper puts it, "For people who are passing through the dark night of the soul, turnaround will come because God brings unwavering lovers of Christ into their lives who do not give up on them."[24]

Young Adults and Community

"They're usually not uncomfortable in religious services – they often describe their religious congregations, when they have one, as being 'friendly' – but they really don't feel much actual belonging or sense of being at home."[25]

There is a profound hunger among our friends and neighbors for genuine community and meaningful relationships. For instance, Ed Stetzer has shown how strongly people desire to belong, noting how this is especially the case among young adults. Within unchurched younger adults (ages eighteen to twenty-nine), 58% are more likely to attend church if people at church cared for them, as compared to 38% of older adults (aged over thirty years).[26]

Christian Smith has extensively researched the religious and cultural state of young adults, backing up Stetzer's findings by showing that belonging is a vital component of the typical young adult worldview.

Citing many of the interviews conducted in the research, Smith draws attention to the finding that many emerging adults speak of finding deeper belonging outside church. In this example, which refers to being part of a rugby team, note the link between belonging (community) and a common goal (mission):

"On the team, everybody's going after the same goal, and it brings people together. At the same time there's a game going on, something that's distracting, so I don't have to carry a conversation, just anything that you thought of could go. I could have said anything, and it wouldn't be weird while I was just watching or playing the game."[27] What an incredible description of feeling truly accepted within a community that shares a strong and defining missional focus! This is why linking mission and community is such a potentially powerful and transformative process.

The need is pressing. For the book *unChristian*, David Kinnaman and Gabe Lyons also undertook extensive research among the eighteen to twenty-nine-year-old age group. "We consistently find that the vast majority of teenagers nationwide will spend a significant amount of their teen years participating in a Christian congregation. Most teenagers enter adulthood considering themselves to be Christians and saying they have made a personal commitment to Christ. But within a decade most of these young people will have left the church and will have placed emotional connection to Christianity on the shelf. For most of them, their faith was merely skin deep. This leads to the sobering finding that the vast majority of outsiders in this country, particularly among young generations, are actually de-churched individuals."[28]

Kinnaman and Lyons noted that young people find Christians to be "anti-homosexual, judgmental, hypocritical, too involved in politics, sheltered and insensitive to others." In the tradition of good missiology, the authors don't just crumble before the critique, but rather suggest we find ways to engage and challenge that worldview where it needs that, in a manner and tone that aren't just going to prove our critics right! We believe that Missional Communities provide a framework for making an important contribution toward redressing these problems, moving beyond just an image makeover toward substantive transformation of our missional competency.

So how can we overcome the cultural hurdles of individualism, isolation, and consumerism, to build authentic community?

Human Connection

People want to be related to and be a part of something.

> **"The opposite of belonging is to feel isolated and always (all ways) on the margin, an outsider. To belong is to know, even in the middle of the night, that I am among friends."**[29]

Starbucks understands this. In a CBS 60 Minutes interview, CEO Howard Schultz declared, "We're in the business of human connection and humanity, creating communities in a third place between work and home."[30]

I (Alex) was struck by this afresh when I went to U2's 360 Tour in 2009. Sixty thousand people packed into the stadium to experience amazing music, an incredible circular video screen descending from a 37-ton "claw," and overall an awesome stadium rock concert. Bono unashamedly led the crowd in worship, singing the refrain from "Amazing Grace" that then kicked into the anthemic "Where the Streets Have No Name," which is about our longing for heaven and for the fullness of God's Kingdom to come about in the here and now. The presence of God was so tangible. Even if people didn't yet know the name of the God who was there, they were being drawn into his presence and having their hearts softened by the Holy Spirit.

Yet a few days later, several people from church dismissed any possibility of such a concert being an opportunity for people to encounter God. "Worship in a rock concert? U2 – Christian? You're kidding me!"

George McCloud wrote, "The cross must be raised again at the center of the marketplace as well as on the steeple of the church. I am claiming that Jesus was not crucified in a cathedral between two candles, but on a cross between two thieves; on the town garbage heap, at a crossroads so cosmopolitan they had to write his title in Hebrew, Latin, and Greek. At the kind of place where cynics talk smut and thieves curse and soldiers gamble, because that is where he died and that is what he died about and that is where churchmen ought to be and what churchmen should be about."[31]

If we can break through these barriers and begin doing mission in community, God will show us ways to serve and witness as a group to a particular people. MCs seem to be the size that ensures a high level of support (people feel it is big enough to work), while remaining small enough that others can imagine being part of the community. And there is nothing like shared battle stories (and battle scars!) to enhance a community's sense of togetherness, so the very action of going out in mission strengthens the group's life with one another.

Speaking at the *onething Conference* in Kansas City in December 2009, YWAM founder Loren Cunningham said he believed that the church will increasingly move back to a model of discipleship that flows from house to house. As a result, he added that the largest ten or so international Christian non-profit organizations have joined together and decided to radically focus their energy on the United States in the area of discipleship.

Why Can't We Do All This on Sundays?

We love Sunday celebrations. It is an amazing thing to gather at the church building with hundreds or even thousands of other believers and be inspired as we share in corporate worship, to respond to challenging preaching/teaching, and to be reminded that we are part of a bigger movement of God way beyond our personal ministry context. For all these reasons, and many more besides, big Sunday celebrations are wonderful and worthwhile.

Don't hear us wrong. Public worship gatherings are incredibly important.

However, this one gathering cannot be expected to fulfill the New Testament descriptions of deep, challenging, life-changing relationships that should exist between followers of Jesus. We need to realize that when Paul and other New Testament writers addressed the early churches, they only conceived of churches meeting in homes, not public "church-owned" buildings. As MC-sized gatherings, they shared their lives together and reached out as a community to the lost around them.

In fact, almost all of the letters Paul wrote were to churches with a maximum size determined by the number of people who could gather in a home, which was probably in the fifty to seventy range.

That framework makes sense of instructions such as Ephesians 4:25: "Therefore each of you must put off falsehood and speak truthfully to his neighbor, for we are all members of one body." How can we speak the truth to someone sitting in the pew behind us, when we barely know his or her name, let alone what might need challenging in his or her life?

When it comes to worship, we read in 1 Corinthians 14:26: "When you come together, everyone has a hymn, or a word of instruction, a revelation, a tongue or an interpretation. All of these must be done for the strengthening of the church." Paul was envisioning a more intimate occasion where (without microphones!) everyone in the room could hear what everyone else was saying. He was thinking of (what we would call) a Missional Community–sized gathering.

The Historical Evidence for *Oikos*

The early church gathered in what the New Testament Greek calls *oikos*. This word, meaning "house" or "household," included the householder's family, slaves, and, through their network of relationships, friends, neighbors, and even business associates. As the major social structure of Rome (and previously Greece), the early church followed these established sociological and relational pathways.

Interestingly, the word *oikos* was also used by the Greek-speaking Jews to refer to the tabernacle or temple, the original place of Jewish worship. Thus, when Paul and the early church started using this word to describe their gatherings, they brilliantly mixed the two meanings.

J. W. C. Wand's standard textbook on the early church explains the way the *oikos* worked. "The church in a particular house would include the members of the family, the slaves and dependents, together with other Christians situated conveniently near."[32] The gathering was relational, and while the gathered group was from a variety of social classes and backgrounds, the pre-existing social networks were the major way in which people came to faith.

Clearly the *oikos* strategy worked well, since Rodney Stark has shown how the early church (meeting in homes) grew exponentially in three centuries. Beginning in AD 40 with around 1,000 believers (around 0.0017% of the population of the Roman Empire), Stark shows how by AD 350 the total size of the church had multiplied to roughly 33,882,000 (56.5% of the Empire).[33]

This incredible growth all took place in a context where Christianity was illegal. Although persecution ebbed and flowed depending on the whims of the different emperors and local governors, nevertheless it was always liable to break out. It was not until AD 313 that Emperor Constantine began to stop the Roman persecution of Christians, and subsequently allowed the construction of church buildings. Some dedicated meeting rooms were built before then – the earliest we know of dates back to the early third century in Dura-Europos on the Euphrates, which could hold around a hundred people and included a baptistery.[34] Nevertheless, fierce persecutions still occurred, until the worst one of all between AD 303 and 311, under Diocletian and Galerius, when enormous numbers of Christians died.[35]

All this leads us to see that, for at least the first three hundred years, Christian community was based in the home, in the context of the *oikos*, and not structured around dedicated buildings and public services. The same period also arguably saw the most rapid and prolific growth of any period from church history.

The Biblical Evidence for *Oikos*

The Bible is full of extended households. In the Old Testament, we can see the principle of *oikos* in operation, for instance, at the first Passover, when everyone in the household was "covered" by the lamb's blood on the door posts. This included family, slaves, hired workers, friends, and neighbors.

Many New Testament books are not written for one specific congregation that met all together in one place. In Corinth, given that city's highly urbanized situation, the church there met in numerous homes as *oikos* communities, which is why Paul spends five chapters of 1 Corinthians dealing with some of the practical issues of worship and community life in the *oikos* setting.

In Romans, Paul addresses different communities, namely the Gentile Christians and the Jewish Christians, who would have followed the pattern of contemporary Judaism by organizing themselves into different synagogues depending on the language spoken. Thus, Jewish Christians, who spoke Aramaic, met in one place, while Greek speakers, or the Gentile Christians, met in another.

In Jerusalem, this issue had been the cause of the conflict recorded at the beginning of Acts 6, when the Greek speakers found that their widows were being neglected in the distribution of food. This text shows us that, even before the first persecution following the death of Stephen, a variety of churches were already meeting in different contexts across the city. Interestingly, the response of the apostles to the food distribution conflict is to radically revisit their leadership style and structures – in other words, the apostles were prepared to change any structure in order to reach a new harvest (in this case, Gentile Christians).

We can see the multiple *oikos* model by turning to the end of almost any of the epistles to specific cities. Romans is the classic example, where in chapter 16 Paul addresses different *oikos* and sends numerous greetings to churches that gathered in distinct *oikos*. He repeatedly uses the term *ekklesia* (most commonly translated as "church," but literally meaning "gathering") to describe these various communities of faith, all of which were addressed by his letter. He also greets other people by name and (what the English translation calls) their family or their brothers – in other words, he is repeatedly using the concept of *oikos* and is recognizing many different household churches across the city.

Read from a literary perspective, Romans 16 is directed at a variety of different households. This includes the household (*oikos*) of Priscilla and Aquila (v.4-5), the household of Aristobulus (v.10) (literally, it reads "the ones of [i.e., belonging to] Aristobulus," which is clearly an *oikos* concept), and the household of Narcissus (v.11). Verse 14 says, "Greet Asyncritus, Phlegon, Hermes, Patrobas, Hermas and the brothers with them." This references a distinct community, with the term "brothers" (*adelphous*) simply a different way of saying ekklesia or *oikos*. This is then directly followed by verse 15, "Greet Philologus, Julia, Nereus and his sister, and Olympas and all the saints with them," which again directly implies another *oikos* community. (Interestingly, a number of researchers have suggested that as those names were all well-used within Caesar's household as slave names, this could well have been a greeting to a church meeting in the Imperial Palace.)

Leading New Testament scholar James Dunn comments on Romans 16:3-16: "The groupings indicate at least five different Missional Communities in Rome (v. 5,10,11,14,15)."[36]

We can cross-reference the Roman decentralized *oikos* pattern of church life with a reference Paul makes in the letter to the Philippians, which is generally thought to have been written from Rome in around AD 61, when Paul was a prisoner there awaiting trial. In 4:22, Paul writes, "All the saints greet you, especially those of Caesar's household." Again, it is that *oikos* word, in this case indicating that a community of Christians, presumably many of whom were slaves and prisoners, met and worshipped where they lived and worked – in Caesar's palace.

Michael Green, author of E*vangelism in the Early Church*, agrees that the *oikos*, "consisting of blood relations, slaves, clients and friends, was one of the bastions of Greco-Roman society. Christian missionaries made a deliberate point of gaining whatever households they could as lighthouses . . . from which the Gospel could illuminate the surrounding darkness."[37]

Put another way, it seems that, from a biblical perspective, *oikos* evangelism is God's natural method for sharing his supernatural message.

It is trans-historical and trans-cultural. *Oikos* is integrity-based evangelism, since it stands or falls on the quality of the relationship, which of course reflects the relational core of the Gospel.

1 Peter 2:1-5 talks of how we are being built into a spiritual *oikos*, centered on the cornerstone who is Jesus, in order to serve God as a holy priesthood. In Ephesians 2:14-22, Paul reflects on this principle of Christ restoring peace between God and humanity, bringing us into a new community together, which he describes as being the *oikos* of God. That is what we are co-laboring with Christ to see – people coming with us into the Father's *oikos*.

When Paul and Peter talked about us being the *oikos* of God, they did so deliberately. Their call into Christian community, into *ekklesia*, was into sharing life together throughout the week, in natural networks of *oikos* relationships. They were highly decentralized units, held together by traveling apostles and prophets who were invited to speak into the community on an ongoing basis. The wider church's unity was neither created nor expressed through all meeting in one place at one time.

The New Testament's instruction and pattern reveal a church that can be called a household of people on a mission.

Fortunately, in twenty-first-century America we live in a time and place where Christians are not persecuted by the state, and so we are free to gather openly and publicly in large numbers. We should have a Christian public presence on Sunday mornings, but we also need to read the Scriptures about church life through the eyes of believers for whom church meant *oikos*-sized Missional Communities. When we do so, all sorts of interesting challenges and possibilities spring up!

When Sally and I (Mike) moved to America, we brought an extended household with us. Six families moved to Phoenix, Arizona, from Sheffield, England. Later, when we moved from Arizona to South Carolina, although with a smaller team, again we moved as an extended household of four families. This Missional Community became the gathering point for others who were called to share in our mission. Now we have a three-generational *oikos* of at least thirty people. Together, we function as an extended family but also as a mission team with a passion to fulfill the calling of our lives.

Interestingly, Frank and Joan, who moved from England to be closer to their daughter (who works with us) and grandkids, joined us with very little knowledge of God or experience of organized church (and certainly no idea that they were joining an *oikos*!). Within weeks of living in the extended household, simply by interacting with us on a regular and sometimes daily basis, they had come to know Jesus. This is the tremendous power of the extended family on mission together.

Oikos Reflected in Culture Today

Sociologists teach us to look at the artifacts of our culture, that they can reveal what culture thinks, accepts, rejects, and yearns for. When we step back and observe what artifacts our culture is producing (books, movies, television, music, other forms of art), we can clearly see this hardwiring toward *oikos*, a household or extended family of friends, natural family, neighbors, and colleagues.

Because so many people are living in the aftermath of the cultural earthquake of the second half of the twentieth century, a time when so many biological families completely broke down, they are starting to rebuild their own extended families. And even in the artifacts of our own culture we see that happening.

In 1994, the number one show on television was *Home Improvement*, a show about the trials and travails of the nuclear family. In 1995, a new show hit the tube and became the new number one: *Friends*.

This show was about six people, some related, some not, who were trying to rebuild themselves and a new community because their own families had gone so terribly wrong.

Ross and Monica were children of Jewish parents. Ross was his parents' favorite, while Monica was always forgotten and never quite good enough for her mother's standards.

Chandler was the product of a "deeply conflicted" parental relationship. We'll leave it at that.

Phoebe grew up without a father, and her mom committed suicide when she was a teenager. Phoebe later finds out the woman was not actually her mother.

Joey is a struggling actor from a large Italian family, whose father has been cheating on his mother for years, but he comes to find out his mother knew all along.

Rachel was destined for a life of luxury before walking out on her own wedding and landing with these five future-family-members in the east Village. Her implacable father, possibly alcoholic mother and two neurotic sisters regularly orbit into the growing family that is Friends.

These six people meet in 1994, devoid of any real identity, carrying the scars and wounds of broken families, and in 1995, these characters are on the number one show on television.

The show ran for ten seasons, and at the conclusion, it is no longer six single people trying to recreate a family. *They have created a real family.* Some are married; some aren't. But now there are children. Phoebe's brother, his wife, and their triplets are a recurring theme in the show and are part of the extended family. Rachel's sisters, Gunther, Janis and her husband, the list goes on. *Friends* didn't go about repairing the nuclear family; the show re-created an extended family.

We see this in ABC's comedy *Modern Family*, the number one comedy in 2010. It's a collection of three families, representing three generations that are all curiously, and quite comedically, related to each another. It's the extended family.

We see it in the entourages that movie, sports, and music stars gather around them – a mix of friends, family, and employees that make up their recreated extended family.

Perhaps there is no better or more explicit example of our culture's hardwiring than in the fantastic and award-winning Walmart commercial, created by The Martin Agency, from 2008. In it, an average, young twenty-something is walking around his Christmas party, singing about the people who've come out:

> The holidays are here again
> So I'm inviting all my friends
> The people who are close to me
> They're my extended family
> You've got my mom, my sis, my brother
> My surprisingly cool stepmother
> And the two kids that she had
> Before she ever met my dad
>
> Next you've got my aunts and cousins
> They showed up with several dozen friends of theirs
> It's fine with me; I've got enough for all
> Here in the hall you've got my office mates
> My best friend and his online date
> They've all come here to celebrate
> This is my family!
>
> My judo coach, my allergist
> My MySpace friends and Twitter list
> And the first girl that I ever kissed
> You're beautiful, I love you
> 'Cause there's one truth I've found
> And it's never let me down:
> When you stock up on joy, there's enough to go 'round, singing:
> Joy! Enough to go 'round, enough to go 'round and around and around and around.

Notice that he's identifying his extended family as the "the people who are close to me." Then he reels off all the different types of people who are close to him, related and not.

Barbara Lippert, an ad critic for *AdWeek*, called the ad "exactly right for the zeitgeist," as it is filled with "clever shout-outs to stepfamilies, online dates, office mates and the latest technology."[38]

And if you recall (and even if you don't), zeitgeist simply means *the spirit of the age*. There is something about people recreating their own extended family that hits the right chord. That is, somehow, simply what our culture is already doing.

The Person of Peace

As Christians, we tend to think that evangelism is really hard and that our job is to focus on the meanest cats in the neighborhood! At the same time, we feel more than ill-equipped to do such a thing, recognizing that the methods that sometimes used to work a generation ago seem even less applicable today.

Or scary.

Or, for some, simply frustrating.

Yet, interestingly enough, how we've seen evangelism done is not how Jesus did evangelism.

Jesus shared the Good News in a very relaxed manner. He didn't hassle or harangue or chase after people, so neither did he expect his disciples to do the same thing. In Luke 10 (there are similar passages in Luke 9, Matthew 10, and Mark 6), Jesus teaches his disciples to search out the man (or woman or child) of Peace.

A Person of Peace is someone who:

- Welcomes you
- Receives you
- Listens to you
- Serves you
- Responds to you.

In other words, a Person of Peace connects with you, and implicitly, you almost certainly connect with him or her.

Think about it this way: Paul says there is nothing good in him to such a degree that even when he *wants* to do good he can't do it. So if this Person of Peace sees something he or she genuinely likes in me, something he or she thinks is curiously good, well, that simply must be Jesus.

That means that, while he or she likes me, who the person really likes is Jesus.

Which means the individual is actually demonstrating spiritual openness.

Interestingly, Jesus tells us to stay with a Person of Peace, which means we invest in that relationship until either we see fruit or we realize that he or she is not a Person of Peace for us. So our role is to be obedient to Christ and look to see where he is about to visit. We'll know that place by the presence of one or more People of Peace – if there are none, then we simply move on.

The entry point for this comes when we intentionally allow Jesus into our seemingly everyday interactions with people we meet (the exchange of "peace," or *shalom*, simply being the standard greeting in the culture of Jesus' day), whereby we look and listen to discern where the Holy Spirit is already at work, as we go about our lives.

One of the markers of a Person of Peace is that the individual often becomes a gatekeeper to his or her community. In other words, as Jesus moves through you to change that person, he or she will then introduce you to his or her network of relationships, granting you favor, access, and opportunity with those people.

Think about it from Scripture. Peter goes to Cornelius's house, and *his entire household comes to know Jesus*. Paul meets Lydia, spends time with her, she comes to know Jesus, and then *her entire household comes to faith.*

Both people were gatekeepers to a wider community.

Not only Cornelius and Lydia became Christians. A slew of people followed.

In the book *Organic Church*,[39] one of the things that Neil Cole is very strong on is the power of turning converts immediately into workers, particularly by enabling them to reach their networks of relationships. He very effectively shows how when one person is found as a beachhead, a Christian community can be started virtually on the fly, as conversions and transformations can potentially become epidemic. He encourages us to think of this as a viral way to spread Christianity.

That seems very much in keeping with the experience of the early church.

Hence, his use of the term organic – his point is that the church grows best through natural organic relationships, rather than through institutional structures.

The invigorating part of the Person of Peace strategy is that it stops mission being yet another thing to cram into our busy lives.

Instead, this strategy is about bringing the Gospel where we already are – as we shop, play sports, collect the kids, go to work, meet the neighbors, etc. Thus, the very healthiest Missional Communities are reaching out to their context in ways that feel natural and life-giving. By focusing on People of Peace, the missional investment is not emotionally taxing – in fact, it can easily become highly life-giving, even for those who are quiet and reserved.

The Person of Peace principle ties very naturally into the understanding of *oikos* that we have already looked at. As we seek the Lord for who and where our *oikos* is to be, we take that principle and then apply it in practice by observing where our People of Peace are. Your Person of Peace, and the people he or she introduces you to, are very likely to be part of your *oikos* for the next season.

So, quite simply, build a Missional Community there!

Maps + Cracks

This brings us to a subtle shift happening within the United States and one that we believe is a major reason Missional Communities have been so successful.

Much of the history of the United States is one of expansion and pioneering. We obviously see that in the discovery of a new world and the founding of the colonies. But for the first two hundred years of the United States' history, people pushed further and further, claiming more and more territory (land) until the whole of the country was settled. Whether this was seen in "manifest destiny" in the taming of the Wild West and the Oregon Trail, the Gold Rush of the 1850s, or pushing out the cities into the suburbs in the 1950s and 1960s, the story of America was one of open space with people slowly coming to inhabit these spaces.

Because almost exclusively Protestant Christians formed the United States, whenever people moved into a new place, it made sense that a new church began. At some point, Oklahoma City didn't exist, and as people moved there and they reached a critical mass, all that was needed to start and grow a church was to construct a building and put up a steeple. There was a vacuum, and this structure filled it.

For quite some time, this worked incredibly well.

What we saw with the rise of the seeker-sensitive movement of the 1970s to 1990s was a similar kind of philosophy. With the mass suburbanization of America, combined with the homogenizing pop-culture influence of television, seeker-sensitive capitalized largely on a massive group of suburbanites who were now seeing culture differently. There was a vacuum, a need for another kind of church that spoke more fluently the language of a changing culture, and this model was very successful in speaking this language.

One of the primary reasons this worked was because "contemporary" had very few meanings. Because culture in the suburbs was largely homogenous, most everyone liked the same kind of music, dressed the same way, and aspired to the same kind of things.

However, there has been a massive but subtle shift in our culture.

There is no longer a homogenous suburban mass.

The advances of the digital age have *tribalized* our culture, creating in every city hundreds if not thousands of "tribes" or people groups.

We propose that, in addition to using **maps** to determine our course of action (in that we choose where the church meets and who it reaches out to based on density, demographics, whether other churches are doing similar things), we also implement **cracks** as a way of becoming the church.

One phrase to describe this shift is that the church needs to move and seep into every crack and crevice of our culture.

With worship services, this is a tall task. But with Missional Communities, this task suddenly becomes far simpler and easier.

A Missional Community is an extended family of people on mission together, seeing the Gospel come to life and incarnated in whatever crack or crevice of society they find themselves in (i.e., mission context).

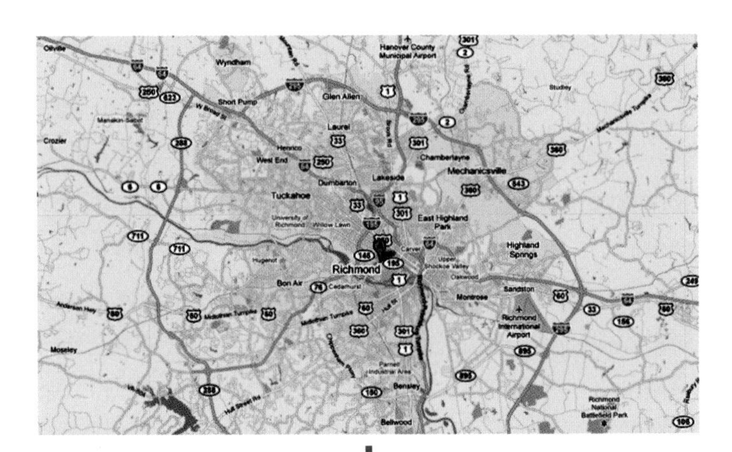

+

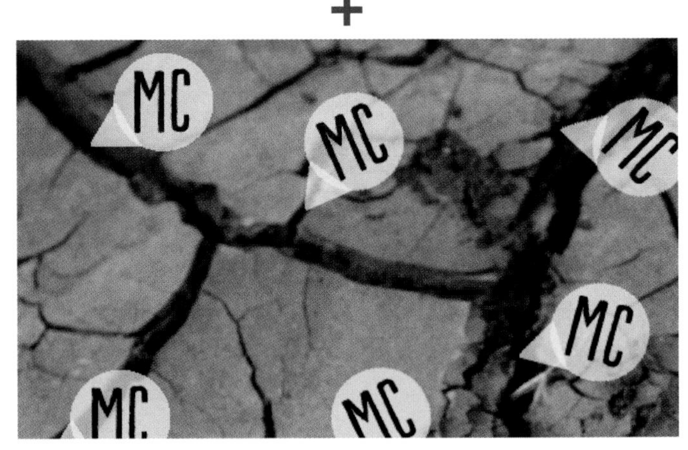

This is why People of Peace are so fundamental to Missional Communities and seeing evangelism happen. The Person of Peace *gives you credibility and access* to the sub-culture crevice he or she is in.

How does this play out?

A few years ago in Sheffield, in the United Kingdom, there was a large Iranian Muslim population. Obviously, a worship service was not going to be the way to reach this population, due to all the cultural hurdles and social pressures in place. However, one

Christian became very engaged and connected with *one* person in that community. Eventually, that person came to know Jesus. He was the Person of Peace. So what happened next? That existing Christian was able to work with this brand-new Iranian Christian, and as relationships were built over several years, more than sixty Iranian Muslims came to know Jesus. Now they are a thriving Missional Community within the body of Christ connected to St. Thomas Philadelphia, Sheffield.

Does this Missional Community look different from one that is focused on suburban parents with babies? Of course. But that's the point. It's Christ incarnated in that specific community.

This person entered and incarnated himself into that crack of society, he found favor with a Person of Peace, and the result was an extended family now following Jesus. We have seen this play out over and over.

When we start to see it this way, we see that the opportunities are endless. How many sub-groups, sub-cultures, people groups, neighborhoods, cracks, and crevices are there in your city? Each has the potential to see the Gospel incarnated in a very specific, contextual way that is true to who Jesus is calling them to be.

All you need is a Person of Peace.

The Seeds of a Movement

If you build a church around Missional Communities (households of people on a mission), what you end up with is a movement. This will be a network of networks, with leaders at every level who are passionate about seeing the Kingdom of God infiltrate every crack of society, planting authentic expressions of church that draw people back to their God and Father.

Reaching the world requires us to release the church to penetrate society, rather than simply offering more centralized services. Such a church, gradually infiltrating subversively through all the networks of society, will birth genuine city transformation. As church history proves, this is the sort of movement that people will give their lives for. This network of tribes will share common values and the same dream, yet each will find unique and tailored ways to express and live them out in their place of service.

2.3 | THE FOUR SPACES

Why Not Groups of Six to Twelve People?

You have probably noticed we keep coming back to this idea of the extended family. We see this in historical and biblical analysis, but we also see the extended family emerging in our culture today. People don't immediately try to rebuild their nuclear family; they rebuild their extended family.

Even with that being said, why not use the number commonly associated with small groups (six to twelve) as the building blocks for communities on mission? Most churches already have small groups. It would be an easy fix. Simply make small groups more missional.

The quick and easy answer is that we did. More than twenty years ago, this path was the first one we walked down. For several years, we experimented, tweaked, maneuvered, and cajoled our small groups into being more missional. Sometimes it worked, but most of the time it didn't. In the few cases when it did work, the multiplication of the small group was incredibly painful, and no one wanted to grow the group again only to have to go through the multiplication process once more. In the end, we found that, when trying to make small groups missional, one of two things happened:

1) They often refused the call and continued to stay inwardly focused, or
2) There was never enough momentum due to the size, and burnout soon ensued.

Furthermore, the latest research on small groups shows that, at best, the top small groups can multiply only three times and then the group is done. People refuse to do it again; it's simply too painful. *And that's before we've even added a mission focus to the group.*

What we have found is that small groups of six to twelve are important, but they simply aren't the best size for doing mission and growing a group on their own. There is something almost magical about the extended family size, something that just *clicks* with groups growing to twenty to fifty.

This section, Part 3, explains why that's the case. What comes to the surface is that it isn't simply a cultural snapshot of what is happening right now. It's how we are and have always been hardwired as human beings.

We can't help but re-create the extended family.

Spaces Thinking and Missional Communities

If the historical and biblical data and analysis are correct, namely, that the early church gathered in an extended household, or *oikos*, and essentially was a community on a mission, then we should also expect to see some similar principles appear in subsequent sociological and anthropological research. In particular, we would expect to find some clear patterns that demonstrate some of the variances between different sizes of gathering, thereby helping to highlight the strengths and weaknesses of the various scales of connecting with others.

Perhaps the most significant work in this realm came in the 1960s, when Edward T. Hall developed a theory based on the relationship between space and culture, coining the term "proxemics" for how we as humans use space and build communities.[40] He concluded that we use four spaces to develop personalities, cultures, and communication:

- ***Public Space*** is where we share a common experience and connect through an outside influence.
- ***Social Space*** is where we share an authentic "snapshot" of who we are, which shows what it would be like to have a personal relationship with us.
- ***Personal Space*** is where we share private experiences, thoughts, and feelings.
- ***Intimate Space*** is where we share "naked" information about who we are and are not ashamed.

Hall's research also indicated that we have a natural comfort level for physical proximity within the difference types of space. Thus, he concluded that, in public space, the person or thing we are interacting around needs to be at least 12 feet away, in social space we need 4 to 12 feet of room, in personal space we desire a gap of between 18 inches and 4 feet to be most comfortable, while intimate space is anything between 0 and 18 inches.

How We Regulate the Spaces

To illustrate, imagine yourself at a formal reception for two hundred people. The person giving the welcome speech will ideally be at least 12 feet away (i.e., in public space). People will gather in small knots of companions, each group being 4 to 12 feet away from the next group (if the room is too crowded to allow this and proceedings look like they will last a while, people feel very uncomfortable and may start to move into alternative spaces, such as corridors and staircases).

Within the little groups of friends or known colleagues, the distances will be 18 inches to 4 feet apart, since together you will share private thoughts and responses to what is going on around you (for instance, whispered comments about what the speaker is saying or what others are wearing).

Even in that semi-formal context, a married couple would still be able to break into intimate space, with a tender touch or a subtle holding of hands – but not too much, or they would be criticized for inappropriate PDA (Public Displays of Affection). Other than for marrieds or very close relationships, in such a situation we would feel touch from another person to be uncomfortable even if the only explanation we could give was centered on a vaguely defined notion of inappropriateness.

When our behavior is described like this, we may be amused, but intuitively this is how we tend to behave (usually offering the defense of, "They were invading my personal space!").

We know how to maneuver these spaces without even thinking about it, and it is a source of conflict when others violate these social norms. For instance, when someone comes too close too early, we can feel intimidated or violated. Cultures define these distances differently. I (Alex) have experienced this traveling within Russia, where the norm is that everyone comes and sits by you, even when there are plenty of seats elsewhere! Likewise, a striking thing for a visitor to India is how that culture allows people to come much closer than in the West before personal space is felt to be violated.

Another common misconception occurs when we meet someone who is highly competent in the public and social spaces, and we automatically assume that he or she is equally at ease in personal or intimate space. Just because someone presents as warm and gregarious when on a stage in front of hundreds does not mean that he or she is good at interacting with individuals in private. If we stop to think, we will realize that we know many people who are competent only in some, but not all, of the four spaces. Factors such as extroversion and introversion also play a part in our preferences and competencies.

Spaces and Belonging

Now all this talk about distances is not some abstract theory, for this discussion forms the very foundation of how we interact with others in different-sized gatherings.

Because this idea defines what we do and do not do in distinct places.

"Thus Hall's spaces are helpful categories not only for culture and communication, but also as they relate to community – our sense of belonging. We experience belonging in the same four spaces Hall describes: public, social, personal and intimate. How we occupy physical space – whether through actual real estate (the shopper standing next to my wife and me in the supermarket line) or through more subtle "spatial language" – tells others whether we want them to belong."[41]

The Four Spaces in Church Life

As we are thinking about this primarily in terms of church life, we can look in the Bible to trace the four spaces and how they affect our culture and relationships.

SPACE	OLD TESTAMENT	NEW TESTAMENT
PUBLIC	Temple festivals	Jesus proclaiming the Kingdom to the multitudes
SOCIAL	Synagogue	Jesus and the 72 Parties/weddings, etc.
PERSONAL	Family devotional life	Jesus and the 12
INTIMATE	Husband and wife e.g., Song of Songs	Jesus with Peter, James, and John

In public space, we see an open encounter between two Kingdoms. Often, though, the church in America either has abandoned this territory or misunderstood what this means in practice. The journey of modernity into post-modernity has squeezed faith in Christ out of the public space, or discourse, assigning faith to smaller spaces (ideally, faith remains just a "personal and private" thing).

In response to this, many Christians assert that the Gospel is a public message, but wrongly assume that this means that the church should run the government and direct all public policy.

We would do well to learn from the early Christians (and the parallel journey of the modern-day Chinese church), who responded to the Roman state's idolatrous declaration of Caesar as lord by declaring that "Jesus is Lord." Yet they did so from the margins of society, operating as yeast, infiltrating every aspect of the culture without resorting to the tools of the system (high control of society and being the dominant voice in the land). The 1,700-year experience of much of Christianity since becoming legal in the Roman Empire – where the church gradually became synonymous with the state and owned the tallest and best buildings in town to prove its status – is a salutary lesson in correctly aligning our interaction with public space.

The synagogue gathering was developed during the Babylonian exile, when the Temple was not physically available as a center of worship and community life. For Jesus, there was a significant disconnect with life in the (rebuilt) Temple, since the folding together of political, royal, and religious power around this center meant that it was not spiritually available as a center of worship and community life. In both cases, God brought cleansing by removing his people from the influence of institutions that had become spiritually polluted.

Yet for the people of God, the question was how they should worship and gather. "How can we sing the songs of the Lord while in a foreign land?" What does faith look like beyond the existing institutions? What are the good values that underlie the original founding of those ways of meeting with God and being a light to the nations?

For the early church, the answer to the challenge of being excluded from Temple worship was to draw from the synagogue – or *oikos* – life and do what the people experienced there. Thus, they gathered in natural relationships around food, Scripture, worship, and listening to what the Lord was specifically saying to them and their context. They sought to be a blessing to the wider world through service, especially to the lost, the last, and the least and found authentic ways to proclaim the Good News of God's Kingdom.

Learning from Social Space in Scripture

Today, Christians are once again on the margins of society, and in many contexts, the inherited modes of "doing" church are increasingly proving inadequate for reaching the lost. While we are not advocating a simplistic deconstruction of all existing church gatherings, we can learn much from how the people of God in the Old and New Testaments developed their lives in social space, in response to massive cultural (and spiritual) shifts going on around them. As we gather with our families and friends, our household and *oikos*, we can turn again to the Scriptures and see how the Lord will shape our community in their light.

As we reflect upon the four spaces, we see clear parallels in church life.

TYPE OF SPACE	CHURCH PARALLEL
PUBLIC	Celebration (i.e., large "Sunday" services) *Over 100 people*
SOCIAL	Missional Community *Ideally 20 to 50+ people*
PERSONAL	Small Group *Approximately 3 to 12 people*
INTIMATE	Accountability Partner(s) *1 or 2 people*

One of the most important things to realize is that people can belong to any of the different types of gathering. The journey of connecting with others involves all four types of space, so churches need to consider carefully how people can access all four. People belong to one another at different levels of intensity, and healthy churches enable people to belong to all four gathering sizes.

The Idol of Intimacy

A complicating factor is that in recent years Christians have tended to idolize the notion of intimacy, as if that should be the goal of all (or at least most) relationships. When we study the principles of the four spaces, we realize what complete nonsense that idea is. Intimacy is not the over-riding goal or the most important level (imagine being married to someone who was completely terrible in any of the other three spaces!).

All connections are significant and bring value and belonging. This also challenges what our expectation should be of an encounter with God: should we be experiencing "intimacy" as the sole hallmark of authentic worship in every gathering size?

In practice, the smaller the group, the harder it is to organize the group on behalf of someone else. Social engineering may work to some extent at a celebration-level gathering (we "force" a wide variety of people to mingle and worship together), where arguably it is to some extent a pragmatic necessity. However, we can't organize someone's closest and most intimate relationships (unless we are trying to form a cult), so church leadership and community can only model, encourage and, maybe, resource deeper relationships.

Belonging in Four Spaces

When someone comes into our church community, at whatever gathering size, that person is hoping for some level of relational connection. For this to be fully expressed, we need to enable people to come to the place where they experience this in all four spaces (or the top three at least, since those are the ones that we can organize). This is not usually an overnight occurrence, but nevertheless, this should be our goal, as this will provide the various contexts required for all individuals to gain and give the most.

We also need to recall what it is like to come into a very large institution. People who come into public space can still feel desperately lonely, because it takes time to find others you can trust. In public space, we should welcome strangers as belonging, whether they are participating in a single or ongoing gathering. For example, using humor allows us to offer a degree of detachment that helps relax people. Recognizing the physical distance component, we should also expect little physical contact, especially without permission.

I (Alex) recall visiting a church on vacation where we turned up late (a treat for a church leader!) but had to run the gauntlet of sweaty, deodorant-free men insisting on trying to hug all of us before they would allow us entry into the school hall where the service was taking place. Needless to say, that was not a terribly welcoming experience and not a wise course of action in public space.

Now that doesn't stop us doing physical things (e.g., taking communion, laying on hands when praying for healing, a welcoming handshake, a helping hand with toddlers or strollers, conversation over coffee, etc.), but people should be given room to stay in public space and not be jumped through the different spaces (especially not to intimate space!).

The challenge for church leaders is to offer high-quality experiences in the different spaces, notably weekend services, Missional Communities and smaller groups. We need to consider what that looks like and how it is achievable in our particular context, without exhausting ourselves in the process by building overly high-maintenance structures.

Restoring Social Space through Missional Communities

Obviously, the main purpose of this book is to look at social space, or what we call Missional Communities, since this is very much the missing link in the church today. Western churches tend to offer only two ways to belong: public space and some kind of blend of personal/intimate. If we are to develop church in social space, how are we going to use it smartly in order to reach the lost and extend the Kingdom? How can a church in social space build deeper and stronger relational ties and a sense of identity for those who want to belong? The nuances of these solutions vary across generations and in different cultures, but our 3experience is that MCs provide a structure that can bring many of the answers to light.

Some churches will protest that they do already operate in social space, but it is important to do an honest analysis. For instance, do your gatherings that are that size genuinely foster a sense of connectedness, or do they actually function as dialed-down public space where the focus is still on a presentation from the front?

Setting the Right Outcomes

A couple of other practical points: with leading at any size, it is important to aim for the right outcomes for the group. In other words, don't expect (or build expectations for) things to occur that won't happen in that size of gathering. In particular, there is always a provider-client pressure, to give to people exactly what they think they want. Pandering to this provides short-term conflict relief, but in the long-term, such compromise will inhibit growth.

As many leaders in churches know, eventually we may easily end up serving the machine of church and, left unhindered, it becomes all-consuming.

We know this. We've seen it. We've experienced it.

Thus, for MCs, the classic pressure is to provide a small group experience, especially when the Missional Community is new and emerging and perhaps the size is still somewhere in the teens. People, especially evangelical Christians, seem to love the idea of sitting around in a circle of fifteen people sharing their prayer requests or having Bible study after Bible study (or watching NOOMA after NOOMA!). Apparently, that is authentic community.

The problem is that such a group size is already way too big to work effectively in personal space (can you really remember fifteen prayer requests?). Thus, what is shared will be shallow (or dominated by the emotionally demanding person), because, major crises aside, subconsciously people will know not to share private information in that size of gathering. Thus, running an MC like a small group is a sure inhibitor for any sort of growth. Instead, we should always break down into small groups (personal space) to share private thoughts, needs, and requests.

Another way to tackle this dilemma is for the leader to have the group act "up" to the social group size. When a group grows from one space to another, there will always be a transition phase. At that time, the group must start operating in its new space. Thus, a new MC in the teens should act as if there are already twenty-five people there, doing only social space activities. Although people will put pressure on for the small group experience (particularly if the MC has grown from a small group), the leader must firmly resist that pressure.

For a Missional Community that is in the teens in size, inviting more people to join needs to be the top priority. The danger of a group settling at twelve to eighteen people is that it will operate like a big small group and won't have the resources and momentum for effective mission. It is hard to form a leadership team out of this sized group, and most of the people will default to thinking the leader will do everything, which leads, of course, to consumerism. One practical idea is for the MC to spend some time at the next gathering brainstorming names. Have each person write down the names of at least two or three people he or she could invite. Make sure you have several MC gatherings coming up that will be good for those new people to have an authentic taste of your community and its mission. Shoot for twenty people as a baseline to build the social space momentum.

Define Your Gatherings by Values

"If you focus on principles, you empower everyone to act without constant monitoring, evaluating, correcting or controlling."[42]

In developing MCs (and, indeed, each of the four spaces), we have a natural tendency to define the gatherings by structures and the specific details of what we do (e.g., Sundays are 25 minutes of guitar-led worship, then we share Communion, followed by 5 minutes of announcements and a 30-minute talk; mystifyingly, Acts 2:42-47 is usually be cited as the rationale for this). Now, none of those things are wrong – personally, we enjoy all of them – and that may well be an accurate listing of what we do. However, if we define the gathering by such a description, then we will quickly set those structures in stone, leaving little freedom to innovate and try better ways of doing things, particularly as the Lord leads us in new directions.

Instead of defining gatherings by structure, a better path is to define them by the undergirding values. This allows room for flexibility in ideas and new ways of doing things to occur without causing huge fights!

Here's what we need to think through: what is the measurement that will guide what we say yes to? Is our goal really "25 minutes of guitar-led worship," or is our goal a deeper value?

We strongly encourage you to take some time to define the three gathering sizes (celebration, MCs, and smaller groups), asking yourself, what are the unique outcomes that you are looking to see at each size? What are the core values that must be present on an ongoing basis at each size for it to be successful? Once you have those nailed, it is much easier to know where there is room for experimentation and where there isn't.

Will this frustrate some of your MC leaders at first? Probably.

More than likely, they are used to you tightly defining every detail of their meetings. But in the long run, it will allow far more creativity to bubble up in their particular mission context.

To help you on your way, here is an attempt to record the values for each of the three gatherings in just three words for each one. You don't have to do it this way, but we urge you not to write lengthy statements.

No one will remember them, and they will become functionally useless.

Try the discipline of deciding what are the three most important and distinct things for each level of gathering. Keep it simple, memorable, and clearly focused.

GATHERING	DISTINCTIVE VALUES/OUTCOMES		
CELEBRATION	Inspiration	Momentum	Preaching
MISSIONAL COMMUNITY	Community	Mission	Training
SMALL GROUP	Support	Challenge	Closeness

When we gather in a large setting with hundreds of others, it is inspirational to worship God together and unite under the banner of Christ. Momentum builds as we hear stories and teaching that remind us that we are not isolated but actually are part of a movement of Kingdom-minded people who are seeking to transform our city. We are envisioned, fed, and stirred to response by outstanding preaching from people who are gifted and able to devote the time to prepare thoroughly.

MCs, at their core, are a community of people who love to be together and know how to have fun, as well as being a place of identity and generosity. This community is on a mission together to impact a particular network of relationships or neighborhood, by incarnating the Gospel into that specific context through words and deeds. This community is also a place of training, since an MC is the ideal size for people to try something (whether it's hospitality, leading worship, teaching, organizing, innovating – or anything else that could happen in an MC) while having a safe context to risk failing in.

Small groups have enormous value, too, for they achieve things not possible in larger contexts. We each need a place of support, where we can be encouraged and loved through the details of our lives, where we really do not want to be alone. However, this is no bland affirmation – it is a place of challenge, too, where we know someone will look us in the eye and ask about our hidden attitudes or call us out on inappropriate behavior. Yet there is a closeness that enfolds the support and challenge, so that we have a genuine depth of relationship there.

As we take these values, we can release individuals, leaders, and groups to put them into action as they see fit for their context. It is not the job of the main leaders of the church to run everything. Instead, they set the values and outcomes by which groups will be measured, providing tons of encouragement, wisdom, and practical support, thereby letting the Lord express himself in all manner of creative and wonderful ways.

As you wrestle with this idea of defining your structures by values (instead of vice versa), here's the question: What is it that you are hoping to see occur at each of the three gathering sizes?

Our starting suggestions for each space are listed above – we expect you will think of better words. Once you have those values defined for your context, you do still need to set out a default structure for living them out, since most people will find that helpful. If you don't, they'll be paralyzed and won't know how to act.

The reason we like building around values is that it makes it far easier to say yes or no (or yes but . . .) to new ideas in a more positive and gracious manner. So often we do church by defining things by meetings or specific tasks. When we break new ground, the structures may well be full of life, but with a different generation, culture, or context, those same structures can stifle rather than innovate.

Of course, values are not necessarily universal and will need reviewing from time to time, but they will prove to be more long-lasting building blocks for mission, community, and worship. Values seem to reduce the likelihood of what we do becoming stagnant, allowing a smoother transition to new and different forms of church life that represent the same core values.

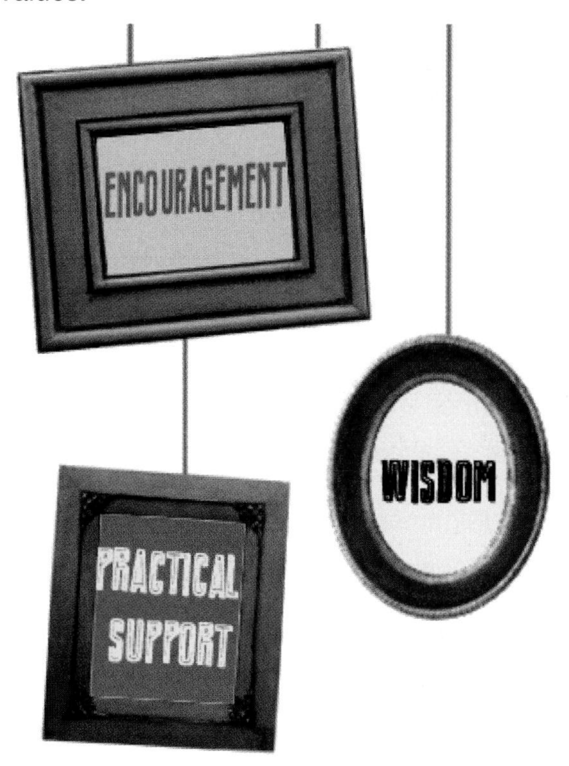

2.4 | ATTRACTIONAL VS. MISSIONAL

The debate continues to rage: *Attractional vs. Missional.* Is one model better? Worse? Which is more effective? Can they work together? Do they have to be separate? While the debate itself can be a bit overwhelming and heated at times, the interesting thing about all of this is that this isn't the first time we've seen this conflict play out in church history. In European history, we see this question being raised and answered in *Minster* churches (or monastic mission centers), which we have come to call "resourcing churches."

What we see is the two dominant church models of the day, the Roman and the Celtic, combined to great effect to evangelize Europe.

In the **Roman model**, there was a very "if you build it, they will come" mentality (this is pre-Reformation). You establish a new mission base in the church and then invite people into it.

Now what happened is that many of these missions grew. In fact, some grew to be very large. In almost every way you can think, they developed into the mega-churches of their day. They were the event-driven Pilgrimage sites of the Middle Ages. The pivotal festival weeks turned into massive occasions, which are where Chaucer's *Canterbury Tales* take place – on Pilgrimage!

These Pilgrimage sites (which later turned into cathedrals) were less about outreach and far more about *in-drag*.

Notice we are not saying this is wrong. In the Jewish and Christian traditions, there has been a strong place for the event-driven Pilgrimage. Think about it this way: a Jew in Jesus' day went to the Temple only twice a year, with the local synagogue (a group usually consisting of fifty to sixty people) the regular place of worship each week. That's what we're talking about here. The festivals at the cathedrals in the Middle Ages usually took place only a few times each year. The festivals were never meant to be an every-week thing.

As it turned out, these cathedrals had all of the problems that people attribute (often unfairly) to mega-churches: nominalism, consumerism, and accusations of growing disciples a mile wide and an inch deep. It's not that the cathedrals wanted it that way; it's just that it happened that way. People wanted the "cathedral" experience more and more.

However, we also have the **Celtic model**.

The Celts had something very organic happening. It was mobile. It was agile. It was missional. *Perigrination* (meaning, "the wanderer"). The Celtic Christians were known as "Wanderers for Christ." They left the island and simply wandered around Europe and evangelized the fiercest people you can imagine: Germans, Vikings, wild northern tribes of England. The Celts were constantly in fear of death. It's hard to really grasp how barbaric these tribes were that the Celts "wandered" into.

The strength of the Celtic approach was that all sorts of people were being reached who otherwise would not have seen how following Christ could make sense in their context. However, the critiques often made of the more radical missional forms of church were made of the Celts as well: a lack of accountability, being judgmental toward the wider church, a tendency to compromise the Gospel for the sake of connecting with the society.

Now, a pivotal turning point for both models was the Synod of Whitby (AD 664). The Celts made a decision to join in with everyone else, creating a *combination* of Roman and Celtic models into one. In other words, they began to work together. The missional churches that were being started were no longer just outposts for the missional frontier but a place of invitation and in-gathering. This combination of mission and invitation proved to be a killer combination for the evangelizing of Europe.

The story of the Romans and the Celts coming together in the Synod of Whitby is basically saying, "My weakness is your strength. What if we could figure out a way to work together?"

Here's the question we would pose: What if the purpose of attractional celebrations isn't to make disciples in the same way that Missional Communities can? What if attractional celebrations serve a profound purpose, but it isn't the everyday, ins-and-outs, life-on-life of making a disciple? What if we shouldn't expect attractional celebrations to do this?

The killer combination for evangelizing Europe was understanding what each group did, what each group didn't do, and then figuring out what was necessary for bringing them to work together. Basically, neither did everything on its own, and they needed each other.

With cathedrals, you create natural in-drag. The cathedrals that dotted the larger cities in Europe became places of Pilgrimage for believers, a chance to experience the transcendence of God but to do so with a really large number of believers. We often forget that the majority of Europe was made up of very small, mostly agrarian villages, so the opportunity to worship with a large number of people together was a rarity. Thus, you have people journeying to a Pilgrimage site where they would worship our Risen Lord with more people in one place than perhaps they had ever seen before.

Lesslie Newbigin said that the church is to be "a sign, instrument and foretaste" of the reign of God.[43] We can see that happening here with these experiences. If you are used to worshipping with a few dozen people in your village and suddenly you are worshipping with hundreds or maybe thousands of people, then that is a pretty powerful sign and foretaste of the life to come.

People recognized that these journeys were important, that in them people gained a real picture of being connected to something much bigger than just their local village and extended family. However, lasting transformation is found in the day-to-day and is only *reinforced* by the Pilgrimage experience.

So when we talk about the merging of the Roman model and the Celtic model, the merging worked when each understood its unique purpose. The small village missions that people attended locally were pioneering the missional frontiers and discipling people and reaching into un-evangelized villages. At the same time, people were connected to a cathedral where, every once in a while, everyone gathered and saw just how big and glorious the Kingdom of God was. When these models worked in tandem together, they evangelized the whole of Europe. The combination of a missional, sending center (the cathedral) and the smaller, missional outposts won the day.[44]

However, obviously there have been some massive shifts since this time, haven't there? It's not as if Europe is the epicenter of brilliant mission and radical discipleship. So here's the million-dollar question: what happened?

And, honestly, this is really where we find ourselves today, isn't it? We are looking around at the landscape of the church in our culture and asking, "What in the world just happened?"

The answer for the Middle Ages is ours for today: over time, the pilgrims went to the cathedral and wanted the cathedral experience in their home churches every Sunday. They saw the choirs, the orchestras, the smoke, the light pouring through the giant stained-glass windows, walls painted with scenes from Scripture, gorgeous tapestries, listening to the famous bishop preaching. It was a lot like going to Catalyst, really. Honestly, that's really what it was in the Middle Ages.

So they saw that, took part in everything the festival experience had to offer, and went back to their local parish church, looked at their priest dressed in his shabby, brown cassock, and said, "You know, you really ought to dress like they do in the cathedral! Maybe put on some nice robes! And their choir – well, all we've got is this guy who, when he sings, it sounds like a dying cat. Couldn't we have a choir, too?"

Essentially, things started to drift.

Now actually, we know the guys who put on *Catalyst*, they're good friends, and we know that's not what they are hoping to do. They are simply trying to pull together the best input on leadership in the most accessible environment possible. But for medieval Europe, we think slowly, over time, there was a real misunderstanding of the purpose of the cathedral and the purpose of the local parish mission. And slowly, over time, the local parish missions became mini-cathedrals (or at least as best they could). But when they did that, they lost the powerful missional engine into the local context and, consequently, the ability to disciple people.

Before this transition, more focus was on the time outside Sunday, whereas this made Sunday the most important day of the week. Community church life became completely about the service. When the Sunday service becomes the center of discipleship and the service is geared more around watching and consuming (which it's almost impossible not to do when it's geared around a "big show"), discipleship becomes really hard. How can we do 1 Corinthians 11-14 in a community like that?

As our good friend Alan Hirsch has said, "We can't consume our way to discipleship." What we see in Europe now is almost one thousand years of that kind of thinking.

What we see in the United States today is churches, by and large, trying to make a contemporary cathedral experience every Sunday morning. When at least 85% of our dollars, energy, and human resources go to that one day a week, how can churches really expect to also engage in meaningful mission and discipleship? There's simply nothing left in the tank to do that with.

And that's really the pulling and the discomfort that we're sensing in the *Attractional vs. Missional* debate. The truth of the matter is that we need both to work in tandem together; we need both to realize their unique purpose. When this is done well, we've seen whole cities start to change. Ultimately, we are about calling cities and regions and countries back to God and seeing them transformed. If that's what we want to do, we really need only to look back into our own history to see how it was done, to look at what went well and where the temptations may be for us.

What we find in Missional Communities is the ability to do both. The ability to have a pioneering, low-maintenance, laity-driven vehicle on the frontlines of the missional frontier being resourced and equipped by a mission center where everyone can gather, celebrate what God has done, look to what he will do, experience a bigger story, and go back into the mission fields. Of course, we recognize the rhythm of this will look different from that of seventh-century Europe, but the underlying principle holds true.

In the book *AND: The Scattered and Gathered Church*, Hugh Halter and Matt Smay write, "The idea of the AND is that every church can find a balance of both scattering people out for mission while maintaining a biblically meaningful reason to gather together."[45]

Jon Tyson, pastor at Trinity Grace Church in New York City, put it this way: "We have Missional Communities that meet during the week and our borough churches (various campuses that meet throughout NYC) gather each Sunday, but every 6 weeks the whole church comes together and it's like freaking *Hillsong United*. We have the lights, the band, the lasers, amazing teaching, the whole show. And we have no problem with that. It's only happening once every 6 weeks."[46]

And there is something to that, right? It isn't that a thousand people getting together to worship God with one voice in an electric experience isn't meaningful. Something in that is a reflection of Isaiah 6 or Revelation 21 and a foretaste of the fulfilled Kingdom to come. But it's meaningful because it's seen through the lens of having done mission. It's meaningful because we are reminded of how big the story is that we are participating in when we all gather together. It's meaningful because it sends us back out into the mission field with fresh energy, vigor, and enthusiasm.

We just need to understand what *Attractional* does well and do it.

We need to understand what *Missional* does well and do it.

2.5 | LEADERSHIP

The Leader

I wanna be the leader
I wanna be the leader
Can I be the leader?
Can I? I can?
Promise? Promise?
Yippee, I'm the leader
I'm the leader.

OK, what shall we do?

Roger McGough

As hopefully has already become clear, you can't move into Missional Communities without first creating missional leaders. While in some ways the bar can be quite low, in others it requires a mindset and attitude of heart that the church has not always been very good at encouraging.

The best MC leaders are completely devoted to following Christ into the mission field, recognizing that, wherever they are, the fields around them today are white unto harvest. If these leaders find themselves in an especially tiring or challenging season of life, they still view themselves as missionaries into those tough places. As the leaders allow God to work through them in those everyday situations and interactions of life, they find rich blessing and fresh grace given to them, by the Holy Spirit, their team, and those they are seeking to reach.

Truly, this becomes a lifestyle that they want forever. They know they have been ruined by this way of living and seeing lives around them transformed. They can never go back to the old ways of doing things.

We honestly believe that releasing leaders who are not paid to live out their calling is a very real and tangible way of embracing the priesthood of all believers.

Team-building Vocabulary

Sometimes the theory of what you will be trying to build can be best expressed through a few simple phrases that form part of your language of discipleship within your church body. A couple of bits of vocabulary we have found helpful in encouraging team-building include the following:

- **Low Control, High Accountability** – One of the key principles behind Missional Communities is that of releasing God's people to do God's work. This means enabling leaders to pursue the creative dreams that God has put on their hearts for Spirit-led, mission-in-community. This applies to how MC leaders lead as well as to the overall church leadership, since all leaders should be aiming to give away as much power as possible. This is what is meant by low control – those with the most power (i.e., those at the center) don't hold onto it but rather release it to those with the mission vision (i.e., those who are on the edge of the church where it touches the wider world).

  At the same time, entrusted people need to be deeply accountable for their character and the way in which they lead. They cannot simply be given access to some money, the church photocopier, and space on the bulletin sheet and left alone to do whatever they like. Even if they are incredibly mature and experienced, they will not be as effective as they could be. And, of course, if they have areas of immaturity or inexperience, it could be a recipe for disaster.

This is what is meant by high accountability.

More generally within the Missional Community, the principle of low control, high accountability needs to work itself out. Thus, with the highly demanding person, the leader will refuse either to be controlled or seek to control but rather will challenge that person to live within accountable relationships. Sometimes this might happen to be with the group leader, but more often, it will be with a few others, generally from within the MC. With regular group members, the leader will release creativity and innovation, holding people to the standard of the underlying values and vision that the group shares. With high-capacity group members, as time goes by, the leader will increasingly freely delegate and allow them to do things "their way," but at the same time giving clear feedback to help hone them into all that they can be in Christ.

- **Low Control, High Accountability in the Marketplace** – In the business world, this principle has started to emerge in some of the most innovative companies, especially those in the knowledge sector (which churches would fall into). They are seeing that relaxation of control by senior managers (leaders) is producing hugely enhanced results. An article in the *Harvard Business Review* in December 2009 reviewed this trend: "In chaotic times, an executive's instinct may be to strive for greater efficiency by tightening control. But the truth is that relinquishing authority and giving employees considerable autonomy can boost innovation and success at knowledge firms, even during crises." The authors give two very dramatic examples (from the consulting and IT sectors) of how "this counterintuitive idea can dramatically improve results."[47]

  The authors conclude the following:

  1. Organizations that are "reliant on knowledge and innovation should abandon the traditional structure in which decision rights are reserved for people at the top."
  2. "We have found that contrary to what many CEOs assume, leadership is not really about delegating tasks and monitoring results; it is about imbuing the entire workforce with a sense of responsibility for the business." They call this mutualism, whereby staff are measured against qualitative values such as trust, responsibility, and innovation.
  3. What is even more interesting is that the companies that are successfully implementing such an approach end up with an accompanying process that facilitates high accountability, often through peer relationships that allow the most effective leaders to come to the fore.

- **Lightweight and Low Maintenance** – This means creating models and structures within the community that are not all-consuming.

  So often leaders within the church develop far too complex approaches that quickly become monsters that demand to be fed with the best resources available. For instance, the children's activities do not need to be to the standard of Disneyland in order to be effective.

Bible studies are great, but we need to model a way of unpacking Scripture that comes out of what Jesus has been speaking to us about during our personal encounters with him that week. Sadly, too often the church has institutionalized the study of Scripture, turning it into a professionals-only area, with the norm being epic hours of preparation and an over-emphasis on academic understanding rather than heart response to the "now-word" of the Lord.

The question is, can someone who dropped out of high school effectively lead a Bible study, or do we condescendingly smile at his heartfelt passion and sharing of what God is speaking to him about, and wait for the "real study" to come back round next week? (For more thoughts regarding *how* this can be done, see the IN chapter of MC Life.)

> **"Can we find ways to equip all types of people, from all types of background, to be Kingdom leaders and planters of Missional Communities, or do our leaders all need to be college graduates?"**

If the Gospel is to be incarnated into every neighborhood, we need flexible and lightweight models that can adapt to the particular cultures that we find there, allowing all types of leaders to step forward.

- **Everyone Can Play** – Let's encourage our leaders to expect everyone in their MC to come ready to give more than he or she will receive. If we are the body of Christ, then we need all members to perform their function freely. Participation increases through intentionality. The leaders and the most gifted need to step back and create the space for others to realize that they can step forward. The challenge after that will be for the teachers not to immediately step straight back in and make sure that the "correct" answer or way of doing things is reasserted! It is OK for things not to be perfect and to be left that way. Family life is messy, and while we want to do as good a job as possible, we will quickly prevent the less experienced/gifted/ competent from sharing if they are, in effect, publicly critiqued and implicitly shown up.
- Multiplication from Day One – The mindset from the outset is that "our Missional Community will one day multiply." The group then talks, prays, and plans toward it. Whether that day comes quicker or slower than expected, with a lengthy build-up or seemingly out of the blue, the wise leader will have prepared the way by building that expectation into the values and dreams of the Missional Community.

Who Can Be an MC Leader?

As we interact with people who are wonder-ing if they can start or help lead a Missional Community, we try not to make the filter too complicated. The following might be a quick checklist:

1) Are they committed to Christ?
2) Are they committed to our church?
3) Do they have a clear mission vision?
4) Are they willing to be accountable?
5) Will others follow them?

Obviously, the exact parameters for being ready for MC leadership vary from church to church, as history and context play a part in how these decisions are reached. In places where there has been a history of leadership failure or abuse, there will naturally be a

> “Leadership is the capacity and will to rally people to achieve a common purpose and the character that will inspire confidence.”
>
> Field Marshal Montgomery of Alamein

concern to ensure that MC leaders are carefully selected and held highly accountable.

In a church that has gone through much change, including external change in the church's cultural context, there may well be strong (if unspoken) pressure for leaders to focus on providing strong pastoral care and support. In a place where people are not used to being released into leadership, there may be a lack of willingness to step forward and offer to serve as leaders.

In other contexts, perhaps a new church plant or a new expression of church within a larger body, the leadership criteria might be much looser, even virtually non-existent. The emphasis may well be on everyone making an attempt, although the danger is that the mindset could become elitist and even proud – "we're going to show how church really should be done."

These responses, while totally understandable, can lead to problems further down the line. So we encourage you to take time to think through where the bar needs to be for your context.

As we look at churches we know with Missional Communities, we do see some criteria generally in operation, some explicitly and others implicitly. These tend to include the following:

- **Being a believer for a period of time before becoming an MC leader** – The most common time lag seems to be "at least one year." While non-Christians are found as part of most Missional Communities, with some clearly having leadership gifts, all of the churches we know would say that a clear and firm commitment to Christ is foundational to effective leadership in the church, whatever the gifting.

  If we unpack this point, we see three main themes emerge:

  1. **Is their character on the path to Christ-likeness?** Clearly, character is the fundamental attribute for any leader, so without making the bar unrealistically high, MC leaders need to be people of godly character if they are to be effective.
  2. **Are they free from any overt or significant bondage to sin?** This doesn't mean that they are perfect, but it does mean that they can reasonably serve as a model to others in things such as self-control, inner healing, and freedom from addiction.
  3. **Do they have a general knowledge of basic doctrines?** While knowing lots of theology doesn't make someone an MC leader, someone who is empty headed isn't much use either, so leaders should have a grasp of orthodox Christian belief.

- **Being a regular part of that church community** – Somewhere around the sixth to ninth month mark seems to be the absolute minimum in most churches (an analogy with pregnancy has been made here!). The rationale is that these things are "better caught than taught," so a potential leader is best trained in a healthy, existing Missional Community. To judge how well someone has "caught it" is something that can be measured only by face-to-face interaction with him or her and his or her current MC leader.

We also recommend an assessment of how committed the person is to the whole church body. It is a nightmare to have an MC where the leaders are constantly tugging against the flow of the whole church, creating their own private fiefdom.

Seriously. Nightmare.

Dealing with leaders who want to be like that takes a great deal of wisdom and energy, with resulting implications for their group and for the other MC leaders watching. This potential pitfall for the Missional Community model is best pre-empted by having a culture of discipleship and accountability.

At this stage, some churches choose to assess how financially committed that individual is to the church. Obviously, this will be influenced by your wider church culture on how you talk about and deal with issues to do with tithing, giving, and finances in general.

- **Do they have a clear mission vision?** – No one can start a Missional Community and expect it to grow numerically if this isn't nailed down. Often the temptation is to let people off the hook with some vague answer, such as, "We are here to love God, love one another, and love our world." Now, obviously there is truth in this, but since it's as true in SoHo, New York City, as it is in Orange County, California, functionally, it's meaningless.

  Our approach is to make people write their mission vision down in one or two sentences. They must be specific to the context. This will enable the group members to know exactly what they are going to put their proactive energy into.

If the mission vision is something that someone in a city one thousand miles away could sign up for, then the vision is too broad. If the mission vision can't be said in one or two short sentences, then it needs further clarification, so that the center of the bull's-eye is unmissable.

At times, we have sent people's proposed mission vision back to them three or four times, until they have refined it into something that will work. They may not always like you for this at the time, but in the long run, they will thank you because the group will have a far clearer sense of identity and destiny. Their approach to IN and UP will subsequently be determined by this OUT focus. Thus, this exercise helps give the leader the ability to know when to say "yes" and when to say "no." (See later in the book for an exercise you can give your leaders in helping them determine their mission focus.)

As an aside, we *never* try to tell the leader what the mission should be, though we are often asked. As leaders, they need to own it fully themselves so that they are responsible for its implementation and outcome.

This is a crucial point, one that will determine how successful MCs are in your community: your MC leaders need to feel like the vision for their MC is something specific that God has placed on their hearts, not something the leaders thought would be cool, simply a good idea, or more detrimentally, *the idea and vision you gave them to enact*.

Missional Communities work brilliantly because the plans, implementation, and ownership belong to lay leaders and their lay leadership teams. You simply hold them accountable to the plans they have come up with and the way in which they operate as leaders and a community.

As leaders, we can offer wisdom and experience on how likely something is to succeed, what some of the potential pitfalls might be, who might be a good person to mine for information, etc., but ultimately, we must let them take responsibility for the focus and shape of their MCs.

- **Are they willing to be accountable?** – You can assess this by directly asking your potential leaders, as well as listening to what others say about them.

  Put another way, how well do these potential leaders submit to those over them? Are these potential leaders loyal, constructive, and servant-hearted, or are they proud, challenging, and disruptive? People who lead the potential leaders will usually be very insightful about this.

  For the churches we have led, this means that potential leaders commit to being fully engaged in the life of a leadership Huddle. All MC leaders need a place of encouragement and accountability where they stop to consider what Jesus is saying to them and what they are doing in response to that word. For our churches, this was a non-negotiable and how we put into effect low control (we truly release people to follow whatever God puts on their hearts for an MC) and high accountability (in Huddles). We have found from experience that we need to make this clear up front, so MC leaders are quite clear about this expectation from the beginning.

- **Will others follow them?** – Often, MC leaders expect senior leaders to find the group members for them. Nevertheless, one of the tests of whether a potential MC leader is ready is whether he or she can gather enough people to make it viable. At this point, we insert lots of qualifying clauses such as it takes time, different personality types, deeply challenging mission contexts, etc., all of which are true. However, a group needs to reach a certain size to be effective over the long term, and some people simply do not have the leadership capacity to achieve that.

  They aren't bad. It's not that others are more important. It's simply that some have been gifted with being an L50 leader (someone with the capacity to lead at least fifty people) and others haven't.

  Ideally, we identify that before they are released, or months later we must be prepared to walk leaders through the disappointment of realizing that the group is not going to be sustainable.

  Sometimes the conclusion might be simple – it was the right leaders and the right vision but the wrong timing. Whatever the case, we need to be honest and candid in debriefing them, so that they are not left bitter and damaged by the experience (see later in the book for practicalities on how to help MCs end well).

Mixing in the Four C's

You might have heard leaders such as Bill Hybels talk about his three C's of team-building,[48] namely Character, Competency, and Chemistry, to which we would add a fourth, Capacity. You can parallel those with our criteria for Missional Community leaders, to make a more complete model:

Are they committed to Christ?
Will they be accountable? = CHARACTER

It's useless to have someone with leadership skills who doesn't have the character to see it through to the end.

If people are flakey, then they probably aren't yet ready. Will they do what they say they are going to do?

Do they have a clear mission vision? = COMPETENCY

Can they seek and listen to the Lord for his direction and then work out how to put that into ongoing, consistent action that bears long-term fruit?

Are they committed to this church? = CHEMISTRY

In other words, do they "click" with the church culture and the church leadership? You don't have to be best friends, but if they are not prepared to submit to authority, there will be problems down the line.

Will others follow them? = CAPACITY

People often intuit whether someone has the ability and anointing to build and grow something of a certain size, and vote accordingly with their feet. This is a way to measure a leader's spiritual capacity at a particular time.

How Leadership Criteria Were Publicized in One Church

Here is an example of how you can establish MC leaders within your church community. The feel is intentionally positive, and the idea is that the major problem is lack of people who feel confident enough to step forward, rather than too many loose cannons who need scaring off. Of course, for anyone who expresses an interest, many conversations will follow. With some people, you know almost immediately that they will be able to do an outstanding job; with some others, you simply need to invest a little in that person, and occasionally, you find people for whom the timing is not right. This was how one church publicly described its core values for a leader:

Who Can Be a Missional Community Leader?

At this point, you may find it helpful to know our core criteria for MC leaders. This is written for a potential MC leader to read and respond to.

1. You love Jesus and are committed to being his disciple forever.
2. You love this church and are committed to being part of things here for the next season of your life (i.e., you need to expect to be around long enough to properly establish, develop, deepen, and multiply leadership in any new group). You will have a track record of service and involvement in the church, so that we know you share our vision and values.
3. You have leadership gifting and are willing to fully connect into our ongoing investment process for leaders that we call Huddles.
4. You have a vision for a Missional Community that incorporates UP, IN and OUT, but can above all be defined by a specific OUT focus. This can be to a neighborhood or to a network (e.g., the urban poor, students from a particular college, business leaders, a specific neighborhood, etc.). Basically, it can be anything that is definable where you could reasonably build an MC.
5. You can gather enough people around you and the vision God has placed in your heart to make something happen!

Leaders Who Build Teams

If leaders are to stay for the long-term, they need to experience leadership as part of the rhythm of their life, rather than a burden to carry. This is especially true for the volunteers who so heroically serve as MC leaders! Additionally, if they can pull this off, then they probably will lead the group into a balanced yet fruitful pattern of growing with God, building community, and going in mission.

To achieve this, leaders of Missional Communities must understand that they are not to do everything themselves or be the "always available with an answer or an assist" person! Their role is more like the conductor of an orchestra and certainly is not that of a one-man band. The leader is there to empower group members to empower others, under the authority and power of the Holy Spirit.

Read again: MC leaders cannot and should not be the only leaders in their MCs.

Like a gifted orchestra conductor, an MC leader brings the best out of his or her leaders (the woodwinds section leader, the strings section leader, the percussion section leader) and brings it all together, in a cohesive way, to make something beautiful.

The traditional model (of a "pastor" who provides religious goods and services to anyone who asks, however unreasonable his or her demands) is neither a healthy nor an effective model. As Rick Warren writes, "The church is a greedy animal, where Parkinson's Law operates in terms of 'needs expand to consume resources available.'"[49]

The MC leader is a helper, coming alongside others to cast vision for a community that goes in mission in the name of Christ. MC leaders recognize that there are others in the group who are better suited to perform most functions. Even if the leaders happen to be the most gifted, they want to train and release others, so those who come after can go further than the leaders have.

In practice, this means that the leader's job is not to pastor and disciple everyone but to make sure everyone has the opportunity to be pastored and discipled. The leaders keep the vision high on the agenda, calling people to a better future as the group brings more of the Kingdom into the context where they are called by God.

When the group is new, the leader plays a more directive role, as is appropriate when the vision is being established in the hearts and minds of those who initially gather. Yet even then leaders don't do everything, and others are very much involved. As the group goes through the different phases of following a call, the leader shifts his or her role from visionary to coach to help people through the inevitable dip, as the scale of the task starts to dawn and the initial energy has dropped away. As the leaders walk people through that, gradually the leaders' role morphs to become more of a consensus builder, enabling the growing maturity in the group to be expressed and the shared ownership of the mission vision to be creatively expressed.

Although this stage is often the most enjoyable and fruitful to be in, leaders at some point shift their focus to becoming a multiplier, preparing the way for the growing group to release new expressions of MCs that the Lord has been stirring up in the hearts of one or more people within the group. The leader at the same time is working out what the next season will look like for the community, as it gives birth and takes stock of what God is saying to community members as they review what has, and has not, been achieved. This process is very much one where the leader's team-building skills remain important.

Different Roles Involved in a Missional Community

As MCs develop, clearly certain roles start to form within the life of that community. This is a natural process, and so long as they remain useful and lightweight, a helpful development.

Examples might include the host for the evening (who oversees room layout, hospitality, etc.), food/drinks coordinator, facilitator for the actual session, children's coordinator, mission planner, newcomers welcome/ follow-up, worship (not necessarily a musical role), etc. You will easily begin to work out the ones that are helpful in your context. Some groups do this in a very informal, ad hoc manner ("Who wants to lead worship next time?"), whereas others are more structured, with some people clearly investing strongly in one particular area.

We encourage all leaders to make sure that the structure exists only to serve and doesn't become the main driver of what happens. For instance, just because you have someone coordinating worship doesn't mean you need to have a formal worship time every time you meet. But the principle is a good one, namely being intentional about making room for many different voices and gifts to contribute to the whole.

The other thing a leader must work out is how he or she is going to offer feedback and coach people. So if everyone arrives for MC and the host's house is a complete mess, that is something to process with them (later!). If someone tries leading some worship and it is done painfully badly, the leader has to decide whether to bring a merciful early end to the proceedings, as well as how best to help that person review what happened. A missional activity that is badly organized and attended is something that should not just be swept under the rug.

In our experience, while many newer MC leaders find the initial journey of learning to give honest feedback a struggle, over time it develops them and those they lead, as well as building their credibility within their community. This is an important value to build into your leaders (which you will model in Huddle).

Some Missional Community leaders have found writing out their expectations of those who seek to be part of the MC leadership team helpful. While not a common occurrence, writing out expectations can be helpful in certain mission contexts in which a high-commitment and high-accountability team is needed. For instance, we have one MC working to reach and impact an urban high school, so the members basically took the leaders' commitment from Young Life and adapted it for their purposes.

Keeping Your Leaders for the Long Haul

One of the issues for churches that develop strong small (or mid-sized) groups is how to prevent leadership burnout. So often, leaders take on groups, but within two years, an astonishingly high number have dropped out of leadership, often feeling sucked dry by the experience and far more reluctant to re-enter a position of leadership in the future. Sometimes this is caused by exceptional circumstances that no one could expect, but far more frequently, the problems could have been countered, or at least greatly reduced, at an earlier stage.

Building a High Invitation, High Challenge Culture

If you are to build a movement of multiplying Missional Communities, with leaders who are committed to a low-control, high-accountability lifestyle, then the aim is to lead in a way that offers

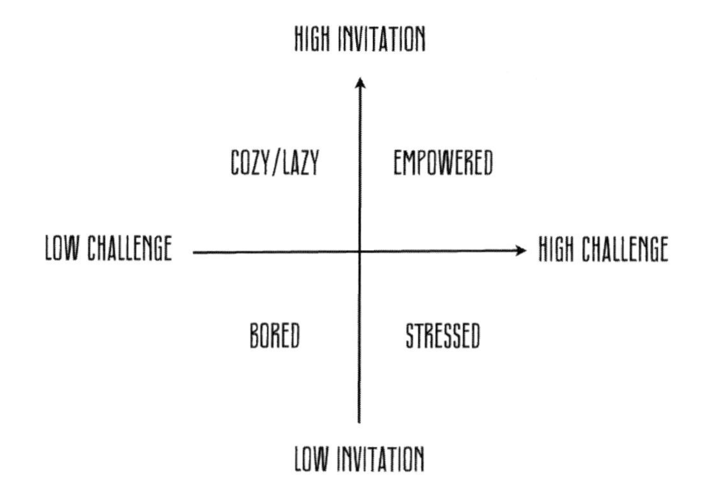

high invitation (or support) and high challenge.

Many churches create cultures that are high in invitation but low in challenge. This creates leaders who, essentially, are lazy – they feel loved and valued, but there is little emphasis on actually achieving anything for the Kingdom.

Other churches go the other way, being low in invitation and high in challenge. This produces leaders who, essentially, are driven – they have lots of goals and expectations placed upon them, and they are brought quickly to account if they don't meet expectations, but they are not valued for who they are as individuals, and there is little care and consideration for the realities of their personal life. These leaders quickly become frustrated and either quit or are on the edge of burnout.

A few really poorly led churches are low in invitation and challenge. For fairly obvious reasons, this leaves any leaders who are unfortunate enough still to be there in a state of boredom.

The goal is to build a church that is high in invitation and challenge. This produces leaders who are well placed to be fruitful and multiply the Kingdom into the lives of others. This is because the leaders are honored and loved for who they are, while also having clear goals and challenges at which to aim. They don't settle for second best and will be significant contributors to the Kingdom of God.

High Invitation: Rhythm of Life

One of the key issues that we see repeatedly with leaders is an unbalanced rhythm of life. Missional leaders almost always work too hard and don't intentionally take rest time – for themselves, their spouse, children, friends, and for their personal walk with the Father. Somehow all the Ten Commandments are valid, except for the one about having a day off, which in our work-ethic-driven culture we have marked with a little asterisk and put a footnote reading, "Optional if you are about the Lord's business"!

Even if we do take a day off, many leaders have an internal sacred/ everyday divide, leading them not to take care of themselves for the marathon we are in. A recent study by Ellison Research showed that 71% of U.S. pastors admit to being overweight, by an average of 32.1 pounds.

Not exactly good stewardship of what the Lord has given us.

David Putnam and Shawn Lovejoy commented on this in an article addressed to church planters but clearly it applies to all leaders: "Planting a church comes with a high price. First of all, let's dispel the myth that you can plant a church without paying the price. Because of this you have to make taking care of yourself a high priority. A church planter must nurture his vitality. This requires taking regular time to refuel your emotional, relational, physical and relational vitality. Paying close attention to these gauges can add longevity and impact to your life and ministry . . . As a leader, if you don't nurture your own vitality and monitor your own pace, no one else will."[50]

If we want to be effective for the Kingdom long term, we must take care of ourselves.

This has to be non-negotiable.

A variety of tools help leaders process this issue and think it through.[51] We must help our leaders balance their lives, so that they can run a marathon, not a sprint. When people "burn out," it is because they have not done this, often with their church leaders being fully complicit in their unhealthy lifestyle in the run-up to the explosion. Our responsibility is to not let this happen on our watch!

Doing This in Community

One of our core values as a community is living with a healthy rhythm of life. This means that we have seasons of activity and busyness, and seasons of rest and renewal. This rhythm of work and rest occurs within a day (it's called sleep!), a week, a season, and a year. This works at a personal level, as well as in our MCs and wider lifestyles.

Consequently, during a twelve-month period, each MC has a month or two when the community significantly dials back on meetings and organization. This pruning time enables you as leaders to be refreshed and to return to the normal rhythm of group life with more energy, vision, and focus. What we also see is that during that rest time, people often gather informally and do more social stuff together, which, of course, greatly benefits the group.

Here is how one church communicated about this issue to their leaders:

For most Missional Communities, the natural time to do this is mid-summer (hence, we don't run leaders' Huddles then), but we recognize that for some groups a different point in the year might be more appropriate. If you are one of these exceptions, then we ask that you let us know so we can support and honor that particular rhythm. For instance, it might be that your best time for missional opportunity is in the summer months when everyone is outside a lot more. In that case, think through in advance when during the year your time of abiding will be.

Jesus says in Matthew 11:28, "Come to me, all you who are weary and burdened, and I will give you rest." This period of rest is specifically a time to abide in him. In Genesis 2, Adam and Eve are made on the sixth day, and we're told God rested on the seventh day. So the first thing that they had to do was rest! While God rests from his work, humanity is to work out of a place of rest.

Our rest and abiding are meant to be a preparation for our work and fruitfulness, not as a last resort after we're already burned out from too much work. God thinks this is such an important principle that he included it in his top 10! In the same way that we wouldn't wish to murder or steal, neither should we ignore the principle of rest and work.

High Challenge: Intentional Feedback

We live in a society that seems to find genuine challenge deeply uncomfortable. We are trained to give regular and gentle words of affirmation ("Oh yes, your cooking is marvelous!"), without ever affirming the truly significant things in a person's character and lifestyle that we admire and try to imitate. We are also taught not to challenge beyond fairly obvious or light-hearted examples ("Not exactly the best parking job!"), since to do so would be deemed crossing the socially acceptable boundary.

As Kingdom leaders, we need to break through both barriers.

We earn the right to speak tough love by doing both those elements. We speak validation into the areas that truly are a representation of the love of Christ, incarnated in that person's character and lifestyle. This then enables us to push back firmly in those areas where that person makes bad calls, and even more significantly, we identify patterns of behavior that are hindering his or her Kingdom potential from being maximized.

CASE STUDY:
Trinity Grace Church New York Leadership Selection Process

Intentionally, the MC leadership team operates very much like a team overseeing a church plant.

At Trinity Grace Church in New York City, leadership of Missional Communities comes after a thorough process of review. Jon Tyson, pastor of the church, explains that this has developed as a result of bad experiences in the past, when MC leaders had very few checks made on them and most of those groups failed to last.

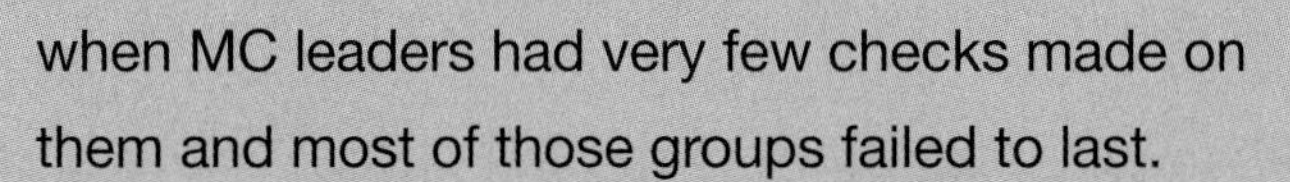

Today, to start a Missional Community, the potential leader needs to have been in another MC for at least six months and have served in some leadership capacity. There is plenty of scope for this, as all the MCs are led by a team of around six to eight people, with one key leader overall. Different members of the team oversee one of the four "Gospel Rhythm" gatherings through the month (worship night, men's and women's night, dinner night, and service night), on the basis that most people have a passion for at least one of these meetings.

After serving within an existing Missional Community, the potential leader can potentially have his or her character vouched for. He or she then enters into a period of testing, with the yardstick being that of a deacon in the New Testament. As part of this testing, he or she needs to establish where the new community will be formed and have that vision affirmed by the church's wider leadership team. Then a series of gatherings, dinners, or meetings occur, to see if others within the church share and will gather around that new vision.

Jon comments that while this might be a slower and more detailed process than other churches use, because of the leaders' experiences, the MC leaders choose to be slower and more deliberate so they can appoint the right leaders from the beginning.

Leaders, Pastors, and the Fivefold Ministry

Since we strongly believe in biblical teaching on leadership, we call those who lead MCs "leaders," not "pastors." Obviously you must choose the right language for your context, but for us, "pastor" is not an accurate description of the leader's primary role. To call a leader "pastor" will ensure that, along with the cultural baggage associated with the term, the individual's role will be viewed above all else as a care-giving, shepherding function.

Although creating a safe, caring, and accountable community is important, MC leaders are there to offer godly, humble yet clear leadership to the community as it goes in mission and builds closer relationships with God and one another. This is not a hierarchical approach; rather, it is about allowing the gifts God gives to his body to be exercised, including the gift of leadership.

It might be that the MC leader is, in his or her base ministry, a pastor, but the leader could also be a teacher, evangelist, prophet, or apostle (see Ephesians 4:11). Each one produces a different flavor in the group and how it is led.[52]

The group leader also needs to be able to identify where the other Ephesians 4 ministry gifts are being expressed in the community and empower those people to operate in those ways. So it might well be that the leaders are not the most pastorally wired, but if they can release and work well with others who are pastors, then the group will feel loved, cared for, and challenged (challenge being an important part of the pastor's function).

Likewise, those who are the prophets will see beyond the horizon of the present and call the group toward God's heart for its missional context. The prophets stir the group to pursue the Lord in prayer and patient expectation and seek his fresh word to direct and guide them. The evangelists are the ones who will keep a passion for those who don't know Jesus high on the agenda, as they equip others to go in mission in ways that are accessible and personally reaching out in fruitful ways. The teachers bring a deep hunger for the knowledge of God, especially through Scripture and clear thinking, thereby helping the group to mature in depth as well as in number. The apostles are the ones who see how to gain breakthrough in stuck situations, since more than anyone else apostles embrace change and the opportunity to take new territory for the Kingdom.

It is important not to just pick people like you to be MC leaders! You want a healthy mixture of Pioneers and Developers with all of the fivefold ministry gifts.

A **Pioneer** is someone who is constantly pushing forward, looking to take more and more ground for the Kingdom and rarely staying in one place long.

A **Developer** is looking to keep the ground that has been won and to develop it so that it is a true and real depiction of the Kingdom.

We need Pioneers so that the Kingdom is forcefully moving forward. We need Developers so that we keep the ground that has been won when the Pioneers move on to the next thing. Without Pioneers, we rarely if ever *gain* new territory. Without Developers, we rarely if ever keep the new territory.

In the Pilot MC, you should have a balance of the different fivefold ministries, as well as Pioneers and Developers, so that everyone feels empowered to participate.

How Leaders with Different Fivefold Gifting Will Grow MCs

Our good friend Paul Maconochie, Senior Pastor at St. Thomas' Church Philadelphia, Sheffield, has been a keen observer, leader, and member of Missional Communities for more than a decade.[53] During that time, he has noticed patterns where different fivefold gifts have different methods and styles of leading MCs, regardless of what the particular mission vision is. Although he is quick to say that these are anecdotal observations, we feel that his insights are extremely helpful and true to life.

Paul believes that one of the challenges for churches starting MCs is that the people who grab the vision first are the early adopters, and within that group are a disproportionate number of apostles. After all, apostles welcome change and new things, so they love something that is so effective in breaking open barriers to the Kingdom while also being so potentially disruptive to the settled order of church life! What happens is that apostles take up the challenge and thus set the model for how to lead Missional Communities within that church. The problem is that non-apostles who follow work off that highly apostolic approach and may not do it as well.

To overcome this imbalance, we need a more sophisticated approach to modeling MC leadership, rather than a one-size-fits-all perspective.

As we go through the typical style of leadership for each of the five areas, bear in mind that these are only broad generalizations, so don't worry if you don't strictly "conform" in all aspects. Nevertheless, you will have a natural bias to one of the fivefold, and understanding your default mode is important. Note also that, while you might be clear about your base in the fivefold ministry, you will also have phases in each of the other four ministry areas, where you learn to access this ministry as a situation arises (even though it isn't your strongest area). God does this to round us out and to meet a particular need in the body of Christ.

- ***Apostles leading a Missional Community***
  Apostle-led MCs are usually highly attractional, orbiting around someone who has lots of charisma and the ability to gather others. Frequently, these groups grow the quickest. Their mode of multiplication is often to split down the middle as a result of the pressure of the speed of growth. A mature apostle should have the skills to manage such a maneuver, even though it can be fraught with pastoral landmines, as multiplying an MC can be difficult for some relationally.

- ***Prophets leading a Missional Community***
  Prophets tend to focus on the mission but not be quite so evangelistic. They often go for high visibility, since they desire an incarnational approach to presenting the Gospel. Generally, this means that they and their groups are very radical, often with the highest demands placed upon members. If you know a group in a tough urban context where there is lots of talk and action about reclaiming the city by their very presence and engagement with the people out on the streets, then that is probably a group with strong prophetic leadership. Such groups can grow by multiplying, but they often keep the core team and allow a new work to bud off into a new context.

- ***Evangelists leading a Missional Community***
  Almost certainly, evangelists love to go straight after the People of Peace in their chosen mission context. Evangelists identify the gatekeepers of that place and stay with them. You often see them

literally going out in pairs, finding some People of Peace, building relationships, and through them reaching a whole neighborhood that was previously unreached. Eventually, evangelists look to hand the group on and go into a new context or send out others in twos to do a similar work elsewhere.

- ***Teachers leading a Missional Community***
  You frequently see teachers go into an existing context where the witness for Christ is struggling or almost extinguished. They give themselves to model how to live the Christian life, whether in worship, community, or mission. Mature teachers do this ever so humbly, so it won't even feel like teaching much of the time. They stay for a lengthy season, but many eventually begin to look for a fresh context requiring their help and then hand on their group. They send out new groups that will be characterized by having been thoroughly prepared with a clear model of how to do things.
- ***Pastors leading a Missional Community***
  Pastors long to bring community transformation, by establishing and then building on long-term relationships. They highly value the integrity of becoming fully embedded in their context. This means that while things are not as spectacular at first, pastors have a slower and longer burn approach to mission. We have noticed that often this model works especially well in the suburbs. As relationships are at the heart of everything pastors do, multiplying can be much more difficult for groups led by pastors. However, they do find it easier to grow as a "bud" or "shoot" off a small group of people and perhaps to take what they are doing into a neighboring area (or even neighboring street!).

  For all of the fivefold ministry areas, taking them through a regular process of goal setting and being accountable for their commitments is important. We find leaders' retreats (see later in the book) to be an excellent context for doing just that that, coupled with ongoing Huddles.

The Role of Church Staff

In a church with Missional Communities, your whole understanding of leadership can be facing change (whether from how your church used to do it, or your experience of your sending church if you are a plant). The conflict hinges on the fact that, if you have come from a programmatic environment, then you have defined leadership by who can facilitate meetings. But now you need a new definition of leadership that is far more focused upon being a discipler and equipper of others as they head out into the battle. What this means is that some who were leaders in the old system won't be leaders in the new system.

The major transition in the role of staff is the change from being paid providers who do everything to enablers of others so they can play their part. The staff's energy will less and less be put into running meetings and far more into building a discipling lifestyle. Staff stop being the hired holy hands and start focusing on resourcing and serving those reaching out through Missional Communities. The mindset shift is one that sees staff becoming a highly skilled resource to help MCs grow in number and depth, so they make and sustain breakthroughs and do only what can't be done by MC members.

Before this sounds totally deconstructionist, we definitely believe in churches having staff, but the challenge is to what end they are there.

Staff are not there to do most of the work of the church.

It is about breaking down the clergy-laity divide, thereby seeing staff as part of the central resources of the church that allow people with mission vision to focus their energies on that rather than on maintaining an institution.

Related to this point, a good challenge to a church (especially with a larger staff team) is for the staff to be released to spend time outside the church building in mission. This should not just be seen as something they do in their spare time, but rather something that they do as part of their role. Such an approach would speak volumes to the church community, as well as encouraging staff to keep on developing their skill set, experience, and confidence on the front lines, thereby enabling them more effectively to coach and lead people into mission. An added benefit is that this would provide plenty of opportunity for the church to be seen by the wider population as being actively engaged in serving and bettering their city.

All this, of course, has implications for hiring decisions. Will a new hire make the church more centrifugal, enabling it to GO with the Gospel more effectively? Or will the new position be centripetal, pulling energy, resources, and people into the center, for the sake of maintaining what goes on there?[54] Now there are central things that go on that do build MC life, whether that's in terms of leader training and resourcing, setting the overall vision for the whole church, interacting with external bodies (from the IRS to other churches to the city council), running outstanding celebrations, building a training-year program for young adults, buying a big whiz-bang photocopier, planning a children's team who not only do great Sunday School but also resource MCs with children, providing the techie guys who build the website, etc.

There are many things that it makes sense to pool resources on and provide centrally, but the point is that the center exists to serve the edge, not the other way round. The staff (and the building and the photocopier) are there to help the "regular" members of the church who are leading in mission to be as well resourced and supported as possible.

The staff exists to serve and equip the body at work on the edge.

Other issues will be thrown up by this journey, many of which we touch upon elsewhere. If a church member has a week where somehow three church gatherings (small group, MC, and Sunday celebration) are on and that is too much for his schedule to remain balanced, which one will be skipped? Which will you as the staff most mind him missing? Will you run an Alpha Course (or similar), and if so, will that be centrally or within MCs? Will you do a centrally organized youth program, or do it all in MCs? What is fruitfulness in this new paradigm?

There are no universally right or wrong answers here, but these are the sort of questions that a staff team wrestles within a church with Missional Communities.

2.6 | DISCIPLESHIP LEADS TO MISSION

Countless books have been written on the priesthood of all believers, and rightly so. But we'd propose another "of all believers" has not been adequately addressed:

The Missionhood of All Believers.

If God is the Rescuing God and we are made in his image, that means that buried deep within each of us is the same seed of the Rescuing God, the God who is on a Mission, the God who will stop at nothing to put everything back together, the God who wants us to get in on the action.

In his final words to his disciples, he clarifies what making disciples means: *Teach them to do everything that I have taught you.* A disciple is someone who does the same things Jesus' disciples did.

Perhaps Jesus' most detailed and practical teaching for his disciples we find in the synoptic Gospels and is his strategy for mission, which has been coined the Person of Peace strategy.

We see Jesus first instructing only the twelve, so maybe we can just write it off. The twelve were special. It was advanced training. Probably not what Jesus was talking about when he said, "Teaching them everything I have taught you."

But then we see him instructing the seventy-two in the exact same way.

Then we see Peter using the same strategy in Acts 10, Paul in Acts 16, and all of his new churches to follow. In the book *The Rise of Christianity*, Rodney Stark shows the exact same pattern. The Celts in the sixth century do the same thing.

In fact, you can trace it throughout the whole of Christian history.

Two things begin to emerge:

1) Perhaps we need to re-evaluate how evangelism happens (which we have started to examine with the People of Peace strategy).
2) If you aren't missional, according to Jesus, you aren't a disciple. And if Jesus has called us to make disciples, it's a Gospel imperative to teach everyone, not just the evangelists, how to be missional in their everyday comings and goings.

What is apparent is that we have, over time, separated discipleship from mission, as if somehow you can be a disciple of Jesus and not participate in his mission.

So how can we actually create missional disciples who can lead others in God's mission?

We have spent years working on this question, and what we have developed is a discipleship vehicle that teaches and disciples current and future leaders to be missional and to be held accountable to having this kind of life.

We call it *Huddle*.

Huddles

A Huddle is a place where missional leaders, usually a group of four to twelve people, can receive encouragement and accountability in community. In essence, the Huddle leader helps each person answer two questions:

1) What is God saying to you (as you worship, pray, read the Bible, spend time with your friends and spouse, discipline your kids, in the stillness of the night before sleep, play sports, watch TV, interact with your colleagues, etc.)?
2) What are you going to do in response?

Why do Huddles work so well in discipling people?

Simple. The leader.

The leader constantly takes people back to these two questions. What is God saying to me? What am I going to do about it?

Suppose during the course of a Huddle meeting someone really sensed that God was calling him to start a new Missional Community that would reach out to artists in a specific neighborhood of the city.

So that's question 1. What is God saying to this person? He senses God is asking him to plant this new Missional Community for artists.

Question 2: What is that person going to do about it?

Well, obviously it would be a good idea to spend some time in this mission context, getting to know the area, the people, and the places people go to. This person is aware that there is a coffee shop called Globetrotters that many of the artists in this area frequent, so he decides to spend some time there. The Huddle members specifically agree to spend two nights there before the next Huddle happens in two weeks.

They've answered question 2. What are they going to do about it? They have a plan. They are going to a coffee shop to observe, listen, and discern the mission context. The Huddle leader will hold them accountable to that plan.

So what does the Huddle leader do?

At the beginning of the next Huddle, each person shares how he or she followed through on the plans. Did these disciples do what they said they were going to do?

This leader did follow through and spent the two nights at Globetrotters, and because of that, he noticed something. While a lot of artists spend time there, they are mostly photographers. And strangely enough, this leader is a photographer as well.

And the process starts again.

What is God saying?
How am I going to respond?

Jesus says that his sheep know his voice.

Huddle is a continued process of learning to hear the voice of the Shepherd and responding. It is the process of growing in relationship with him and being changed by that relationship, as a disciple and as a leader.

Exploring Huddle

The word Huddle may make some of you think of a sports team gathering together, arms draped over each others' shoulders, receiving inspiration and instruction from their coach as the players come together. Another example is animals coming close to one another in order to share warmth and companionship in otherwise harsh circumstances – Emperor penguins huddling together for warmth in the middle of the Antarctic ice shelf, spending those long winter months protecting their penguin egg from the conditions that drop to -70°F.

Our understanding of leadership Huddles is that they draw upon both perspectives – Huddles are challenging and nurturing, offering accountability as well as encouragement. This means that Huddles are not therapeutic in nature; rather, they help people discern what God is asking them to do and then respond.

Huddles for MC leaders need to meet regularly to build momentum – at least monthly, ideally every two weeks; some even occur weekly.

Honestly, we'd recommend at least every two weeks.

A Huddle generally lasts around 1½ hours. Huddles can have up to twelve members, although that is very much the high end, so groups of around six to eight are a better place to start.

As you will recall with a group this size, Huddle is not a public but a personal space.

A Huddle is:

- For your leaders in mission – it is also a place to draw in emerging leaders, as a place where they can be developed quickly and you can assess their level of maturity.
- A place where they give and receive encouragement and accountability.
- For a group of up to twelve people (but usually fewer).
- Regular and consistent in their rhythm of meeting.
- Led by the leader.
- Accessed by invitation from that leader – this is not something people bring a friend to. If you lead a Huddle, then it is your Huddle and you set the terms, including who is invited in to be discipled by you.
- A privilege, not a right.
- Relaxed and fun – laughter should happen regularly!
- Dependent upon openness and honesty – the bar is set by you as the Huddle leader being equally open and honest.
- For a season only, not forever – we tend to ask people to commit for a church year at a time. Obviously, MC leaders remain in Huddles for as long as they lead a community, but you will want to shake things up from time to time, partly as some stop leading a Missional Community and others start leading.
- Measured by growth in maturity and fruitfulness of members.
- Something that multiplies over time, as members start their own Huddles – your aim over time is to see MC leaders take the principles of Huddle and in turn start to Huddle their emerging leaders in their communities. They should be looking for those who are emerging into leadership, in the MC and out in the wider world, as missionary leaders. Huddles led by MC leaders are selected based upon leadership and leadership potential, so someone doesn't receive an invitation to be in one just because he or she wants one.

Probably your Missional Community leaders will find it easier to Huddle smaller groups than you do. We often work off the 8-6-4 principle, which means you Huddle eight people, who each in turn grow to Huddle six others. Eventually your plan is that those in MCs being Huddled will then each seek to gather four others and Huddle them. If you can do this, you will end up with 248 people being Huddled,[55] with you doing just one Huddle yourself, which is extraordinarily effective and highly reproducible.

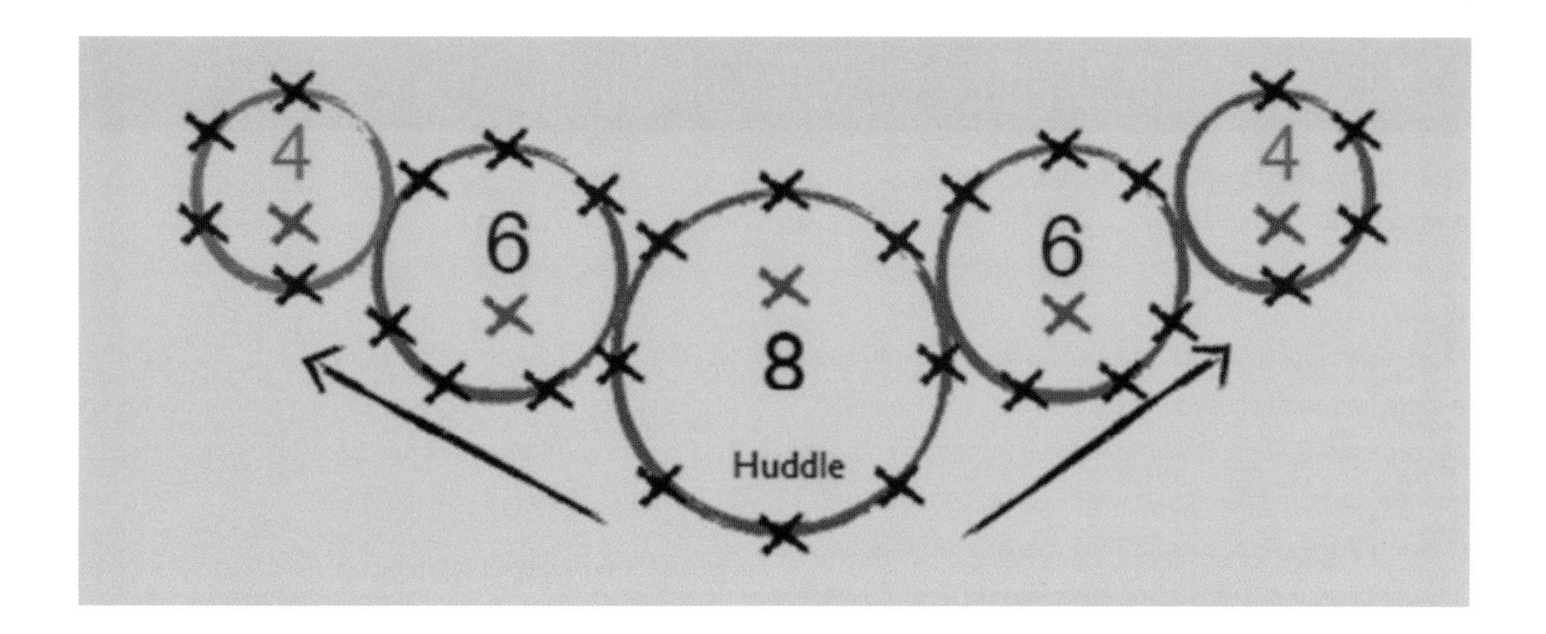

When MC leaders, or those they Huddle, feel unable to start their own Huddle (the "I'm not as good a leader as you" defense), just have them copy what you do with your Huddle and go from there.

- For leaders, language defines culture, and it is so tempting to baptize all your small groups with the name Huddle. But Huddle is your premium brand for discipling leaders (and not the same thing as small group). Thus, be selective where and when you use the term and avoid labeling everything "Huddle."

Far more information and resources are available than we could possibly put here to help you practically with Huddles, including a book we have previously written on Launching Huddles, plus a separate Members' Guide. See this footnote for more details.[56]

Above all, our largest concern is that you are releasing leaders *who actually know how to disciple people* and are held accountable in a loving, supportive environment.

2.7 | CONCEPTS IN ACTION – THE STORY OF ONE MC

Ryan on Planting and Multiplying a Missional Community:

In 2004, our MC started out of a group of five people praying together. The idea was that we would become a Missional Community, but honestly, I didn't believe it at the time. I just went with it because that was what we were asked to do. We started meeting at our house, just getting together, eating and praying for each other. It was a random group made up of one married couple, a single guy, and two girls. We prayed through the vision of our MC – we want to plant and be planted – and shared what we were reading in the Bible. One of the guys was going through Hosea on his own and talked about it often, so one night we all just sat around and went through Hosea, trying to find a name for our newly formed MC. We found Jezreel (which means "God plants") and went for it. It was our vision.

Over the next year, we grew to about twenty-five people and met in lots of different homes. They were friends and people we knew in our neighborhood. We started to have a vision for our neighborhood, known as the Village, and so we began to pray for all our neighbors.

We continued to grow until we were more than sixty-five people in 2007, so that summer we multiplied. When we look back, we sometimes wonder where all those people came from! Really, it was people in the Missional Community gradually drawing in people they knew, whether through sports and outside activities, or people from work, or people who lived nearby. We did have some Christians join, too, but we tried to balance being welcoming with making obvious that we were going to be looking outwards into our community and not be a traditional church group that looks only in.

As we thought about multiplying, God had set it up to where half of the people lived nearer the city center and the others lived in or near the Village. All the city center people went and started meeting together, but even though the people were there, it was hard to find leaders to take that many people. Looking back, I wish we had started to envision several people from that group at the beginning of '07. The summer months were hard; my wife and I were still focused on finding leaders for the new group, while also leading our current group. Nevertheless, after a lot of praying and cajoling, by the fall we had found leaders, and we were pumped that the vision of planting was happening.

What then surprised us was that Jezreel continued to grow. At first, it seemed that we had tons of room, so maybe some of that was just fringe people started coming more regularly. But also new people were being added to the group. We were starting to more intentionally do service projects in our area, so that helped us build more relationships. Several of our MC households cooked out in front of their homes at least once a week. We deliberately cooked too much and invited neighbors and passers-by to come over and eat with us. This consistent presence out in the street really helped cement our place there and possibly gave us greater spiritual authority and impact.

Either way, a year later, in the fall of 2008, Jezreel had grown to sixty people again, and we knew that we needed to start talking about multiplying. This time, we started praying that God would highlight leaders for us to plant the vision in. He did, and so we did! We began in the fall to talk with the two couples about being leaders of new MCs, which gave them time to digest it and prepare for it. In January 2009, we multiplied into three MCs. As we multiplied, we decided to change the name of our group from Jezreel to Village Hope. God was giving us more of a calling to pray and reach out to this neighborhood, so we felt a new name would help to bring more life to that vision. The MC multiplied pretty well, we kept about twenty-five, the second group took about twenty-two, and the third group took about a dozen. We lost a few people in the restructure, but we gained even more in no time! It was a great multiplication that was prayed over, and it was very clear to everyone that God was leading us in it. He was working out the details and gave the new leaders lots of vision for their groups. It was life giving whereas the first multiplication had been a little life draining. We learned to wait on the Lord as well. He was a part of the first one for sure, but I think we rushed it a bit. The second one we mapped out, prayed into, and planned for properly.

In the meantime, the first multiplication, who went nearer the city center, have themselves grown to around fifty people, have spun off one new MC, and are in the process of moving towards multiplying again. They have done very much the same pattern, with a mixture of friends and colleagues being drawn in, plus seeking to serve the local community. One of the leaders of that Missional Community became the chairwoman of the local neighborhood group, which helps organize big art nights (they live in the artists' area of town). So members of the MC have become very involved in that, whether helping run things or, for the more creative types, hosting stalls at the arts nights. This has given them tons of favor and open doors into that whole culture.

It is so exciting to see all that has gone on and how God has taken our faltering efforts and turned them into something so amazing.

What can we say? God is good!

LAUNCH GUIDE
TACTICAL MANEUVERS

If you want to start MCs in your church community, this section will give you the practical steps to do just that. Every church will be different, but this will provide a solid foundation for your ministry context.

STEP 1 | BEFORE YOU BEGIN

"There is nothing more difficult to take in hand, more perilous to conduct or more uncertain in its success, than to take the lead in the introduction of a new order of things." (Nicolo Machiavelli)

This book is designed both to explain the theory of Missional Communities and also to equip you practically to launch and run them in your situation.

The first part of this book gave you a mixture of biblical, theological, sociological and historical rationale for MCs. Now we move into focusing on how to introduce the ideas into your church community, win support from your key influencers, train your first generation of leaders and launch them publicly. Further on in the book we will tackle many of the detailed questions about how Missional Communities work in practice.

While you have been reading and digesting the first part of the book, simultaneously your subconscious leadership wiring will have been constantly assessing everything through the filter of, "Would this work here?"

That is not a wrong thing – in fact, that is probably a healthy sign that you are thinking through what it means to lead a church.

However, even if you have consciously come down on the side of, "I would love to see Missional Communities applied into our context," that isn't the end of the story.

You now stand at the beginning of a significant period of change implementation that over a number of years will result in a significantly different-looking church community. As people begin to grow in their understanding of this journey ahead, you will see different responses.

There will be those in your church who embrace this change the minute you start talking about it. You will have the many who (at varying speeds) will be increasingly open to and supportive of MCs, if they see a clear and compelling vision and strategy. There will also be a few who will view this as ruining their church and who could, if mishandled, make the process of transition as difficult as possible (including for you personally).

John Maxwell comments, "People will not change until they perceive that the advantages of changing outweigh the disadvantages of continuing with the way things are. What leaders sometimes fail to recognize is that the followers will always weigh the advantage/ disadvantage issue in light of personal gain/ loss, not organizational gain/ loss."[57]

Clearly there will be unique circumstances in every church and in every leader's relationship with those she or he leads. At the same time, there are also common patterns that will occur in the vast majority of regular churches, which can be largely foreseen and prepared for. This is not about manipulating people – in fact, it is the very opposite. Good leadership is about leading others through change in a way that fairly pre-empts and addresses fears and concerns, without being held hostage by them.

As a senior leader, or as a member of a senior leadership team, you are tasked with guiding and directing the church into a better future, as far as you can foresee it. Being human, you won't handle everything perfectly, but you can go a long way towards gaining the trust and support of the vast majority of people if they see an open, reasonable and appropriate process in place. Obviously you will already have considerable experience in leading change, including vital local knowledge, which will affect how you move towards Missional Communities in your particular time and place.

Nevertheless, there is a growing body of experience that has been gleaned from those who have already made this journey ahead of you, into Missional Community life. This field guide aims to cover the critical tasks facing you in transitioning MCs into your church.

As you start this guide, we should be honest and tell you our three working assumptions about you.

Three Assumptions We Have Made About You

1. That at the very least, you are seriously considering using Missional Communities in your situation. This is important, as in this section we are giving very practical steps for making MCs happen in your church. Because of this, we are not going to spend a lot of time trying to convince you that MCs are right for you.

2. The leadership structure in your church is in a place to respond positively and in a timely manner to this process. By leadership structure, we mean your board/ council/ elders/ congregational meeting, or whatever way of ordering things that your church has.

   This means that if you do not currently have the leadership capital to make such a shift, you'll want to deal with those underlying issues first. If you don't, not only will you make this an incredibly painful (and probably unsuccessful) process, you will ruin the chances of anyone ever implementing Missional Communities in your church, since at an emotional level MCs will be tied to this broader conflict. So our assumption is that you are in a place of relative peace and unity in your church, where you have the general backing of your wider leaders to propose change and expect a positive hearing.

3. You have little-to-no experience of Missional Communities. If you do, wonderful. This guide will still be enormously useful. But we have tried to write this material so that a first-time implementer can make MCs happen in their situation.

A Health Warning

In an entrepreneurial culture such as the US, leaders will always be excited about opportunities to pioneer new things and the vision of MCs is a compelling one for those who have functioned within a predominantly attractional model. However, before you go diving in, we need to issue a health warning! This process of transition takes time and needs to be seen as a major shift of culture. In particular, this is about moving from a provider-client relationship to one where individuals are being strongly discipled.

For us, a **culture of discipleship is one where there is a dynamic mix of low control and high accountability**. In practice this means that the central resources of the church are easily accessed by those "on the missional edge," but those same leaders are held highly accountable for their character and the way in which they lead.

This is about the vision of the Kingdom being released as Missional Communities are enabled to reach previously untouched people. Yet it is also about doing so in a way that honors the grace-filled values of our King.

Your potential MC leaders may have been used to running programs where the teaching curriculum is laid out for them to deliver. They may have only led under the spiritual covering of senior leaders within the life and confines of the church campus. If this is the case then they are usually inexperienced and ill-equipped for the spiritual battle and engagement on the front lines that Missional Communities often involve. Their initial feelings of excitement and enthusiasm might quickly give way to feelings of inadequacy, incompetence and despondency.

If you try and launch MCs without the foundation of a true discipling culture and a clear structure of high invitation and high challenge, it will be much harder for your MC leaders. If they fail, inevitably it will be much harder a second time round, as you will have to backfill support and direction for leaders who are already discouraged. In addition, you will miss the vital component of advocacy from the initial MC pioneers. Success stories from the participants in the first MCs will provide concrete evidence and testimony for those still undecided on the merits of MCs. So how can you give Missional Communities the best possible chance? What are the foundational building blocks?

The Process Is Crucial

We would strongly encourage you to follow this guide as closely as is appropriate for your church situation. We want to make the journey towards MCs as painless as possible, since with a weak process you may struggle to implement them effectively. Although easy to overlook, our experience is that the process is crucial.

The guidance that we set out here is designed to help you think through the main areas that you will need to tackle. It may be that not every theme is relevant to your situation, so clearly you can ignore those. However, we suspect almost all of them will be pertinent and so we encourage you to use this guide, along with the specific suggestions we make, as a template off which to work. Of course, you will need to tweak and, at the very least, put "local paint" on things. However, our aim is to give you a clear, thought-through process for the main areas of change management with regards to implementing Missional Communities.

Willow Creek founder and senior pastor Bill Hybels records how he responds to eager staff with a dynamic Kingdom vision for change and transition. He looks them in the eye and says, "This really is a thrilling opportunity you are being entrusted with, and I'm happy for you! But can I give you a piece of advice? Don't lose your better judgment in the elation of launching something new. Think things through. Cover the details. Do the requisite follow-up so that you increase the likelihood that this fun new Kingdom thing will actually work over the long haul."[58]

We hope that this section of the book will help you to respond to Hybels' wisdom and do the detailed planning for a successful implementation of Missional Communities.

How to Use this Launch Guide

On a practical note, we have tried to write in an interactive manner. This means that we ask lots of questions that we intend you to stop and think about. Some will be quick answers, while others will be longer, maybe even only coming to clarity over lengthy periods of time. Your willingness to intentionally allow yourself to be challenged and provoked by these questions will directly impact the effectiveness of this material. The prize here does not come from finishing the book as quickly as possible.

You might find it helpful to plan some time away from the office and busyness of life in order to work through what is included here. Allow the Lord to speak to you through what is written, the questions and his own direct guidance and revelation to you. Don't feel at all guilty about creating quality time at this stage, since like a good farmer you are deep plowing the field and preparing the seed for sowing.

After you have done some processing, you might want to take a couple of your closest and key colleagues through the same journey. If you work in a team environment, you might even want to all engage with this material separately and then come together to think through how to implement it in your church.

Whichever route you take, the main point is to emerge with a very high quality, specific and time-lined plan that you can follow and measure against. This is not mechanistic or legalistic. Rather, it is about using your God-given planning skills to ensure that your church are taken through the very best possible process as you depart on this amazing journey of transformation for your city (or town or village).[59]

NOTES

Consider: Bob Biehl writes, "A change can make sense logically, but still lead to anxiety in the psychological dimension. Everyone needs a niche, and when the niche starts to change after we've become comfortable in it, it causes stress and insecurities."[60]

Before introducing change, we have to consider the psychological dimension. How will people respond emotionally to what this shift to Missional Communities represents?

____

____

____

____

____

Ponder: Who in your church has the most to gain – and the most to lose?

____

____

____

____

____

____

List: From a logical perspective, write down the advantages and disadvantages that will result from introducing Missional Communities in your context.

____

____

____

____

____

Write down: What will be the psychological impact, both positive and negative? Answer both from your own perspective, as well as that of church members. What will be the major sources of stress and insecurity?

____

____

____

____

____

The Major Areas Covered in this Transition Process

There are two main strategies that you will be given in this section. The first of these is the Pilot Missional Community. This will be the primary way that you prepare and train your potential MC leaders, as well as walking your church's key decision makers through the journey of determining whether this is the right path for your church to follow.

The second strategy is what we've termed Launch Sunday, which is when you publicly release Missional Communities within your church community. You will be walked through many of the practicalities and given a variety of options that you can either use directly or freely adapt. This will also cover the important task of communicating with the whole church family and doing effective change management with the whole body.

Alongside these two areas, you will also be helped to think through what changes you need to go through in order to prepare yourself. Change always begins internally, so as a leader that is where you must begin.

STEP 2 | PREPARATION

We have found the following questions, practices and resources incredibly instructive in our journey towards launching Missional Communities. Obviously this isn't exhaustive, but we think you'll find it particularly helpful.

What could you be reading/listening to as you begin this process?

Here are a few examples to stir your thinking. See the footnotes for many more suggestions of books and articles that we have found helpful.

- **Being Missional**
  The Forgotten Ways by Alan Hirsch
  The Rise of Christianity by Rodney Stark
  Church Next by Eddie Gibbs and Ian Coffey
- **Culture and Communication**
  The Millennium Matrix by M. Rex Miller
  The Culture Code by Clotaire Rapaille
  Made to Stick by Dan and Chip Heath
- **Organizations and Leadership**
  Good to Great by Jim Collins
  The Spider and the Starfish by Ori Brafman and Rod Beckstrom
  Axiom by Bill Hybels
- **Building a Discipling Culture**
  Outliers by Malcolm Gladwell
  Building a Discipling Culture by Mike Breen and Steve Cockram
  Untamed by Alan Hirsch
- **Blogs**
  Mike Breen | www.mikebreen.wordpress.com
  Alex Absalom | www.alexabsalom.com
  Doug Paul | www.3dchurchplanter.wordpress.com

What should you be experiencing?

1. **Identify other leaders you can learn from**

   Who are the leaders who have already gone ahead and implemented MCs in their churches? Learn from them, whether through their teaching, blogs or other materials. If you can visit their churches, even better. To be able to see and experience MCs and Huddles done well is a powerful thing. Some churches in Europe and the US are starting to host opportunities for leaders to take such pilgrimages. If you would like to be connected to a church which has been through this process, you can contact us and we will put you in touch with a church close to you.

NOTES

Plan: What specific resources are you going to seek out and read or listen to?

____

____

____

____

____

____

Name: Some leaders you could visit or connect with in some way.

____

____

____

____

____

____

2. **Visit local mission situations**

   Scout out the people who are already finding ways to incarnate the Gospel into different contexts in your area. They don't need to be in your church or even doing Missional Communities. Also try to experience a variety of contexts, whether with the urban poor, immigrants, social action, college students, teens, children, families, the suburbs, the rich, businesses, hospitals, the military, farmers … the list is endless! Look at a variety of approaches, such as bold witnessing, servant evangelism, incarnational presence ministries, reaching the political and cultural leaders, prophetic-led approaches, compassion-driven, etc.

   What you are looking for are some of the lessons that people have already learned in your city.

   Are they doing everything the way you would do them? Probably not. But allow them to coach you in what seems to work and what doesn't in your cultural context. They might also be aware of other agencies where there are People of Peace which will be valuable information as you move forward.

3. **Experience places of authentic community in your context**

   Where are the places that people belong and experience authentic community? What does it look like to really belong? Consider your local coffee shops, gyms, clubs and societies, sports, nightlife, etc. Where do young moms belong? How about business people, high-school kids, twenty-somethings, police officers, the homeless?

   Try walking through your city center at different points during the day and observe the different happenings. For instance, a college town is not the same at 11 p.m. on Saturday night as it is at 11 a.m. on Sunday morning! Have you seen both? To help in this learning, ask some people you know – whether in or outside the church – who are well connected with different strata of society. Find out where people belong and experience community.

Helping your Key Lay Leadership Come on Board

Managing change is never simple but there are things you can do to reduce the stress and potential conflict. The strategy of running a Pilot MC allows your church board[61] to evaluate and assess the relative pros and cons of the new approach before having to commit the whole church. Having some of those key lay leaders participate in the Pilot MC is very wise, as their testimony and advocacy will head off potential fears from others that the pastor has had yet another great new idea.

NOTES

Write down: Some local mission situations you could visit or connect with in some way.

____

____

____

____

____

List: Some community building places you could visit.

____

____

____

____

____

In short, the pitch could be: "These Missional Communities are working all across the United States, they are biblically and sociologically smart, so let's see if they could work for us. Maybe they will, maybe they won't. But it's at least worth a try. A Pilot is low risk and will create the context for people to experience things for themselves, rather than simply reading about it in a book."

Remember that advocacy is a core component in managing this change effectively. The Developers will want to know where it is already working, so get connected to churches and leaders who have effectively implemented MCs.

Do you know church leaders who have gone before you? Maybe some of their key lay leaders could hop on the phone with some of your key lay leaders? Is there a church nearby that your leaders could visit to engage with their staff and MC leaders? This type of preparation will greatly reduce resistance to change and allay fears.

In every church community there are wise lay leaders who often function as gatekeepers to the wider community. If they give their blessing, then usually everyone else will trust their judgment. You could invite a small number of these leaders to your house for a meal and give them the chance to ask all their questions. You are not expecting them to become passionate advocates, but simply seeking their blessing to *explore options with the Pilot MC*. By their very nature, Developers need something concrete to build upon and at this stage inviting some of them to be part of the Pilot evaluation team is a great way of gaining "buy in."

Finally, you will need to determine at what point you will formally evaluate the Pilot. We would recommend you do it sometime in the last month of the Pilot MC, at least two weeks before the planned Launch Sunday. You will obviously need to prepare as if Launch Sunday is going to happen, but build in the safety valve that if the Pilot evaluation proves to be a

NOTES

Consider: Who are the key influencers in the church that you want to see buy into Missional Communities?

____

____

____

____

____

Think: What strategy could you deploy in order to bring them along on this journey in a positive manner? Do you need to issue an invitation to the Pilot MC to a few key influencers?

____

____

____

____

____

Plan: What will be the process and timescale for evaluating Pilots? How will a final decision be reached? Put a specific date for the formal review on the calendar of all concerned.

____

____

____

____

____

____

complete disaster, you can cancel it. To our knowledge this has never happened, but having this evaluation process in place will give comfort to those with genuine concerns about the MC strategy.

Counting the Cost

As the senior leader you will need to count the cost personally and settle in your head and heart that the prize is truly worth the price. You cannot just do this because you believe it's a good idea. Faith comes by hearing the Word, so you need to know that this is what the Lord himself has called you to.

Jesus tells us that before a building project is started, the wise person estimates the cost to see if he can finish it. As we read in Luke 14:28-33, a king going into battle will consider whether he has enough troops to win a victory. In the same way, you should consider what the cost will be for you, your family and your team in this endeavor.

Practically you will need to re-adjust your calendar and re-order your priorities. You will have to become very strategic in the allocation of your most precious resource, time, investing it in your key leaders as they seek to lead those in their Huddles. Emotionally, you will need to be prepared to deal with the inevitable consequences of change. Spiritually, you and your family will need extra prayerfulness and prayer support from others, since the enemy will try to derail this process. We write later on that spiritual warfare is a common pattern in churches that make this journey, so you need to go into the fight with your eyes open and spiritual weapons fully deployed.

Never forget that prayer is a powerful weapon that releases so much Kingdom life (as well as having the invigorating side-benefit of deeply annoying the enemy!). However in times of warfare we are tempted to pray less and rely upon ourselves more. Alongside that, the voice of the enemy will try to trick us into self-doubt and second-guessing, usually through the "What if" game.

> What if no one wants to move into Missional Communities?
>
> What if no one is reached?
>
> What if giving and attendance go down on Sundays?
>
> How will we pay the bills if we start releasing people all over the place?
>
> If we aren't keeping a close eye on everything, just think what nonsense they'll start believing!

The antidote, of course, is prayer – for you, your church, your city, those you lead, for the presence of the Holy Spirit and the advancement of the Kingdom of God.

We strongly implore you to ensure that you have excellent prayer support, strong accountable relation-ships and the ability to invest deeply in your family life at this time. Such tactics will help prevent the enemy's ploys from being effective.

Consider the cost –

The Price:

- Most of us have been trained as church leaders to act as spiritual benefactors, where we do it all but retain a lot of control. We receive much affirmation when we function in that way, since that is what most of the church have been taught to expect from their leaders. However, Jesus explicitly says, "You are not to be like that."[62] Making this journey will mean having to learn new skills and we will inevitably experience our conscious incompetence at first. If you want to see your community and leaders fully engaged in mission, it will have to start with you.
- The battle is not against flesh and blood. The enemy will attack us at the points of our

greatest weakness and he will not give up ground without a significant fight.

- Launching effective Missional Communities is impossible without creating a low control, high accountability culture. It means you will have to trust the team you have discipled and recognize that you will no longer know everything that is going on.
- There will be internal opposition from those who want to maintain the status quo of the consumer culture. They may withhold their tithes, stir up dissent or even leave the church. People you know and love may not want to follow you into this new paradigm. But now for the good news –

The Prize:

- With discipleship as your operating system (using a computer analogy), church will become the "killer application" that is capable of changing your community and fulfilling the Great Commission.
- You will be giving your life for a vision you truly believe in rather than maintaining a feudal system, which weighs so heavily on your shoulders and does not create disciples.
- You will be opening the door to unlimited Kingdom possibilities because it will be the Holy Spirit working through other leaders; the future will no longer be limited by your personal capacity and vision.
- More of your leaders will be engaged in front line mission and living a more fulfilling and fruitful Christian life.

And all those who have made the journey say the Kingdom prize is worth any cost.

NOTES

Consider: In what ways does the enemy tend to attack you and your household?

____

____

____

____

____

Write down: How can you pre-empt, and prepare to see off, the attack when it comes?

____

____

____

____

____

Be specific: Name the people to whom you give specific and personal prayer requests. Who else could be added to that list?[63]

____

____

____

____

____

____

____

____

____

____

____

NOTES

Prayer exercise: Use the Lord's Prayer to help you pray into this topic of introducing Missional Communities into your church:

The Father's Character
– He is the giving, generous, going, searching, community-building Father. (What other names of God are relevant for your situation?)

The Father's Kingdom
– His will is for the Kingdom to forcefully advance in your city. (Talk with him about particular people and places that especially need this.)

The Father's Provision
– He WILL provide all that is needed… by you, your church, your leaders, your mission, your city. (Ask for specific needs and expect him to provide.)

The Father's Forgiveness
– He loves to help us to change from old to new ways of thinking. (What specific attitudes and actions need turning from?)

The Father's Guidance
("Lead us not into temptation")
– Where is Jesus about to come? Where is the Father at work and where can we join in? (Ask for help with the specific decisions you face.)

The Father's Protection
– He protects us against the wiles of the enemy. (Talk with him about specific attacks or areas of concern.)

STEP 3 | RECRUITING FOR YOUR PILOT MC

The 40 days which Jesus spent alone in the wilderness battling with his enemy proved foundational for all that was to follow. Upon leaving the desert the first thing he did was to gather his team. We think it's fair to say that they would not have been everyone's first round draft picks. But his retreat had been the context for deep revelation from the Father and it is in prayerful retreat that we should ask the Lord about those he has prepared to help launch the first wave of Missional Communities.

NOTES

Consider: Bearing in mind your mission context, the background of those you lead and the history of your church, what characteristics should be seen in your potential MC leaders? What does a leader of an MC look like in your context?

Brainstorm: As you think about the leaders you are actively investing in, write down all the names of people you sense might make excellent MC leaders.

Revelation: Spend some time asking the Lord to give you specific names of potential MC leaders *who are not on the previous list*. These are often the most successful MC leaders.

To help you think things through: Try using a table like this one to assess potential leaders, especially ones about whom you might not be certain. You can either write in words or simply use a numerical marking system (e.g. 1 = very weak, 10 = outstanding). This might help you identify more specifically what is causing your reservations.

	NAME	NAME	NAME	NAME
CHARACTER				
COMPETENCY				
CHEMISTRY				
CAPACITY				

To help you check the balance: Take the names of the people you are thinking of inviting and see which column they would fit into on this chart. (If necessary, go back and review the earlier material on the Five-Fold Ministry and Pioneers and Developers.)

Don't worry if you don't know this exactly – just take a guess. You aren't judging a person's character here, just trying to assess whether their leadership of an MC is going to be effective. The chart is designed with the idea that you won't know where exactly to place everyone, but usually you can work out roughly where they fit. The idea is to give a snapshot of how balanced your selection process has been. Process your thoughts with your leadership team and gain their perspective.

PINONEERS			DEVELOPERS		NOT SURE
Apostle	Prophet	Evangelist	Teacher	Pastor	

Those who land on the beach first confront the enemy dug in, fresh, and well prepared. Establishing a missional beachhead that others can subsequently land on is not for the faint-hearted. It's well worth asking the Lord who should be invited into the Pilot MC and creating the space to listen carefully.

The Invitation to the Pilot MC

Obviously there is a certain amount of basic information that you need to give people up front, partly to explain the vocabulary. An easy way to do this is with a simple letter, but it's probably worth following up with an email as well. Topics to cover could include:

- A description of Missional Communities.
- A link to a short web article (e.g., the Wikipedia article on Missional Communities[64].
- An explanation that this is an experiment to test the waters, so they are being invited to help see if this is the right thing for the church.
- Setting out the basics of a Pilot MC, including the three main elements: Huddles, community gatherings and missional OUTs.
- A clear timeline.
- A clear explanation of what is required of them. What is the commitment that you are asking for during the life of the Pilot?
- A description of the end-process, notably what their commitment is after the Pilot ends. You should make clear that, while you believe they could be future MC leaders, there is no commitment either way at this point in time.
- "What's in it for me?" This is not as shallow as it sounds! Basically it recognizes that people respond to any request with that as a filter, so be open about what benefits they will gain, both tangible and intangible. Practical benefits range from the high quality investment this will be in them, the invitation to be part of a key group of people who are helping shape the future direction of the church and the excellent food you will be serving! In addition they will have high access to you in this time, which (amazingly enough!) for many serves as a very meaningful opportunity.
- Other practicalities include how you will release participants from other commitments in the church for those four months, flexibility for those with work responsibilities that could sometimes clash, or how childcare will work (will it be provided centrally or might it be refunded out of church funds for sitters at home?)

The other thing to remind you of is to keep a lightness of touch in giving the invitation. Those of you who cook know that baking powder is really important when you bake a cake. Without it the cake will collapse under the weight of its own ingredients into something heavy and inedible. What is interesting is that not much baking powder is needed to create that lightness, although some batches of ingredients require more than others and even geographic altitude affects the amount of baking powder needed! This means that you need to keep the Pilot enjoyable for everyone – it's a big process of change that could become bogged down in its own self-importance, so keep adding fun and lightness to keep the "cake" rising.

NOTES

Think: How are you going to pitch your invitation into the Pilot?

Consider: Are you stronger or weaker at creating a sense of fun and lightness? Who can help you with this as you run the Pilot?

STEP 4 | SETTING OUTCOMES FOR YOUR PILOT MC

Purpose of a Pilot Missional Community

Now that you have gathered a group of potential MC leaders and key influencers, you can look to start the Pilot MC. This will serve as the framework within which you can train and equip this group of pioneering leaders, as you build towards the public release of MCs on Launch Sunday.

In particular, Pilot MCs have three main purposes:

1. They create a context for you to cast the vision for Missional Communities and MC life with your key leaders and influencers.
2. This group of leaders will be able to experience a taste of the three-dimensional MC life for themselves:

   UP: Through Huddles – looking at their character and skills, as people process what they are learning and experiencing.

   IN: Pilot community gatherings – tasting the possibilities for *oikos* life together.

   OUT: On mission and service – engaging directly with the community that exists beyond the church campus and learning how to recognize and pursue People of Peace.
3. Helping the first wave of MC leaders to feel equipped and ready to go, especially as they clarify the mission vision for their MC.

Pilot Practicalities

The lifespan of a Pilot is usually around four months, although obviously you are free to adjust as you see fit. It is difficult to do the process properly in much less time without exhausting everyone, while if you drag it on for too long you end up drawing on energy that should be being released into planting the new Missional Communities.

We would recommend that each member of the Pilot MC have the opportunity to experience:

1) Four Pilot Community Gatherings (IN)
2) Four Pilot Community Huddles (UP) (These could be part of the Pilot Community Gathering)
3) Two Missional Out Activities (OUT)
4) A public Launch (COMMISSIONING), where you celebrate together and release the leaders you have trained to start forming MCs.

Be aware that Pilots do have inherent weaknesses, primarily those to do with the fact that the group has a very limited lifespan. This lack of ongoing relationships – in both the community and the mission aspects – is difficult to work around, but in our experience the benefits definitely outweigh those drawbacks.

NOTES

Ponder: What are the most important outcomes that you hope for from your church's Pilot MC?

STEP 5 | RUNNING YOUR PILOT MC

Below we explain in more detail what we mean by the three different types of MC Pilot meetings:

a. Huddles (UP)
b. Gatherings (IN)
c. Mission (OUT)

However, before we do that it is probably helpful to understand this: The life of an MC is very much like different puzzle pieces coming together to form something. The community that people experience and the vibrancy that it brings aren't stuffed full into one gathering time, rather, they are dispersed throughout the month. In doing this, it allows all the beautiful, organic things to happen in between that are truly the lifeblood of the community. It is the consistency of coming together regularly with an expressed mission over a longer period of time that makes an MC work. So the following example calendar will give you a bird's eye view of how these pieces fit together.

Is it simple? Yes.

Is there tons going on each week? Not really.

But know that it is the relationships that start to form in these organized times that lead to unbelievable mission, friendship and spiritual growth *outside* these organized times. As we mentioned at the end of Step 4, the weakness of the MC Pilot is that because it has a limited lifespan, you won't see this concept fully flourished. But given the proper time in the MCs you will be launching, it definitely will.

Please note that the Appendix has a full Pilot Calendar that covers all four months of your Pilot MC, with details on how you could guide each week.

Pilot MC Huddles

Pilot Huddles provide the perfect context for you and other senior leaders to invest directly at a formative stage in the lives and vision of your key MC leaders. They will take what you model for them and invest it directly in the lives of those who subsequently join their MC. Thus you have a hands-on way to define and build the culture for MCs in your church.

Don't forget the core of a Huddle is incredibly simple. Huddle is a place where leaders in mission receive encouragement and accountability. Two fundamental questions are returned to repeatedly:

1. What is Jesus saying to you?
2. What are you going to do in response?

We suggest that your Pilot Huddles meet a minimum of once a month. You will see in our pattern of meetings that we have placed the Huddles at strategic points in order to give people a place to think about, process and apply what they are learning and experiencing. This is a deliberate approach and we would encourage you to stick with this plan.

Huddles are also excellent places to help future Missional Community leaders to develop their mission vision. This is one of the specific tasks that we will have you address in the Huddle plans below, since they are an excellent context for such activity. Make sure you have some good strong challenges as well as support going on, so that leaders are truly confident in what they are aiming at and know they have thought through potential pitfalls. The other members of the Huddle should be encouraged to be very much part of this process of iron sharpening iron.

To help everyone in this, we strongly encourage you to use some of the Huddle resources that are available. See this footnote for links on accessing the very latest materials.[65]

Once the Pilot gatherings come to an end, you will see that the Huddles continue on. This is crucially important, since this will steer your emerging MC leaders through the process of Launch Sunday and the public release of Missional Communities. Subsequently, you will have a good rhythm of Huddles established, so that you can then continue them on into the future.

You also need to think through who will lead the Pilot Huddles. If you are a larger church and have more than ten or twelve people in the Pilot, you will need to turn to your core staff team and your closest allies on the church leadership, who are fully on board both with your leadership and also the MC journey. These other leaders can each run a Huddle, even if it is a smaller one (such as a group of six) for a less confident or experienced leader. This will change your role, though, since now your most important function will be as the Huddler of the Huddlers (at another time in the month). Once your actual MCs are launched, you will want to continue to Huddle the Huddle leaders, as that will be a quick and effective way to keep aware of, as well as influence, what is going on across the church.

One of our continuing expectations of MC Leaders that is a non-negotiable: Every MC Leader is in a Huddle.

This ensures that they are receiving the investment and discipling that every Christian needs, but it also ensures that they are being held accountable for the groups of people they are leading. What we have found is that Huddling becomes an addictive thing for these leaders. Not in a co-dependent sense, but in the sense that they are constantly seeing spiritual breakthrough in their own lives, which is then seen in the people they are leading.

One item to note, here. Leading a Huddle is a skill that is developed over time. As we mentioned before, the elements of a discipling culture are High Invitation and High Challenge. Encouragement and Accountability. Relationship and Responsibility.

NOTES

Dream: In four months time, what do you want your Pilot Huddles to have accomplished?

____

____

____

____

Be Specific: What will be your markers of success that you will use with the Pilot Huddle(s)?

____

____

____

Brainstorm: Who else could be a Huddle leader in the near future?

____

____

____

____

Consider: What equipping do they need to make their Huddle a success?

____

____

____

Everyone is born with the ability to do one of these (Invitation or Challenge) better than the other, which requires you to learn the other. This will take some time. In this way, leading a Huddle is a bit of an art form. In some ways it resembles a Small Group, but in many ways it is nothing like it.

We have found that the best MC Leaders tend to be the best Huddle leaders.

They have simply worked and developed the ability to bring the best out in people and disciple their leaders incredibly well.

Pilot MC Gatherings

The Pilot MC Gatherings have two main purposes.

Firstly, they model something of how a Christian gathering in a social space operates.

Starting with food and hospitality, the Gathering models what Paul talked about in 1 Corinthians 11–14. People share thanksgiving for what God is doing in their lives. There is the breaking of bread and the opening of Scripture around the table, together bringing fresh bread that satisfies both body and soul. Worship, prayer and the ministry of the Holy Spirit are welcomed, as people look UP to the Father, IN to their life together (e.g., in healing for the sick and prophesying over those in particular need) and OUT to their city in prayer and planning for mission.

The Pilot Gathering will often break into smaller sub-sets for personal prayer and ministry time. There will be a strong sense of the saints being equipped and released for ministry in the here and now. As you look at the schedule we suggest below, note the balance between UP, IN and OUT, and try to reflect that in y our own unique Gathering.

Secondly, the Pilot is a context where training can occur that is focused especially on MC leaders. While regular MCs do not usually feature long training or teaching inputs, a Pilot may have extra training (that we have labeled "equipping"). Into that mix you might want to add some stories and reflections, maybe some input from another church or leader who is further ahead than you are, or perhaps creative ways to tie this in with your church's existing vocabulary of discipleship and vision.

NOTES

Consider: What outcomes are you looking for overall from the Pilot Gatherings?

____

____

____

____

Plan: What special things do you want to do at the first Gathering to build excitement and expectancy?

____

____

____

____

Write down: How can you build an atmosphere of both celebration and commissioning at the final Pilot Gathering?

____

____

____

____

____

____

One further note is to make sure that the senior leader doesn't do everything. MCs are about body ministry, so in the Pilot make sure that other people are involved in leading parts of the evening.

Pilot MC Mission

Mission occurs in two main ways – through witness and service. Through both, we need to learn how to identify and pursue People of Peace, following the strategy that Jesus gave us for evangelism.

In the Pilot, the main purpose is to give people a taste of doing OUT as a group operating in social space. They need to realize for themselves that it is not as difficult as the enemy would suggest. In fact, very often it is a lot of fun!

To make it effective, we suggest focusing on a mission day, when people in the MC can devote at least half a day, if not more, to a great project. Tied in with prayer (including a prayer walk) in advance, equipping on the theology of the Person of Peace and a Huddle afterwards to learn from the experiences, this should be an effective strategy for building confidence and faith in your leaders. They in turn will speak with more courage and confidence to those they end up leading in their MCs, sounding like seasoned old pros at doing mission in community.

Be aware that this is the element of the MC journey that people will be most likely to try and skip! To overcome this, your role is crucial. Make sure that you:

- Cast a compelling vision for what people are going to learn and experience.
- Do proper planning for the mission prayer walk and action day.
- Organize things really thoroughly, so that people feel secure and that their time is being well spent.
- It's better to set your goals a little lower and make sure you meet them. You want people leaving saying, "That was really good and probably we could have done even more!"
- Be an enthusiast for the specific mission activities you have planned.
- On the half days build in some (unexpected) fun and lots of laughter. It is okay for mission to be enjoyable!
- Make very clear that this is not an optional part of the process – people are expected to be there unless they have an amazing excuse.
- For people with children, try to have some OUT options that are family friendly. We have taken our children from a very young age into all sorts of mission situations. They tend to not mind dirt or poverty to the same degree that adults do, so long as they feel safe and included. Just put them in old clothes and let them loose!
- Make sure you debrief, celebrate well afterwards and tell the stories of what the Lord has done. You can use upcoming Huddles to talk through observations and reflections more deeply.

Selecting a suitable OUT for your Pilot MC is important as you are not really seeking to build long-term relationships. You are seeking real engagement in a mission situation and yet you want to do so without letting people down at the end when the Pilot concludes. There are ways around this.

We suggest that well in advance the Pilot leadership team brainstorm a number of specific OUT ideas, which have a mixture of witness and service. Look for situations where your church already has an influence that a burst of people on a particular day could enhance. If nothing is obvious, can you partner with an existing ministry, like a soup kitchen or children's home? How about talking with a key part of your geographic community? Examples of this are a local school where you can clean up or redevelop a playground, or a nursing home that would welcome some investment of labor and conversation, or taking part in a one-off community event.

Perhaps there are individuals who are People of Peace

to some of the more effective evangelists in your community who could be served, for instance by fixing up a needy person's home. It might be that you personally are a leader in these things – could the Pilot help you with your People of Peace?

The other point to note is that even though you are setting up a very short-term involvement, it might be that there is a genuine opening that a future MC could continue to develop for its mission.

Below is one simple example –

Involving Children and Families in Inner City Mission:

For our missional focus, we volunteer at Cross and Crown Mission in Oklahoma City, which offers food, clothing, medical services and more to people in need in a very poor inner city area. On Sunday nights they offer a hot meal and have a worship service, so our Missional Community, including the children, goes to worship with the folks there. This had a humble beginning:

One Saturday our families, including kids aged 1 to 13, decided to do a neighborhood-wide trash blitz, by walking through the area and picking up the (considerable!) trash along the street. We made our way to the end of the first street and one of the houses had a lot of trash in the front yard. The door was open and a woman was standing in the doorway looking suspiciously at the weird people collecting trash in front of her house. We told her what we were doing and asked if it was alright for us to come into her yard to clean up. She said it was fine, but she still looked unsure, so we were very surprised when she and her two little girls came out carrying their own trash bags and began to help us! We finished her yard quickly, but the little girls wanted to go with us and help in the rest of the neighborhood, so they latched on to the other kids in our group and stayed with us for the rest of the morning and even shared our picnic lunch. In doing the simple task of picking up trash, we helped a family take pride in their home and sparked a desire in them to help the rest of their neighbors. And it gave our kids an opportunity to make new friends and make a difference in our community.

NOTES

Think: What neighborhood or network of relationships does your church already influence? Are there local community projects with which you could meaningfully partner? Is there someone in your church who is already leading out in these things and could use some additional resources?

____

____

____

____

Consider: What specific objectives do you have for your Pilot MC mission?

____

____

____

____

Reflect: Are you personally comfortable in identifying and building relationships with the People of Peace in your own life? If not, you need to engage with this principle before you start teaching others! Ask the Lord to show you who your People of Peace are at this time.

____

____

____

____

Suggested Plans for the Pilot MC

We have written some outlines for each of the sessions for your Pilot Missional Community. They are there to help you as you see fit – please use as much or as little as you choose to!

However, we have spent some considerable time reflecting and trying to come up with plans that will take your leaders through the journey of the Pilot MC. We have intentionally put things in at strategic points, so we would encourage you to follow their format fairly closely unless you have a lot of experience with Missional Community life. Our hope also is that this takes the pressure off you as the leader in planning the content of the different sessions, freeing you up to concentrate on your leaders and sensing what the Spirit is saying to you all.

The suggested plans for the Pilot meetings can be found in an appendix at the back of this book.

CASE STUDY:
Church of the Good Shepherd, CA

The Lutheran Church of the Good Shepherd, in Torrance, California,[66] went down the route of running a Pilot in order to bring a number of people onto the same page. Lead Pastor Bob Rognlien kindly shared his reflections on what they experienced and learned.

As we look back on our Pilot:

- It was great to widen our circle of Christian friends by meeting new people and connecting in a Missional Community.
- It was so helpful to get input from others to help us discern what God was saying and then get the support we needed to respond and follow through.
- There is something refreshing and powerful about being together in a simple environment with friends, the Word of God and the guidance of the Spirit – kind of like the way Jesus did it with his disciples.
- The Pilot MC was a bit artificial since we didn't form organically through relationships around a common missional purpose.
- For those who didn't know a lot of the people, it was fairly overwhelming to come into a group of 60 at the very start. Also, this didn't leave any room to invite new people.
- For the reasons stated above we never really got much traction to do mission together.

We agreed that God was speaking to us through both the successes and the shortcomings of our Pilot Missional Community so that we could be better prepared to help pioneer this "new" (old?) way of doing life together for the sake of others.

As we moved into "real" Missional Communities, here are some lessons we applied:

- Be very clear about the missional OUT of the Missional Community from the start.
- Make sure Missional Communities develop organically by building relationships.
- Don't start with too many people, so that there is room to grow.
- Be sure the leaders have lots of support to effectively meet the challenges of leadership.

STEP 6 | EFFECTIVE COMMUNICATION IN PREPARATION FOR LAUNCH SUNDAY

Assuming that your Pilot MC leaders now have a clear sense of their Missional Vision and have given their MC a name, it is now time to coach them in effective communication of what the Lord has placed in their hearts. This can take place as part of a Pilot MC Gathering or Huddle, and we recommend that you include the following in your coaching:

1) Be Concrete

Interestingly, 70% of the population prefer to gather and processes information using their five senses. The more they can touch, taste, see, hear and even smell the vision of your MC, the more real it will become for them and the easier for them to commit to it. (The other 30% prefer to see the big picture first and work their way back to the details.) When you describe your MC, use the five senses to help craft your communication. A visual presentation is essential for Launch Sunday. Who are you seeking to reach? Who are the leaders? When is it going to meet? How do people sign up? Where can they ask their questions?

2) Be Realistic

Don't set the bar for initial entry too high. Invitation to relationship should always precede the Challenge to do something! High-octane Pioneers (Base Ministry apostles, prophets and evangelists) who want to change the world can always gather a few fellow revolutionaries who are happy to be all in no matter the cost. However, the long-term success of their MC will depend on whether they can recruit and empower the Developers (Base Ministry teachers and pastors) to build on the new frontiers.

3) Be Accessible

People follow a leader before they follow their vision. The vast majority of the people who join your MC will do so because you personally invite them! The first disciples on the beach did not have a clue what "I will make you fishers of men" meant, they simply accepted an invitation to walk with Jesus. You are not holding yourself up as the perfect example, but you are inviting people to join you as you follow the vision the Lord has given you. It is usually the combination of passion for the Mission Vision and personal vulnerability that creates the context for others to trust and follow you.

Investing such wisdom in the life of your first MC leaders will pay huge dividends. Make them work hard at their communication skills and get them to practice sharing their Mission Vision and the process of invitation within the safe relationships of the Pilot MC. Make a comprehensive visual presentation a condition of their participation in Launch Sunday.

Examples of How Some Churches Define Their Approach to MCs

When senior leaders are considering communication with the wider church, it might be helpful to look at a few other churches' definitions of MCs taken from their own publicity. There are links to sections on their church websites that focus on Missional Communities in the footnotes at the end of this book. Here is a small selection.

Lutheran Church of the Good Shepherd, Torrance, CA

Missional Communities are known as Clusters[67]

"A house-full of friends on a mission!"

If you want to make a positive difference in the world and do it with a group of friends, then Clusters are for you! Clusters are groups of 20-50 people who gather regularly in homes to do life together and carry out a common purpose beyond themselves. They have fun, share meals, pray, have fun, read the Bible, have fun, welcome new people, serve those in need, and – you guessed it – have fun! You are invited to come and try out any Cluster until you find one that fits you. Just call the leader and find out how to be part of their next activity.

St Philip's Church, Moon Township, PA

Missional Communities are known as MSCs[68]

Mid-sized Communities (MSCs) are closely connect-ed groups of people who are actively calling people to faith in Jesus while serving the community and the world. Within MSCs are smaller groups of people who are growing a deeper relationship with Jesus, while building deep lasting relationships with each other. When small groups combine and share a common purpose or mission, efforts to reach out to those in need and those longing for Jesus can be accomplished. Think of it this way – MSCs are small enough to share a vision and large enough to do something about it. Ready to bear fruit? Explore our MSCs.

Love Canton, Canton, Ohio

Missional Communities are known as Villages[69]

Villages are the main way that we live out relationships UP, IN and OUT. They are the environments where we can become disciples of Jesus together if we are intentional about it. Each Village is centered around a common mission to reach out to a specific neighborhood, sector or demographic in Canton in Jesus' name. So proximity is a big deal.

Villages are relational environments of around 15-50 people that feel kind of like a family reunion. Villages are small enough to have a common mission together but large enough to do something about it. They are communities where we'll be missed if we are gone and where we all can be a part. Villages are made up of smaller accountability groups where we are able to really be known and encouraged to keep running after Jesus – kind of like immediate family. Villages are always led by at least two people who are accountable to being a part of a Leadership Huddle. The vision and direction of the Village primarily come from the leaders with the input of the rest of the community. Each Village will have a unique identity and rhythm for doing things, and will be a part of the larger Love Canton community when we all come together for Celebration.

Trinity Grace Church, New York City[70]

Missional Communities are groups of 30-50 people that work together for three things: first, to grow in our relationship with God and understand our identity in him; second, to grow closer together in fellowship and relationships; and third, to serve our city in mercy and justice projects. Each Missional Community consists of a number of smaller groups known as Lifegroups designed for accountability, discipleship, prayer and communion.

Generation Axis, Willow Creek Church, Chicago

Missional Communities are known as Missional Community Hubs, or MCHs[71]

MCHs are at the epicenter of everything we do in Axis. These are communities based out of someone's house, apartment or condo in a neighborhood throughout the Chicago-land area. They exist to bring redemptive change to their neighborhoods through gatherings, serving initiatives, social events and discipleship opportunities. This is where life happens in Axis and our dream is to see Missional Community Hubs launched all over our city…

Life Transformation Groups (LTGs) are seasonal, gender-based groups of three or four people that seek to live out the teachings of Jesus in intimate community with focuses on Scripture, prayer and accountability. These communities are generally born out of relationships within your Missional Community Hub.

Eikon Community Church, Richmond, VA[72]

Our community life and strongest expression of "church" is found in our Missional Communities. A Missional Community (MC) is a group of 20-50 people who share a missional identity. Each MC has a specific flavor as each is creating a community with different people and in different places. As you can imagine, our Artists' MC is quite different from our MC that is geared towards young families which is quite different from our MC that is emerging in the homeless community.

Our end goal is that people will find their primary identity of "church" within this group about the size of an extended family. Are we still connected to a deeper and wider movement that is Eikon Community Church? Of course. But this allows our church to exist more as a movement than the institutional church most of us are familiar with.

MCs are small enough that people can know you and know if you're missing, but large enough to actually do something substantive in the world. We work to build strong relationships that support and encourage each other through the good times, the tough times and each MC regularly gathers together to serve the world, making it a better place in Jesus' name.

In this way, we can be true to our calling: *We exist to be a movement of people joining Jesus in the renewal of all things.*

Norman Community Church, Norman, OK

Missional Communities are known as House Churches and small groups are known as Discipleship Groups[73]

House Churches are composed of Discipleship Groups that share the same or very similar vision. Often, they have resulted from the multiplication of a single original Discipleship Group. Two or three Discipleship Groups together would usually be considered an "emerging" House Church, and by the time Discipleship Groups were multiplying from four to six or eight, the House Church itself would usually multiply into two new House Churches.

House Churches allow us to do certain things that are not possible in either the Discipleship Groups or the Celebration. They provide a greater context for encouraging every-member ministry than Discipleship Groups alone. In particular, they provide the bridge between these two other groups that allows members to grow in their giftings and ministry it's a big gap between leading worship for 10 people to doing that for 300! House Churches also provide the structure for church growth through mission across the whole city, not only by raising up leaders but also by increasing the "surface area" through which people can enter the church.

STEP 7 | PREPARING THE WIDER CHURCH FOR LAUNCH SUNDAY

All of us at some point have been "strongly encouraged" to join a group, being told that it will be a wonderful, life-giving experience. We go along, only to discover that while you may share a common faith, you don't share a common life with the other group members. You might keep going for a while out of loyalty or a desire to grow in Christ, all the time hoping that there must be a better way of doing life together.

Generally, such socially-engineered groups don't create a healthy platform for dynamic community life to emerge. We may create a meeting, but programming an event into our calendars does not produce a sense of shared connectedness and purpose.

Jon Tyson comments that, "Despite its good intentions, programmed community often feels like a small group version of eHarmony. Fill out a life stage/felt need profile and you are matched up with other people at a similar stage of life and loneliness with the hope that it all works out." Of course, such a foundation means that there is very little trust or energy to release missional life. Tyson continues, "These inward-facing, need-based groups often fail to take into consideration the Kingdom of God at large."[74]

So as we move into thinking about how to deliver this in your church, our plea is not to do so in a heavily programmatic manner. Missional Communities work best when they have a deftness and lightness of touch about them, so that they seem to emerge out of the very fabric of the church's life, reflecting both the vision and values that you all hold dear. People need to feel wooed rather than driven into the community, so that they are held there by relational rather than organizational bonds. If you can achieve this, MC members will genuinely feel a high level of ownership to the group, which is when the energy, effort and persistence required for significant growth will occur.

Communicating to the Whole Church

Alongside the Pilot, which is where you prepare and train your leaders, you also need a strategy for communicating to the whole church, so that you win hearts and minds for the experiment of Missional Communities.

We encourage a mixture of process and event for doing this. The process includes the training of the leaders in the Pilot. With the whole church, it is about finding ways to drip-feed the ideas and to speak into the underlying principles of using MCs. This gives people time to think things through for themselves and talk about it in their relational networks.

The one thing to be aware of is that when the senior leader of a church announces something on a Sunday morning, people's tendency is to HEAR it as, "this is a done deal," however much the leader insists it isn't! So you will need to work hard to communicate clearly, especially if you are using Pilots to genuinely assess whether or not Missional Communities could work for you. Think through what key terms you will use, such as "experiment" or "testing lab."

As you communicate to everyone, be conscious that you are engaged in high-level change management. This means that you need to frame this transition in grace-filled and positive ways. For instance, make clear that the old way the church did things was not wrong or bad. Affirm that those things were started for excellent reasons at that stage in the life of the church and you are simply building on those values.

You don't want Missional Communities to feel like a hostile takeover of the church. Take the time to think through how to demonstrate that MCs build on the past, not disown it. Make sure you know your history, as consequently you can show how it fits with the long-standing vision of your church (for instance, if it was originally planted to impact a particular neighborhood or network of relationships). If the specifics of your context have changed, show how MCs can help you honor the principles that lay behind the original vision for the church, even if the out workings have developed over time.

The event part will include certain points along the way where information, vision and testimony are shared, culminating in what we call Launch Sunday. That is the weekend where the whole focus of the church's service(s) is to publicly launch MCs and invite people to find out as much as they need to in order to commit to trying one out. The goal is coming out of Launch Sunday with the ability to engage tangibly with the process of building and developing a variety of MCs led by those who were in the Pilot MC.

Communication Strategy

At what stage does the whole church hear about the vision for launching MCs?

While there is no right or wrong here, we recommend that you start talking about Missional Communities in broad terms early on, perhaps a couple of months into this six-month process. This would be fairly soon after you have gained the approval of your board for the Pilot MC and have recruited the first wave of MC leaders for the Pilot.

Preaching

In many churches, the primary way of steering the whole church will be through sermons. In this build-up period, some of these topics would be great to cover:

- Community
- Mission
- People of Peace
- Balancing the relationships of life between UP-IN-OUT
- How the New Testament presents church life (*oikos*, etc.)
- Romans 16 (on *oikos* in the New Testament – see earlier in this book for details on that)
- God's heart for the city
- What the Bible says about the lost, the last and the least
- The principles of MCs, including how they fit into the vision of your church
- Some church leaders have simply chosen to preach through one of the synoptic Gospels (often Mark) during the six months or so of the Pilot phase.

Here are some themes you might like to include in your communication strategy with the wider church during the Pilot MC process:

The Challenge:

- The priority of being witnesses.
- We all want to do OUT, but struggle so much with it.
- To understand how our society has changed (e.g., globalization, post-modernity, less religious and yet more spiritual, fragmentation of families and community, etc.).
- People are far more relationally based in how they do life, so they want to know that they are valued

and accepted for who they are before they consider whether the claims of Christ are true and valid.
- Sunday services will only reach some of the lost (as a huge generalization, those who are middle-class or aspirational middle-class, more culturally conservative, de-churched as opposed to unchurched). However, we need to do something more if we are to reach all of our city/community.

Our response:

- Going as a group to where the lost are.
- Studying the early church.
- Explain the concept of mid-sized MCs and how they relate to the Minster Church (the resourcing central church).
- Explain the core elements of MCs.
- Being different from small groups (see further on in the book for more on this).
- Being lightweight/low maintenance and flexible.
- Having Sunday services that serve the Missional Communities, not everything serving the center.
- The measure of success is not whether everyone reached will come to a Sunday church service, but whether the lost are being saved and appropriate expressions of church are being formed.
- Talk about the values of the three different sizes of gathering (celebration, MC, small group). Explain how these will be your yardsticks for decision making.

Examples:

- What does it look like? When does it take place? (The answer is that it depends. There's a huge variety; give a few examples.)
- 1 Corinthians 11-14 as a model for life together. This includes praise, thanksgiving, breaking bread, stories, studying Scripture and applying it to our lives, intercession, practical support, gifts of the Spirit and training opportunities etc.
- The Person of Peace strategy is central, as we look to do *oikos* evangelism, through missional houses of Kingdom life infiltrating our city life.

Alongside public teaching, written documents are clearly also going to be important. You'll probably want to include more than just information. Find stories that stir their hearts and cast a vision of what your MC could be. You can also link people to more information and perspectives via blogs written by a number of leaders specifically on their experiences of launching MCs (see www.weare3dm.com for some current examples). The Wikipedia article on Missional Communities has been quite helpful for many leaders.

Somewhere in the mix, many churches have found it productive to have a team come in from another church that has already implemented Missional Communities. They can speak into your church community out of experience that carries great credibility, especially if they share their mistakes as well as their successes. Testimonies from the front lines will be stirring and inspirational. One plan could be for them to lead a church weekend for you, whether at home or by going away together. Have them share in your weekend services. Towards the end of the weekend they could meet with your church board, to process your questions.

As you approach Launch Sunday, a constructive next step is to encourage people to join you and the leaders of the church in praying both for the missional effectiveness of the church and your community life. Create a point of contact for people to feed back what they sense prophetically. If God doesn't want you to go down the MC route, then you want to hear him. Alternatively if this is his direction, then having that confirmed from a variety of people is greatly encouraging to the whole church.

NOTES

Brainstorm: What are your ideas for making communication about MCs effective and fruitful? Write everything down, both big picture and small detail.

Consider: What do you think will be the major objections to MCs (however unreasonable) from your congregation?

Reflect: Are there elements of the history of your church upon which MCs could build?

Plan: How can you start to address these concerns?

STEP 8 | RUNNING A LAUNCH SUNDAY

Launch Sunday is your public launch of Missional Communities. It is the simplest way for your wider church family to connect with an MC that particularly appeals to them. It represents the culmination of at least six months hard work and personal investment, so obviously you'll want to be well prepared.

Service outline

As a running schedule we recommend the following:

1) Welcome and Worship (20 minutes) – a brief overview of how Launch Sunday is going to work.
2) Show a video of the Pilot MC in action (3-5 mins).
3) Have three testimonies from the Pilot MC – choose leaders who represent different base ministries and make sure at least one is a Teacher or a Pastor. (Get them to prepare in advance what they are going to say!) (10 mins).
4) A short talk to explain to people how they should approach MCs and what they should expect (10 mins) –
    a. To grow "UP, IN and OUT."
    b. Be willing to serve.
    c. They will be giving and receiving.
    d. Flexibility – it won't be the same every time.
    e. Realize it will feel different from Sunday services.
    f. Be encouraged to actively contribute to the group.
    g. Freedom to fail is a high value, so MCs can be a place where people experiment and attempt new things.
    h. There's no perfect group.
5) Explain the process of the MC Fair and then release people to go and look around at the tables that interest them (40 mins). There will need to be some activities planned for younger children while everyone else is checking out the different MCs.
6) Gather everyone back together and finish with a prayer.

Practicalities

Below are our five non-negotiables for making your Launch Sunday a huge success:

1) Communicate early on with your Pilot MC leaders about the planned date. Give them time to plan, pray and prepare. Make sure they know exactly what is expected of them and have a clear sense of how the process is going to work.
2) Communicate with the wider church in advance through multiple media, emphasizing that this is going to be a significant day in the life of the church. You need to make a big deal out of this day, showering it with energy, profile and importance. If necessary, clear the church calendar surrounding it so that nothing else clashes.
3) Appoint a small team of people to oversee the practicalities of Launch Sunday. Gantt charts and project management may not be your favorite things in the world, but there will be people in your church family who love it and will be only too happy to invest their expertise in making Launch Sunday a huge success.

4) Transform the church building to grab people's attention. We recommend that you give each new MC a space in the building, some presentation boards, a large table and a $30 budget. Create a "Farmer's Market" type atmosphere. Maybe have some musicians spread throughout the building playing, enhancing the energy and atmosphere of the occasion. Make it loads of fun, as this will enable lots of groups to raise their profile and most people to find an MC in whose mission vision they are interested.

5) Celebrate the Pilot MC with story/testimony and video footage of the Pilot MC Gatherings/ Missional "OUTs." This will profile the new MC leaders and also make concrete what actually went on during the Pilot MC. This will involve advance planning but there are often people who love to use their skills to make a promotional video for a Pilot MC.

Preparing the MC Leaders for Follow-up

Here are some examples of items you could include in a summary document to your MC leaders as they prepare for Launch Sunday:

- During Launch Sunday the wider church family will be invited to walk around and engage with you and other potential MC leaders. This is your chance to promote your vision and connect people to your group. You have permission and a fishing license to invite anyone you'd like into your group.
- Every stand needs your MC name, a concise Missional Vision statement and an explanation of what you'll be doing in the next six months. This will give people something tangible to consider and take away with them. You may also want a signup sheet to collect names and email addresses and phone numbers.
- You need a short "elevator speech" to be able to explain your Missional Vision. It can't be longer than 30 seconds and you need to practice.
- Know the event to which you can invite interested persons in order to find out more about your MC. We suggest you have at least two specific dates planned; something with a missional flavor to it and something more social.
- Every MC will have a table at which to be based. You have been given a $30 budget to use to make your table attractive and interesting. This can be for decoration, food, balloons and giveaways; anything that will attract people to your table and help start a conversation.
- Have plenty of information available about your group. Use laptops, posters, flyers, maps, mission statement, prayer request sheets, etc. Centrally we will provide business cards and the MC Family Tree informational board.
- Please feel free to use the workroom at the office to make any copies for handouts, etc. (but please don't wait until that Sunday morning!).
- Decide who will represent the MC. Will it be just the MC leaders, or include others on your core team? Make it about two to four people so you don't intimidate people.
- Please ask those who are already committed to your MC not to clog up your table, in order to leave room for people to browse who are not already connected to your MC. This would be a great time for them to find out what's going on in other MCs, so that they can pray more knowledgeably.

STEP 9 | GROWING YOUR MC

So the new MCs have been launched. Launch Sunday and all of the associated excitement are now a faint and distant memory. You now have MCs of varying flavors, representing different types of leaders and sizes.

Some groups have more than twenty people in their Core Team, already making it the size of an extended family.

Some groups have ten to fifteen in the Core Team, making it the size of a large small group, but still under that extended family size.

With other MCs, the Core Team is relatively small, with maybe four to eight people.

For all of these new MCs, though there are questions of what it looks like to contextually do UP and IN, the driving question is about OUT: **How do we grow our MC?**

Now we have devoted a whole section to OUT a little later in the book, but we think it is worth digging into on a more general level before we get there. How do Missional Communities grow and sustain their increased numbers?

What we'd like to discuss is not the way that it always happens, but the way that often happens. In other words, this isn't prescriptive, rather, it is *descriptive*. Much of this section is largely taken from a gem of a book, *Sowing, Reaping and Keeping* by Laurence Singlehurst.[75]

If you have ever read much on church growth and evangelism you have probably heard of the Engel scale, which is meant to be a descriptive tool that tracks where people are in relation to faith and maturity. Where the Engel scale gives a window into how people are *feeling* or *experiencing* things, Singlehurst's inverted triangle (very similar to a purchase funnel) gives a window into what seems to be a normative process for people outside of a faith community experiencing community and eventually coming to faith and maturity.

The progression is simple and is seen in Jesus' Parable of the Sower:

1) The seeds of the Gospel are sown to many, many people with varying levels of depth (Sowing Stage. In the original book there were two phases of Sowing, S1 and S2, but our good friends Bob and Mary Hopkins shrewdly showed why an additional Sowing Phase, S3, is necessary).
2) The seed sprouts in some people's hearts, grows, and they respond, decide to follow Jesus and step more fully into the Kingdom (Reaping Stage).
3) They continue to grow deeper roots, become more mature and sow and reap with the others in community (Keeping Stage).

When given a picture, it becomes a lot clearer how this can be effective for MCs.

You will need your Missional Communities to have many People of Peace. These are people who like you, want to spend time with you, are interested in you and your life (and more than likely your friends' lives as well). How do People of Peace move from

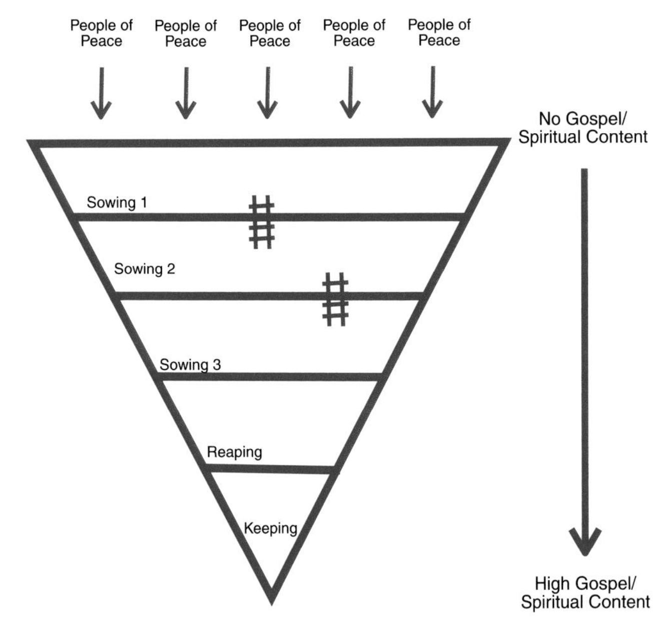

being disconnected from community to being fully integrated into the life of community and the Kingdom of God?

What should by now be the obvious answer is that it happens best through relationships.

They are exposed to more people who know Jesus, have an opportunity to see his power at work, see the extraordinary lives of his disciples, hear the Gospel and want to respond to it. This inverted triangle of Sowing, Reaping and Keeping is the descriptive process of how this often works.

With a cursory glance you'll notice that there are more people at the top of the triangle than at the bottom. You'll also notice that as Gospel/Spiritual content increases, the number of people moving further into the triangle decreases. These two things are obviously related. The higher the Gospel content, the lower the number of people. It was true with Jesus, and it is true today.

Sowing 1 (S1)

In this stage, People of Peace (POPs) interact only on a relational level with you and whatever people they might also be spending time with in your community. They probably know you're a Christian and that you know the other people from "church," but there is no Gospel/Spiritual content involved in this stage (unless, of course, they happen to ask any questions). The only thing you want them to walk away thinking is:

1) I like those guys.
2) I think God might be good.
3) Maybe Christians aren't that weird.

In his book *The Tangible Kingdom*, Hugh Halter remarks, "Sometimes I wonder if evangelism is simply defying people's expectations of Christians."[76] That is what S1 is all about. They are probably surprised they liked you and "your friends from church" so much. They are surprised they want to spend more time with your community.

What are some S1 examples?

A lot of times the organic ones are the best (remember, Missional Communities have formal times together, but they are simply the springboard for some of the best stuff, which is often organic).

+ Dinner with you and a few other friends who are also in the MC.
+ Watching a football game with a few people in the MC.
+ A shopping trip with a few people in the MC.
+ Golf or a game night with a few people in the MC.

On a more organized, all-MC level:

+ Big party with everyone from the MC where everyone invites their POPs.
+ White water rafting trip with the whole MC and people's POPs.

+ Large, open room where artists can come and artistically express themselves and then share their work. It would include people in the MC and their invited POPs.

In essence, S1 is about creating space (with a few or a lot of people) where people can connect relationally in very easy ways.

Sowing 2 (S2)

This stage is still relying very heavy on the relational (as each stage will), but a little bit of Gospel/Spiritual content is added into the mix.

And when we say a little bit, we mean just a little bit.

What are some S2 examples?

+ A story time with a few friends and their kids at Barnes and Noble where the books being read have spiritual content and POPs are joining in with their kids.
+ Watching a movie and then talking about the spiritual implications – everyone can join in, nothing is off limits, people can say what they like!
+ Serving the homeless by giving out street survival kits but the occasion also includes a brief Bible study and quick prayer and POPs are present.
+ An MC meal with the whole MC and before eating, each person says what they are thankful to God for, a prayer is given and then everyone eats together. POPs participate.

Often in the S2 phase, stories and personal narratives are the most compelling Gospel/Spiritual content. POPs walk away and think, "Wow, their faith actually means something to them, and they are different because of it. That's really interesting."

You'll notice when looking at the diagram that there is a bridge from S1 to S2. This is a very important dimension to understand. When people move further down into the triangle from S1 to S2, *they must choose to go there*. In other words, you don't want to surprise them with spiritual content when they are not expecting there to be any. It is up to you and the people in your MC to ask them if they want to go to that place. That bridge represents a bridge of trust that you cannot afford to burn.

Because once it's burned, it's really hard to rebuild.

Bob and Mary Hopkins tell a story about a Missional Community that was reaching out to young moms and they had a monthly playgroup that had been going for about a year. It was really well attended with 25-30 moms, very few of whom knew Jesus, and the women were quickly becoming good friends. The pastor of the church, who was an evangelist at heart, was a little frustrated that only a few had become Christians over the previous year, so he stepped in. For their December playgroup he hired a specialty Children's Evangelist and sprung it on the playgroup. Needless to say, it landed with a dull thud and that next January fewer than half of the women came back.[77]

NOTES

Brainstorm: As you think about your specific MC and your mission, what could be S1 ideas?

____

____

____

____

____

____

Letting people choose to engage with spiritual content is really important.

How might you do that? Take our example of working with the homeless. Many people who don't know God are very open to participating in God's mission.

You could easily say to your POP: "Hey, I know you've done some work with the homeless before and thought you might like to join me and a few friends on Saturday morning. We're handing out weekly survival kits and just hanging out, drinking coffee with them, nothing too crazy."

POP: "Yeah, that sounds really good."

You: "Just an FYI, usually when we go down there, we read a piece of Scripture to the homeless guys that come out and pray with anyone that's had a hard week. Obviously you don't have to pray for anyone, but just wanted to give you a heads up. That alright with you?"

It really doesn't need to be a big thing, but you'll want to make sure they have a heads up and have the opportunity to bow out and say, "No." Not everyone will move from S1 to S2 and not everyone will move at the same rate of speed.

Sowing 3 (S3)

Up to this point in the process, there hasn't been any explicit telling or sharing of the Gospel as a whole. A big reason for this is a principle that Jesus seemed to use most the time: **He let people experience something before explaining it.**

In the framework of Luke 10, People of Peace meet someone, spend time with them, taste community, see the power of God in a very real way, and *then they are told that the Kingdom of God is near to them*. People experienced and tasted the goodness and power of the Kingdom, and then they were told the Gospel.

In many ways this is what is happening with S1 and S2 if our POPs spend enough time there. They get to experience the goodness of God through you and the beauty of real community and perhaps through the power of community or God's power shown in other ways, they experience the Kingdom in an almost visceral way.

S3 is when they hear the full Gospel *but are not asked to give a response*. The simply hear it and are given a chance to process, ask questions, let it sink more fully into their spirit. Once again, there is a bridge of trust from S2 to S3 where people need to know what they are walking into and aren't surprised by the level of spiritual content and have the opportunity to say, "No."

NOTES

Brainstorm: With your specific MC and your mission, what could be some S2 ideas?

____

____

____

____

____

Brainstorm: With your specific MC and your mission, what would be a few S3 ideas?

____

____

____

____

____

What are some S3 examples?

+ A Christmas Eve service. Often these are beautiful services that fully explain the Gospel but usually don't offer a forced or awkward response time.
+ A conversation you have with them that naturally leads there because they are asking questions about what they have experienced. That is why Peter tell us, "Always be ready to give a reason for the hope that you have, but do so with gentleness and respect" (1 Peter 3:15).
+ A neighborhood Vacation Bible Club your MC is throwing at someone's house during the summer (a slightly more incarnational approach to VBS).

Again, notice that these examples cover the gamut of natural conversation, church-wide event and an event that involves the whole Missional Community.

Reaping

The Reaping stage is not much different from S3, except that you sense through the Holy Spirit that the POP is ready to receive an invitation to respond to the Gospel and become a disciple of Jesus. At this point the person is probably a regular attendee and participant in your Missional Community and no longer needs to be asked if they are OK with hearing more. They've heard it all and they are still coming back for more.

The Reaping stage is when the seed has been sown, it has taken root in good soil, it has received water and nourishment, it has grown and is now ready for harvest.

What are some Reaping examples?

+ You have a conversation over coffee with a few friends in the MC, and you ask the POP if they want to become a disciple of Jesus and live more fully in his Kingdom.
+ Your MC goes on a two-day retreat that is full of fun, laughing, down time, teaching and worship followed by a chance for everyone to respond to what God is saying to them.
+ You have shared the Gospel with your POP for the first time, and they are clearly ready to respond.

Keeping

It's not enough to have someone make a decision to be a disciple of Jesus. We want them to actually *become* a disciple of Jesus. Yes, they have come in with the harvest, but now they can join in on the fun! They scatter seeds and walk their own POPs through this process. Not only will they often bring an entire new network of people with them (POPs generally serve as gatekeepers to wider communities), but they will mature, develop, see healing and restoration, serve and lead in the Missional Community.

NOTES

Brainstorm: With your specific MC and your mission, what might be workable reaping ideas?

In other words, crossing a line in the sand isn't enough. We want to keep them. We are not called to make converts, we are called to make disciples.

In the last twenty years, much of the work we have done has been focused on this Keeping phase, as we have developed Huddles and Missional Communities that we believe are instrumental to making disciples instead of converts.

Everyone Plays a Role

As we have seen this play out, there is a unique opportunity for everyone to get in on the action of evangelism in your Missional Community. Most people assume that evangelism is a pressure packed, awkward, sweaty experience where we are called to "witness" to unsuspecting victims. In contrast, the beauty of this Sowing, Reading and Keeping process is that within MC life it allows people to play to their strengths.

More than likely you will have a few people in your group who are better at doing S1 than anyone you've ever seen. They throw parties and half the city shows up. Theirs is the house that everyone goes to and the couple that everyone wants to be around. They have an almost magnetic quality to them. They do fun better than anyone you know. They love Jesus, people love being around them, but they are also more than a little nervous about sharing their faith. It's not because they are ashamed, it's because they seem to stutter, get nervous and suddenly get very awkward.

Should they work on getting better? Absolutely.

But what if they understood that they have been gifted with gathering large numbers of people? They enable those people to relax, have fun and can create community by being generous with their time and resources. They should be encouraged to realize that this is vital to allowing other relationships inside and outside the MC to flourish. What if S1 was their home turf for your MC's plans? What if S1 was how they fulfilled their role in evangelism until the baton is passed on to someone in your MC gifted with the S2 phase?

The same is true of the other stages.

Some people may not be great at gathering people, but they have a gift for sensing when people are ready to hear an insightful spiritual remark (S2) or are able to share the Gospel in a warm, welcoming way (S3).

If you can help people find their sweet spots as leaders and servants within your MC you will see remarkable growth and transformation in the life of your Missional Community.

The Center, the Fringe and the Inverted Triangle

More than likely your experience is similar to ours: most churches, over time, become quite insular, creating a type of bubble and as more time passes, more relationships with people who aren't Christians fall by the wayside.

There is the Center (people in church/MCs), and there is the Fringe (relationships with people who don't know Jesus yet).

For most churches, it looks like this:

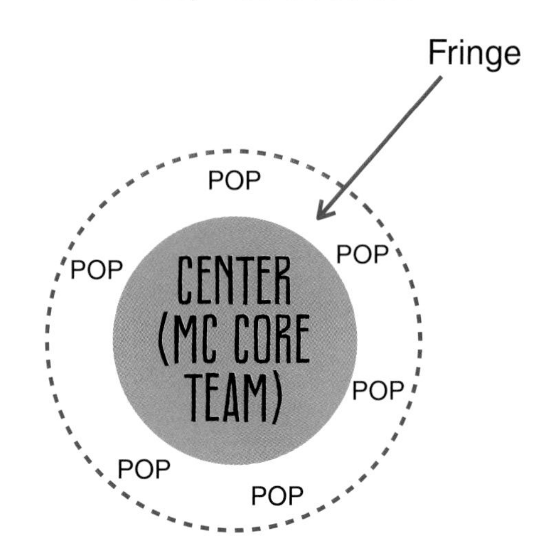

When you look at it in light of what we just covered, you realize what needs to happen: We need a bigger Fringe. There just aren't enough People of Peace to really grow the group.

If our MCs only collectively know five to ten POPs, and even those relationships are dodgy at best, we will need to spend more time doing S1 type activities. In other words, be where the most people are. As your Fringe grows with your S1 OUT activities, you will be able to start attending to your S2, S3 and beyond. Moreover, as your Fringe grows, you will have access to even more networks as more people are becoming missional disciples.

The good news is that if you have a small Fringe, the antidote is your MC spending quite a bit of time having fun together and inviting others into the fun! Find the people who are magnetic, who do S1 better than anyone else, and let them run wild.

Eventually this will build relationships with POPs who will begin to move further down the funnel towards being committed disciples of Jesus Christ.

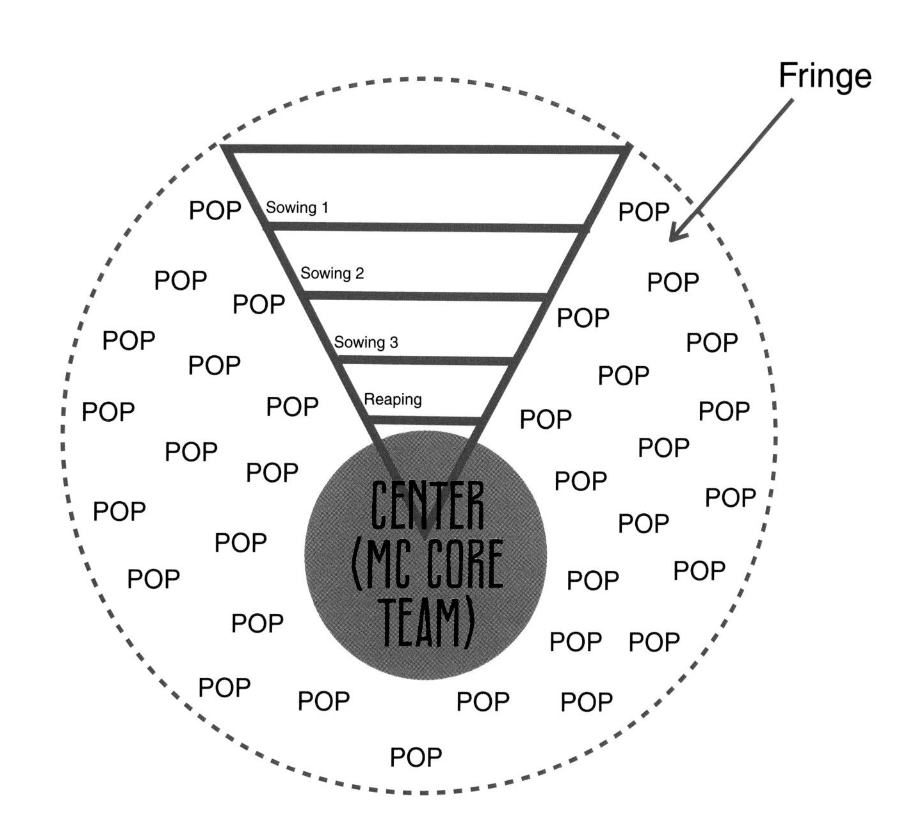

ADDENDUM | CHURCH PLANTING WITH MCS

While most readers will be in already existing churches, where using Missional Communities will involve a process of transition, we also realize that some of you will be in what we term pioneering contexts. These fall into two main categories.

1) You have the opportunity to plant a new church and build from the ground up, which means that you have the option of using Missional Communities from day one.

2) You are part of an existing and (probably) a large church where you are being released to start a new expression of church, again giving you the possibility of utilizing MCs from the beginning. This might be a vision to reach a new demographic (perhaps college students) or a geographic area with clear openings. You will be part of the whole church, but within your area of responsibility you are being given considerable freedom as to how you will build.

Clearly most of what we have written in this Launch Guide still applies to some degree and has probably been helpful, but we wanted to speak to some of the unique issues that you face.

This Addendum isn't meant to be a formula. Undoubtedly your context will create variations off of this template. However, it is the general path we have seen many, many churches/new ministries use as they are starting from scratch.

Process for Planting: Discipleship Leads to Mission

+ Start a Huddle

You (the leader) plus eight people. We understand that the inclination and current way of church planting is to get as many people as you can in your Core Team. The idea that a total of nine people is one of the best sizes to plant a church feels somewhat counterintuitive.

In fact, in the current mode of church planting where even the more missional expressions still try to get up a Sunday service as quickly as possible, there are three magic numbers:

45 If you have forty-five people in your Core Team to start the church, you have five to six times the likelihood of succeeding.

2 If you have two pastors on staff from the get-go, your chances go way up.

70 If you have seventy people in your Core Team, your chances of failure are virtually non-existent.

Ed Stetzer and his team at Lifeway have done a fantastic job examining things like this and are even now researching different avenues for planting viable missional churches. Without dismissing their insights, we would want to say that a long-term multiplying church plant in the culture today is most likely to occur through turning everyone into disciple-makers. In our experience, discipling people so well that they become multipliers, or missional disciples, works almost every time.

As our good friend Mick Woodhead says, "It's not hard to grow a church. It's just really hard to make disciples."[78]

If you can make missional disciples, your church will grow. The real battle is in discipleship. If you are going to play the odds, if you are going to play the numbers, play the ones with the highest rate of success: missional disciples = success.

If you can disciple people who know how to disciple people who know how to disciple people, well, that's a church growth plan the way Jesus did it. How does that play out practically? People know going into a Huddle that if you're in a Huddle, one day you'll start a Huddle. It's actually about raising the bar, not lowering it.

The real problem, as Dallas Willard has talked about, is that people don't know how to make disciples. We see people engaging in community and often becoming "nicer" people in Small Groups, but we rarely see the type of movement towards being a radical, missional disciple that Jesus seems to be talking about.

For us, after years of experimenting, honing and practicing, we have found a discipleship vehicle in Huddles that seems to actually make disciples. (It probably should come as no great surprise that, in the end, the Huddle looks a lot like the way Jesus discipled his disciples.)

Does this process of gathering eight for a Huddle take more time than the "gather a Core Team and throw up a weekly worship service as quickly as possible" route?

Definitely.

The numbers aren't going to be that impressive after one year.

But we'd say almost every time we overestimate what we can accomplish in our strength in one year and vastly underestimate what God can do in his strength in five years.

What you are aiming for is exponential growth, not growth by addition. To get exponential growth it takes time for things to build until you hit a *tipping point.*

So grab eight people you feel God is calling you to invest in and disciple, and start a Huddle. Make sure they know this is high commitment and that your ultimate goal isn't to form the trendiest church they've ever seen. But this will unlock the life they've only dreamed of.

+ **Do life with this Huddle: Create the mid-sized, extended family experience.**

While you have a formalized Huddle every other week, this group will, over time, become like extended family. So you'll want to hang out a lot. What you will quickly notice is that the language of discipleship you learn in Huddle makes its way very naturally into other conversations. So while Huddle is formalized discipleship time, every time you hang out with people there is an ever-growing spiritual depth to the conversations.

One church planter we know opens up their house every other Friday night to the people in their two Huddles. They provide drinks and snacks, while everyone else brings their own meat for the grill.

You'll naturally do dinner, breakfast, and coffee with these people a lot. Why? Because they are people you are intentionally investing in.

Eventually, the other people in the Huddle learn to do this with each other outside of just you, and slowly you start to see a spiderweb network of relationships developing. People are starting to act like extended family.

They go to kids' plays that aren't those of their kids.
Birthday parties.
Moving days when people move.
Dinners for people with new babies.
Spur-of-the-moment coffee.
Late-night car problems.

Everything you'd do with close friends begins to happen.

What you see is community and intimacy develop, but it is the *byproduct* of good discipling, not the aim. Ronald Rolheiser says, "People who love community always end up destroying community. People who love relationships always build community." If you make community an idol, it will self-destruct. If you make relationships the focus, community will naturally follow.

+ **Develop balanced rhythms for community and mission early as you gather weekly.**

You'll want to pattern everything you do around UP, IN and OUT. We want all of our lives and communities to revolve around the UPward dimension (God), the INward dimension (relationship with the body of Jesus), and OUTward dimension (people who don't know Jesus yet).

Obviously Huddle has a very strong UPward dimension. There is teaching, discussion, scripture, prayer, accountability. It's great for the UP.

So what about IN and OUT if we want a balanced community from the outset?

Here is a suggestion for a monthly rhythm to begin with (and then obviously all of the organic stuff is happening in between).

+ **Week 1** - Huddle

+ **Week 2** - Meal with Huddle, spouses, kids. Everyone brings something. The only set "spiritual" time is for people to share what they are thankful for and take time to pray for:

   a. Is anyone sick?
   b. Is anyone worried/anxious?
   c. Pray for People of Peace.
   d. Pray for your community.

+ **Week 3** - Huddle.

+ **Week 4** - Mission. This can be as simple as doing a big party with everyone and inviting People of Peace who don't know Jesus, exposing them to the supernatural quality of the community that is almost tangible, it can be serving the homeless and inviting friends who don't know Jesus, it can be very, very bold mission where you do something like Treasure Hunts. The possibilities are endless.

The point is that you are developing a community that is balanced, with an eye towards personal discipleship, family and growing the family. In fact, what you are doing is launching a Pilot Missional Community: a mid-sized community that is experiencing UP-IN-OUT together, but not looking to grow the group just yet. It's just testing the waters out. It's about letting people see how good life can be with a group the size of an extended family.

+ **Teach the people in your Huddle to sow seeds of mission into everyday life.**

This is relatively easy to do.

For a few Huddles, have people bring their calendars for the next week or two and then draw the Triangle on a whiteboard. UP. IN. OUT.

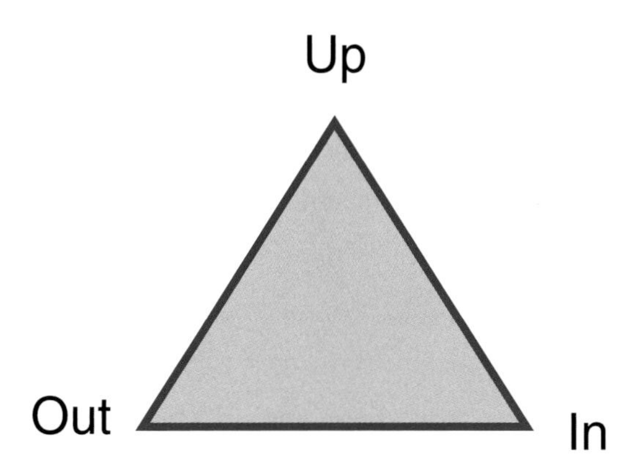

Then have them look at their schedule.

How is it weighted?

What you will quickly see is people are quite selfish with their time. My schedule, left to my own devices, revolves around what I want, when I want it, almost exclusively to the people with whom I want. But I should be able to look at my week and clearly be able to see:

a. When am I resting this week? When's my day off? When, each day, am I pulling away and spending time with God? What about my family? Are they getting my best? (UP)

b. Am I spending time with people in our spiritual *oikos*? Breakfast? Coffee? Lunch? Dinner? Movie? Gym? Basketball? Am I spending time with the people who I can encourage and be encouraged by outside of just Huddle? (IN)

c. Who am I spending time with this week that doesn't know Jesus? What if I had dinner with that couple who are People of Peace along with the other couple who is in our Huddle, so that way we are doing OUT and IN together at one time?

What most people see is they are reasonably strong at IN, maybe decent at the UP, but are woeful at the OUT.

So, we simply use Huddle to teach people how to fold OUT into their natural, normal lives. Many Christians claim they don't have non-Christian friends. OK, well, change that! Huddle gives you the vehicle to teach people how to do mission and hold them accountable to doing it.

By doing this for a few months together and talking about it regularly in Huddle, people start to see more and more People of Peace who are open to them. This is sowing the seed for a harvest in the future.

+ **Spend six to nine months in this rhythm.**

Don't try to grow the group. Just sow seeds. As many seeds as possible. Become healthy. Huddle will give you the opportunity to teach them how to do the basics of what Jesus said disciples should do.

Experience mid-sized, MC life so you know what it feels like, what it's like to live in a community that isn't tied to the identity of worship service or building. Yes, there are times that you intentionally meet, but the best stuff is usually coming out of the organic that has developed from the intentionality of the organized.

+ **Start talking about creating Missional Communities, communities that grow to be 20-50 people, which are targeted at a certain group of people or geographical place (network or neighborhood).**

This is probably six to eight months into this. Ask people in the group to pray for vision, that God would put something specific on their heart. You are looking for two to three sets of leaders, each with a specific vision for a MC, who want to pioneer the missional frontier. In our experience, after months and months of discipling, of experiencing life, community and the vibrancy of knowing Jesus, you'll not only have people that want to step up, they will have a clear sense of what God is asking them to do. You won't have to beg. You've taught these people, via Huddle, to hear the voice of God and respond. This first group stepping up in this way is an *amazing* experience.

+ **Work with those leaders to clarify and hone their plans, determine details, start dates for everyone, etc.** (See the leadership section in *MC Life*)

+ **Work with the people who aren't leading the future MCs, who will serve as the Core Team, and help them discern the Missional Community they want to be a part of.**

How do you know which you are called to?

a. You are called to the specific vision of the MC, or

b. You are called to serve a specific leader of an MC.

+ **Take the entire group on a retreat for two to three days before the MCs launch.**

Make sure you have lots of down time and fun on the retreat. Prayer. Worship. Teaching. Discussion about details and the future. Lots of celebration for what God has done. This is putting an "Ebenezer" up. This is a huge marker in the life of your community.

+ **Each MC leader starts a Huddle of his/her own.**

Their Core Team (the leaders within this new MC) are in the Huddle and additional People of Peace who are drawn to the vision of the MC. Grow the MC by balancing UP, IN and OUT within the life of your Missional Community.

+ **Decide the rhythm of the wider community now that you are a networked community.**

How many times a month will everyone gather together? At this stage, you probably need to get everyone together twice a month and maybe even every week. God will make this clear to you. Remember, when people hit the missional frontier for the first time, when they are in a small Core Team of four to eight people where they have to grow (and it can feel like it's sink or swim), they need a lot more official gathering time. This eases the chaos in their minds and spirits and serves as a constant reminder that they are participating in a bigger story. It also starts to slowly shift your understanding of why we gather for worship services in the first place.

+ **Start a Leaders Huddle where you are Huddling MC Leaders.**

Each MC will have two, possibly three leaders. So this Huddle is a collection of those MC leaders (and will more than likely have both men and women in it). Continuing this rhythm at every-other-week Huddles seems to be the rhythm that has worked for most people.

+ **Decide what your role in this multiplication is.**

Are you starting an MC of your own? Are you simply pouring tons of yourself into your MC leaders and jumping from MC to MC to MC each week? One thing you'll want is times when your place is open and your leaders can just come and relax. Some have called this the Leader *Oikos*, a time when we can just be, enjoy each other, tell war stories, laugh, and take care of each other, all without trying to grow the group. There isn't any structured time, it's just friends being together.

Your top job will be investing and equipping your leaders. But remember, make sure you are doing all of the things you are asking them to do. If you want them to be bold in mission, you better be doing that and leading the way. You can't take people to places you haven't been yourself.

+ **Every six months gather all of your MC leaders for a retreat for several days.**

This retreat is a combination of teaching, stories, discussion, worship, team exercises and planning. This is the track we've learned:

a. What is? (honest assessment of the previous six months and where we are now)

b. What could be? (dreaming, inspiration, revelation)

c. What will be? (six-month detailed plan)

At this point, groups grow and multiply, or stall and don't make it (not every MC succeeds and that's OK, that's part of the nature of it). You continue to resource and equip and discern how to best guide your leaders and the rhythms of the greater community.

As you continue to grow and groups multiply, you will continually be adjusting your systems and processes so that the center continues to serve the edge and not the other way around. (See the previous section, Step 7: Growing your MC for more details.)

We do think it's important to note: For all of this–which, by the way, is simply the beginning of the amazing growth you'll see–you're looking at probably a minimum of a two-year process. Like we said at the beginning, this isn't a quick thing. Investing in people and discipling them never is. But from the beginning you create something that's worth imitating and worth multiplying. There is nothing worse than being three to four years into a church plant and realizing the DNA is wrong.

What you are doing is creating something that has the potential to see exponential growth, but something that remains incredibly substantive. Rather than saying "church growth" and "deep, substantive church" are mutually exclusive, it says they are integrally connected. After four years you could have four to five MCs, after six years, twenty MCs, after eight years, sixty MCs, each representing a bucket of about twenty to fifty people. Every person being discipled. Every person feeling like they have a family fighting for them, to whom they belong. You start doing it from the beginning, and it never really changes. It just contracts (multiplies) and expands (grows). Contract and expand. Contract and expand.

You don't need a ton of people to start it, in fact, you don't want a ton of people. Like Jesus, you start with a handful.

MC LIFE
BUILDING INFRASTRUCTURE

So you've started Missional Communities. What do you do now that you're on the front lines? How do they grow? How do you disciple and teach people? Kids? How do you develop leaders? This is the nuts-and-bolts to Missional Communities.

RECAP | WHAT IS A MISSIONAL COMMUNITY?

A Missional Community is a group of twenty to fifty people who have united, in the name of Jesus, around a common service and witness to a particular context. Friends, family, neighbors and colleagues are invited to come and be a part of this extended family of relationships.

Together, they follow Jesus as His disciples, even if not every person may yet describe him/herself as a Christian (although the leaders will happily do so). There is no test in order to come; simply a desire to discover more about God, whatever someone's journey has been up to that point. MCs aim to offer a grace-filled, non-judgmental welcome in the name of the Father. This is balanced by the belief that it is only as we submit our whole lives to Christ that we can experience forgiveness, transformation and real purpose in life.

Within MCs, people seek to share their lives with one another day-to-day, so that this overflows into their formal meetings, rather than being solely expressed there. The relationships in MCs have to blend into 'normal life', or else they become yet another thing to clog up our schedules. Structures, such as formal meetings, do not create life, but they can be helpful in sustaining it. The Lord told the Israelites to build a tabernacle that was flexible and easy to move, so that it could go easily with them on their journey. Missional Communities take the same view towards their structures, with the function being more important than the form.

The group balances its energies between an UPward movement towards God, an INward movement towards the MC as a place of identity and an OUTward movement to represent Christ to their mission context. When they gather, they express this in creative ways that are appropriate to their context. There will be great diversity between groups in how this looks, with a variety of faces and voices being given room to step forward and contribute what they can. The only rule is that they do not try to do a miniature version of a Sunday church service!

MCs recognize that their measure of success will, above all, be the stories of lives transformed, of the wider community being impacted and reached for Christ, of people being drawn closer to their Heavenly Father. Such change happens in community rather than in isolation, since every aspect occurs with the love, challenge and impetus of others, as everyone tries to live with one another as Jesus would.

In short, they are a community on a mission.

Another Way of Describing MCs

One church that we know uses ten key principles to describe Missional Communities, saying that an MC:

1. Has its own distinct vision for mission; for example, by age group, neighborhood, network or some other specific area of common interest
2. Has a name—key to building identity and belonging
3. Is a community of up to fifty adults who meet regularly
4. Is led by members of the church family, preferably with a leadership team
5. Seeks to identify emerging leaders

6. Is committed to forming new small groups from within its membership that share its distinct vision for mission
7. Has a heart to see the MC multiply
8. Is accountable to the sending church and its ordained leadership
9. Remains part of the gathered church
10. Is lightweight/inexpensive/not bound by building or maintenance[79]

MY NOTES

HYPOTHETICAL MONTHLY MC CALENDAR

The following is a hypothetical calendar and certainly not intended to operate as a strict template.

We have tried to give some indication of how the monthly rhythm *might* look. However, we can only list the more organized or formal gatherings, whereas the best Missional Communities will be seeing lots of informal interaction happening throughout the week (including with their People of Peace). This calendar would work well earlier in the life of an MC, since it gives the most priority to time as a whole community, which is key to long-term growth and health.

	SUN	MON	TUES	WED	THURS	FRI	SAT
WEEK 1	Celebration		MC gathering including time for accountablity groups				
WEEK 2	Celebration			Huddle for MC Leaders			Mission Day
WEEK 3	NOT at celebration free space after Mission Day		MC gathering		Accountabilty groups meet (sometime during week)		
WEEK 4	Celebration			MC Leaders Huddle their key leaders		Party Night (invite People of Peace)	

THE UP, IN, OUT HEALTH CHECK: IS YOUR MISSIONAL COMMUNITY BALANCED?

This is a simple tool to use with MCs that are established, in order to help leaders to honestly review their areas of strength and weakness.

For each sentence, give your Missional Community a score from 0-10 in response to the extent to which you agree with the statement. This is not compared to other groups, but a relative comparison of how your community is doing in different areas of life. Answer from the perspective of the group as a whole (i.e., it's not your personal responses). Don't agonize over each question—go for your intuitive gut response!

UP

- Group members make regular time to retreat, reflect and pray
- Together you have found a way of praying regularly that suits your life and community personality
- People in the group feel close to God at the moment
- Your group worships God in numerous creative ways
- You hear God's voice when you gather and put into practice what He is saying
- As a group, you observe both regular and occasional Spiritual Disciplines
- Together you find relevant ways to learn from and be shaped by Scripture

IN

- Everyone has someone in their life who knows everything about them—there is nothing being carried alone in darkness
- Within the group, both marriage and singleness are supported with a healthy and balanced perspective
- People are comfortable both giving and receiving mentoring
- People feel that they belong to a group who together form an authentic expression of church
- The group is characterized by regular and gracious hospitality
- You all feel loved emotionally and supported practically by the MC—it's not just going to meetings
- People regularly discuss with each other how they are seeking to be better followers of Jesus
- Overall, people feel surrounded by meaningful community

OUT

- Your group has a clear missional focus towards which you devote time and energy
- Your community spends time with lots of friends and contacts who are not in church
- In the last month, your group has found ways to lovingly demonstrate the power of the Kingdom to people who are not Christians
- Your group has seen people with whom you are in contact start to follow God in the last year
- Members are involved in lots of activities beyond church life
- The place where many MC members spend most of their time (at work, study, play, etc.) is predominately in relationships with non-Christians
- As a group, you are excited about your involvement in serving the wider missional context

- In the last three months, each member has offered to pray with someone who is not a Christian
- Your group has a name that reflects who you are
- Your group is actively involved in an area in which injustice exists

Now add up your scores to create an overall number for each area. Obviously, you can dig a little deeper by studying specific questions that are most pertinent to your Missional Community.

There is no secret formula for growth in ministry. If your MC/church is healthy, it will grow. To be healthy, you must be in relational balance as pictured in the triangle of UP-IN-OUT.

MY NOTES

LEADING MC LEADERS

Leaders' Meetings

As Huddles are not leaders' meetings, you might need to think about holding these. Different churches will have different patterns, depending on the season in which you are.

In order not to overburden leaders, we have had seasons during which we ran a central leaders meeting, with food and childcare, with say forty minutes of training/information sharing etc., followed by a Huddle. This model was developed by our close friend Mick Woodhead[69], who is a fantastic developer of Missional Communities and their leaders. The advantage for people is that it just takes up one evening, and they don't need to find childcare (which again may or may not be a big issue for your leaders). It also gives the senior leaders of the church the regular opportunity to reinforce vision, hear from and interact with the MC leaders.

Some churches that have church councils are working on shifting the make-up of those councils to include a number of MC leaders. If your Missional Communities are your key expression of church growth and life together, this seems to be an eminently sensible direction to take. Once you have lots of MC leaders, you could have them select however many representatives you need for the council for that year.

Leaders' Retreats

An intensive but fruitful way to impact your leaders and their communities is to pull all your leaders together for 24 hours twice a year. Whether you go away to an inexpensive conference center (budget for it—people won't appreciate having to pay much, if anything, for the experience!) or stay 'at home', this can be a key time. There is something powerful about time over meals, hanging out, playing together, worshipping and praying together, and having high quality input to shape and train your leaders.

In recent times, we have started to use these times away to run communities of learning. In that model, we move leaders (who come with three or four key members of their MC) through a three-stage process. We look at what is (current realities), what could be (we stir up their thinking way beyond the present situation or their experience) and what will be (where they make specific action plans for the following six months). These headings can also be summarized as what they love, what they hope for and what they have faith for. On different retreats we will bring one major theme, since that helps to focus hearts and minds in a particular direction. The tools that we use for planning are detailed, but are then followed up on in individual conversations and Huddles in the following months. The church resource staff does an excellent job of capturing all the data that is produced, so that we have good record keeping, and no one can simply 'lose' their action plan!

Continuing Communication Strategy

It is almost impossible to over-communicate, so find any and every way that you can to keep a clear line of communication with your MC leaders. As you increasingly become a decentralized community, all of your resource staff exists as a support to your MC leaders. They serve by providing the resources necessary to carry out the vision of a church built around Missional Communities. In this context of high accountability, low control, you must be excellent at communicating to sustain the accountability!

Communicating with Your MC Leaders

- Try to limit the number of different emails going out to MC leaders. You don't want mailings from the church office to become like spam rather than a beneficial resource. We suggest that you bundle most communication into a newsletter to leaders.
- Have a single point of contact for leaders—one person on the team who is their go-to person for practical help and support, as well as the primary access provider to the MC leaders en masse. This creates great clarity in communication.
- Phone calls–some churches have a member of the central team phone every leader every week, to ask for testimonies, how they can be prayed for and what red tape needs to be taken away.
- Leaders' meetings with a mixture of informal sharing of best practice, prayer, equipping in the areas of theology, skills and personal spirituality. Providing some good food helps to draw higher attendance!
- Periodic visit from a member of the staff/leadership team to the Missional Community when it gathers.
- Taking surveys and collecting feedback from groups and leaders: for instance, at the end of a church year, after a major initiative, or when a leader stops leading a group.
- Making sure that communication is two-way. I (Alex) recall organizing a Spring leaders' retreat where we went from 30 to 250 registrations in the last week, with an extra 50 kids registered for childcare the day before the retreat! We fed back very clearly (but politely) afterwards that this was not being accountable on their part and had caused needless headaches for the resource staff at the very last minute.

Advertising MCs to the Wider Church

- Have a prominent notice board in the place where you do your Sunday services, with well-presented information on every group.
- Try making 'business cards' for each MC, with name and contact information on them, so that people who are interested in trying out a couple of groups can easily take the information home with them.
- Create a significant area on your church website for Missional Community information. Allow groups either to blog there or to be able to easily link to a group page on Facebook, etc.
- Feature different MCs in your weekly bulletin and other printed material.
- Testimony in Sunday celebrations—there is something unbeatable about real lives being changed and the telling of those stories.

Appreciation of Your MC Leaders

While your leaders aren't doing it for the thanks, they will still appreciate being appreciated!

- We run social gatherings for MC leaders twice a year, making them really well done events. They should be well-planned, fun, high quality and refreshing for those who come—otherwise you do more harm than good! Make sure that you either provide childcare (or include children), or have funds available to reimburse babysitting costs if leaders need to arrange their own. In other words, strongly urge people to prioritize being there, then remove as many barriers to attendance as you can.

- At Christmas we give thank you gifts—perhaps a gift card for a meal out and trip to the movies. It doesn't need to cost a fortune, but enough for people to feel special.
- Drop people little notes of appreciation, especially if you hear good things about their group from others. Even a quick text or message on their Facebook page is appreciated.

Helping MC Leaders to Identify Their Mission Vision

We are often asked: "What is the main thing, after prayer and God's initiative, that makes an MC stand or fall?"

Easy answer. Mission Vision.

This is the key subject in which we are asked to coach emerging MC leaders, and your MC leaders will need your help with this process. Remember, all those who come after your first Missional Communities will have had the luxury of being part of an MC.

The practical wisdom and examples that follow should stir up the visionary juices of your leaders. Just being told to come up with a missional OUT can lead some to paralysis and a sense of failure. Invest whatever capital you need to help your first wave of MC leaders to clarify and hone their missional vision. It will be an investment that delivers a significant return.

1) Do You Have a Clearly Articulated Mission Vision for Your MC?

Who exactly do you want to reach? Who do you want to see saved? If your answer is, "the whole world", then you haven't even begun to address this issue! If you say, "the city", then you still have much to do. You need to be able to specifically say who your community will have at the center of its mission.

Remember, vision is always set by the leaders of the MC and not by committee.

One of the core functions of leadership is to paint a picture of a better future and call people to join them in moving towards that Kingdom goal.

Below is the text that one church gave to its leaders to guide them:

Your role as leaders is critical to the process of birthing a new Missional Community! If you are to lead an MC, then you need to have really clearly settled in your heart what your missional vision is that you will call others to follow. This means that right now you should be really seeking the Lord to see if you are to be leading a Missional Community and, if so, what specific mission vision He is speaking to you about. Do not try to make this decision by discussion and consensus in your group—that will be a disaster! Either you will have loads of different visions (all worthy, but you lose focus because you can't do multiple visions all at one time) or, in the group where no one really knows what to say, it will be very discouraging both to you and to the members. As leaders, you are called and commissioned to lead; so, if you are not clear yet, then get on your knees, and ask God to show you what the mission vision is to be during this next season!

As you explain the goals of your mission vision, you may find that some people will say to you, 'I'm busy with work/life, etc… Isn't it enough to do Missional Community values and personally live a missional life?' The response is that 2000 years of church history show us that there is a group size, roughly equating to the extended family that has repeatedly been the key driver for growing the church. This 'extended family' interaction is built into the regular rhythm of life. It is the mid-sized Missional Community that has been most successful in growing the church across time and cultures.

For example:

- Christians meeting in a home in Corinth in 50AD
- A monastic community led by Celtic missionaries in the 6th century
- Local congregations gathering around the teachings of the Reformers in 1540s Europe
- Local chapels formed by communities impacted by the Wesleyan revival of the 1740s
- Groups of new Pentecostal believers in Latin America in the late 20th century
- Gatherings of persecuted Christians in the underground church of China today.

Here's another example of a specific missional vision:

Beth's group is a women-only MC, since that is what she felt the Lord was calling her to build. Naturally, they have sought to do mission activities related to women, but the breakthrough for a sustained approach came when Beth began connecting with a ministry that fights human trafficking.

The city where she lives is located at the intersection of two major highways and is a significant hub for this horrendous problem. A local non-profit runs houses of refuge for women who escape or are rescued by the police, but this is very resource-intensive as the women arrive traumatized and with few possessions. Beth, who loves parties, wanted to find a creative way both to fundraise and also to draw women together in positive relationships. So she founded WRATH—Women Rallying Against Traffic in Humans. Her idea was to host great parties for women, where as part of the evening everyone brings a certain thing that the rescue house needs (whether it's shoes or toiletries or food or whatever). As part of the evening, there is a short presentation, and then people are invited to host their own WRATH parties with their own circles of friends. Beth's aim is for her and the MC to educate, equip and empower women to do this, so that they can build an ever-widening network of women, most of whom are successful and prosperous but together can support some of the most vulnerable and abused women in society.

2) Clarify Whether Your Missional Vision is For a Network or Neighborhood

Your vision might be for a specific neighborhood or a specific network of relationships. Those two inform one another, but one will predominate. You might say that you are reaching the geographic community where you live, but you are probably focused on a particular segment, such as young families, the poor or retirees (the default will be that you will reach people like you).

Alternatively, you might say that you are focused on reaching college students, but that will probably be limited by distance and thus focused on a particular part of the campus or town. Sometimes we are asked if we would organize groups by life stage, to which the answer is, it depends! If that means putting young families together simply because they are all young families, without any sense of a clear missional calling, then the answer is no. Such action will produce a holding tank that is not looking beyond itself in effective mission.

However, a particular life stage makes an extremely good missional focus. So, to use the same example, an MC that reaches young families will have plenty of Kingdom opportunities if it intentionally seeks out those people in appropriate ways, and runs the MC in a manner that engages young families. The emphasis is always upon the mission vision rather than grouping people because they look similar on the outside.

Here are Ryan's Reflections on Determining an MC's Mission Vision:

How do you decide what your MC mission should be? Our minds were flooded with thoughts concerning this topic. We knew that we needed a mission and we were eager to get on board with our church's senior leadership concerning mission. But how in the world would we choose just one thing on which to focus? My husband and I went round and round discussing and praying about our mission, pleading with the Lord to give us one.

Then, we were encouraged to 'look at the natural'. This meant looking to what our focus as a family already was. What is the main thing about which we are passionate as a family? What is the main thing that we are already doing in our lives as far as mission goes? There was our answer! What a relief it was to turn to the 'natural'! God undoubtedly showed us what our MC mission should be. It didn't matter if no one else would be interested in it; that was what God had called us to do in life and that naturally should flow into our Missional Community.

Specifically, our mission is to families with children who have special needs, as well as to those who have critically ill family members. As a group and as individuals, we will be seeking out families that fall into these categories—at the grocery store, at the park, in the city—and intentionally serving them in practical ways such as hospital visits, meals, babysitting, etc. Our desire is to reach out to this special community that so many times feels isolated and alone, even in the Body of Christ.

Our daughter, Ellie Kate, has a terminal genetic disease called non-ketotichyperglycenemia (NKH). Basically, she has too much glycine in her brain, which causes her to have vision problems, heart problems, muscle problems, seizures and brain damage. We didn't know that she had the disease until shortly after she was born. We've spent about six months total in various hospitals here and in Texas, including two and a half months on life support. So, that is why it comes so naturally to us! We are surrounded by doctors, nurses and therapists of all kinds, and we get to come in contact with many families in similar situations. This makes a natural mission vision, in which we are passionate and find life.

3) Can the Person of Peace Strategy Help to Clarify Mission Vision?

For your first leaders who may struggle to define their missional focus through the lenses of either network or neighborhood, it is important to demystify the process. Since the Father loves the whole world and sent his Son to release eternal life to all who believe in him, this means that no people, group or community is off-limits.

The joy of the Person of Peace strategy is that it stops the mission being yet another thing to cram into the lives of leaders who are already too busy. Instead, it is about bringing the Gospel to where you already are—as you shop, play sports, pick up the kids, go to work, meet neighbors, etc. The very healthiest MCs are living in their context in ways that feel natural and life-giving. By focusing on People of Peace, the missional investment is not emotionally taxing. In fact, it can easily become highly life-giving, even for those who are quiet and reserved.

One MC leader, Jayne, started going to a new hairdresser, who was very friendly and talkative. Sitting in the chair, Jayne found that spiritual conversations flowed as her hair was being cut, and she realized that her hairdresser was a Person of Peace for her. Sensing that this was not just a personal thing, she encouraged other women in the MC to start using the same hairdresser. The women would identify themselves as Jayne's friends and more amazing conversations ensued, as Jesus slowly drew this spiritually hungry hairdresser towards Him. The climax came when the hairdresser initiated an, 'I have to make a decision about this Jesus' conversation with Jayne, which led to her committing her life to Christ. A few weeks later, she was baptized and shared with the wider church body her testimony of how she had been profoundly impacted by this obviously caring community in which all the women stood out because there was something distinctive about each of them!

Cathy's Thoughts on Staying with People of Peace:

Our Missional Community, which is in a working class part of town, was trying to work out who our people of peace might be. Not wanting to wait endlessly, we decided to start being a presence in our wider neighborhood and just see what happened.

We began by all meeting in the local park for a big picnic, intentionally bringing too much food so that we had plenty to share. We ended up attracting a bunch of local kids who were hanging out in the park, some of whom in turn went to fetch their families. Various conversations later and members of the MC were starting to connect with some of those households and build relationships with them, including being invited into their homes.

As Christmas approached, we felt led by God as a Missional Community to adopt five of the poorer households, helping to provide Christmas food and simple gifts for the children. Spiritual conversations inevitably followed, with long-term relationships and high credibility being established in the area.

4) Naming Missional Communities

Leaders always get to name their MC because it is an important part of defining its future identity. Not everyone may want to name his/her MC, but lead them to do this. Whether leaders choose something serious, fun or Biblical, they should always be aware of the people whom they are trying to reach and also what God is saying about his plans for that Missional Community. Some group names are prophetic and speak to the vision and intent with which the group was birthed.

Here are just a few examples, with a brief description of their mission focus:

- **Ethnos** – reaching international students (Ethnos being the Greek word in the New Testament for 'the nations')
- **Chosen** – helping women to live out their true identity in Christ
- **The Family Van** – reaching young families in a particular neighborhood (the joke being that you need to drive a minivan to be accepted into the group!)
- **Legacy** – reaching teens and their families, to build a Kingdom legacy in them
- **Soul Mates** – focusing on married couples who want to improve their marriage and singles preparing for marriage
- **Miracles in Motion** – reaching their neighborhood through service projects for the needy

CASE STUDY:
St. Thomas' Philadelphia, Sheffield, UK

The church describes the essence of its MCs through seven core values:

1. **Vision-led Community**
   Each community is founded on a God-given vision or a common purpose that unites the group. This provides a focus for the life of each group and its rhythm and activities. These range from reaching out to the city using the creative arts, serving a local neighborhood, welcoming international students, sharing a passion for the outdoors, supporting individual members in their workplace, working with the homeless, to... anything!

2. **Balanced Community**
   In each group, we give time to growing our relationship with God and all that he would want to do and say to us; to creating open, honest community with each other and those within the body of Christ; to reaching out with love in mission to our city and the places where God has put us. These are the three basic dimensions of the life of each group.

3. **Adventure**
   We believe that community grows best when people are joined or bonded together in a common focus or task beyond themselves. We want our communities to be places in which people are encouraged to step out in their faith, to take risks and to learn from their experiences together.

4. **Community Core Values**
   Each community shares some common core values with the whole church, and each community also has its own distinct values that shape its identity more specifically. They could be things like a focus on releasing the prophetic, a passion for welcome and hospitality, creativity, or inter-generational involvement.

5. **Freedom in Style & Structure**
   Each group is different! And the way in which members express their community life together will look different. We strongly value diversity across the whole church, so we don't have a set program or pattern that we ask communities to follow. Instead, we want to release a mixture of vision, style and structure, allowing each community to shape the way in which its members meet in a way that best fits their vision and call, based around the value of balanced community (value 2).

6. **Making Disciples & Raising up Leaders**
   Missional Communities are places in which we expect people to grow in their relationship with God. We want to grow a church that is full of disciples and learners, people who increasingly look to God for everything that they need, and learn to put his ways into practice. We want to see new people becoming disciples and joining communities in which they will be supported and inspired in their faith. Communities create an environment that gives opportunities and encouragement for members to realize their God-given potential. This can include growing in spiritual gifts and disciplines, skills and abilities and leadership.

7. **Open Community & Kingdom Expectation**
   We believe that God wants to extend his Kingdom here in our city! We want our communities to be hospitable, open and welcoming to new people, and to be places that are expectant that God will move and do amazing things amongst his people and in our city.

UP

Teaching God's Word in MCs

Clearly, it is important to create an environment for people to learn and grow in their understanding of Scripture, as well as helping them to understand the great doctrines of our faith and grow a balanced and grounded theology that serves them well through all the ups and downs of life. A common concern is, how does teaching take place within a Missional Community? The underlying worry is that somehow, the teaching won't be deep or substantial enough in the midst of all this flexibility of form and low control approach.

First, remember the discussion of Minster churches in the Middle Ages. There were mission outposts (MCs) and there were the Cathedrals (wider church community) to which they were connected. Simply because people are spending more time in an MC does not mean that they aren't still connected to and receiving substantive teaching from the Resourcing Center that is the organized church.

However, we also see that Jesus teaches that religious knowledge alone is not our goal (Matthew 7:21-23). Rather, we are judged by God on whether we live the life and walk the talk as we go about our everyday existence (e.g., James 1:22). Put another way, do we love God more as a result of what we are learning? As we have previously noted, Jesus (and Paul) repeatedly sent out disciples to share the works and words of the Kingdom, often in a wildly under-equipped state.

When the disciples returned with the inevitable pressing questions, they were far more open to training and input. The best educational methods teach us the same thing: when people are aware that they are ill-equipped for some practical area of their life (whether it be interpreting their bank statement, relating to their spouse, or praying for someone), they will listen eagerly and learn deeply. MC teaching needs to be helping people to live their lives better, particularly as they seek to be effective as missionaries in the world.

In Missional Community, we would encourage leaders to respond to the key question that they learn in Huddles: What is Jesus saying to you (both individually and as a group), and what are you going to do in response? Now to unlock that, you might take on an in-depth Bible study, or watch a DVD, or have someone come in to stir the group up with his/her specialist knowledge and experience, or take time to brainstorm responses to a recent OUT activity.

The point is that you allow God to set the agenda for learning, working out the most effective and creative ways for people to learn and respond. To clarify, this is not to denigrate in any way the classic spiritual disciplines. If God speaks to a group about growing in holiness, its members might well find spending several months in Leviticus to be of great benefit, along with days at the beginning and end set aside for prayer and fasting. This is not an anti-intellectual call; but it challenges the idolatry of study for the sole goal of increasing knowledge, of a puffed-up pride in academic standards and 'deep' teaching.

So, teaching is an important function in Missional Communities, but it is a teaching that is grounded, applied and incarnated. It is decided upon in response to what God is saying, either to the leader personally or to the group, with the goal being to see growth in Christ-likeness and effectiveness in mission. Great teachers who never reach the lost are probably not so great after all.

Michael Frost and Alan Hirsch comment, "Some critics of the missional church ask, 'Where is the Bible taught? How do people learn doctrine?' We recognize these as valid questions. But we believe such learning takes place more effectively when the Christian faith community is involved in active mission... like Jesus' first followers discovered, learning occurs when we need to draw on information because a situation demands it."[80]

The other balancing component is the role of celebrations in teaching. Elsewhere, we wrote about the values for the different sizes of gathering, and put preaching as one of the three core values for celebrations. Our experience is that a celebration-size gathering justifies preaching input from people who have been able to set aside the time required to come up with high quality biblical preaching that changes lives. Whatever your church's rhythm of meeting at celebration size, outstanding preaching should be a key component of those gatherings. This, in turn, takes some of the pressure off MCs.

Sometimes churches will produce study guides for use mid-week by small groups in response to the sermon. This may well be something that some small groups would like to do, as a way of stimulating fresh sharing and accountability in personal space. The point is to be ruthlessly honest in applying what has been taught the week before, so that growth occurs as the Word is put into action.

Easy Teaching Process for MC Leaders

Sometimes we tell our leaders that all we want them to do is breathe...

1. Inhale - you can't give to those you lead unless you are yourself receiving from the Lord (Psalm 23, "He anoints my head with oil..."). Make sure that you are meeting with God daily and giving him a chance to speak to you. It is out of this that you will have fresh bread to break open and share with those whom he has asked you to lead.
2. Exhale - give freely what you have received from the Lord, but remember that you are not the provider. Do not take upon yourself responsibilities that belong to God alone (Psalm 23, "My cup overflows...").
3. Repeat - be faithful and accountable to one another and, most of all, to the Lord (Psalm 23, "The Lord is my Shepherd...")

Another great resource for helping MC leaders and their groups to delve more deeply into scripture is *Covenant and Kingdom*, a book that I (Mike) have written to help our 'regular' church people to really understand and immerse themselves in Scripture.

Confidence as a Disciple Maker

One of the best things for leaders of Missional Communities is to have their confidence built up, particularly in their capacity to be a disciple maker. Most people doubt that they are worthy of being imitated by others, yet imitation is very much the basis for discipleship. In Matthew 11:29-30, when Jesus invites his disciples to, "Take my yoke upon you and learn from me", the image is of an older ox paired with a younger one, sharing a yoke, where the younger one learns how to plow by following the older one. Jesus is our lead ox, and there is a space beside him for us to learn by imitating him.

In the same way, we are to lead those who follow us by inviting them to walk alongside us and imitate our lives. Thus Paul writes in 1 Corinthians 4:16, "Therefore I urge you to imitate me." This is not meant to be an impossible bar but rather an encouragement to our Missional Community leaders to see that who they are, far more than what they know, is what will most influence others.

We are not giving people the perfect example, just a living one.

A key function of the main leaders of the church is to encourage and speak faith into the hearts of our leaders who are out on the front line; to keep affirming that they have heard from God, that the dream on their heart for reaching the lost is a great one, and that they do have the capacity to lead their group into that context and see people won for Christ.

This is not about hyping things up or saying things that are untrue. Rather, it is about helping people to keep on pressing on into all that the Lord has for them. A humble yet confident leader of a Missional Community is a mighty and powerful weapon in God's hands, so we can help birth and sustain that in those whom we oversee.

MCs as Centers of Training

Church structures can struggle to find ways to train and give room for people to experiment and to try serving God, without creating cumbersome and centralized training programs. An overly programmatic approach can mean that a church is way behind the ball in terms of what God is doing in the church body, as the center struggles to keep up with the current needs. This is simply not the Minster's purpose.

Missional Communities are a more flexible and fluid context for training and development of individuals. They are a place where people can try, where they can have a go in a safe environment. The traditional model of church can usually only offer people the chance to do things on a large scale on Sundays (where, because the cost of failure might be very high, excellence is highly valued) or at the micro scale in small groups (where it can feel equally pressurized but in a different way, since this is private space). Both practically and sociologically, Missional Community is an excellent size gathering for someone to have a go at learning how to exercise his/her spiritual gifts.

A Missional Community is large enough to dare and small enough to care.

What this means in practice is that someone can try (for instance) to lead worship, and if he/she completely messes up, it is not the disaster that it would be in a Sunday morning Minster Celebration; but it is also less acutely embarrassing for all concerned as it would be in a small group setting.

There is also the advantage that once your group size is in the 20s or 30s, there is a greater range of spiritual gifts present (and experienced practitioners to help those just setting out), yet the group is small enough for anyone to step forward and contribute without things becoming out of hand. When Paul writes in 1 Corinthians 14:40, "Let all things be done decently and in order", we tend to focus on imposing the order and structure, quickly slipping into high control (because, of course, my personal boundaries for what is decent are synonymous with what Paul had in mind!). While doing things with appropriate leadership is right and proper, let's not forget that Paul encourages us to do ALL things (that the Spirit inspires, to take the verse in context). Missional Community is a really good context in which people can live out this verse, enabling leaders to spot genuine giftedness in a context in which character is also known.

Thus MCs can quickly become a key component in a church community's Leadership Pipeline—the phrase used by Drotter and Charan to describe how an organization plans how leaders at all levels will be intentionally developed[81]. MCs are a context in which people can be trained, grow into leadership, and, in turn, learn how to develop and train others. Most churches fail to create a clear process for leadership development, but along with Huddles, MCs enable huge amounts of leadership development to go on in a way that is peer-assessed and validated. If we as church leaders can learn to trust our MC leaders and members in this decentralized process, not only do we stop having to be the source of all training but also, those who do grow through to a wider level of influence and leadership will come with tremendous credibility and support from the people of the church.

Adriene on Releasing Spiritual Gifts:

Our MC has always focused on our spiritual gifts, including speaking encouragement when we see them present in others. We spend each fall and spring re-exploring this, perhaps taking a few nights to read the Word and pray for each other.

We have had nights together where the presence of the Holy Spirit has been very tangible, which creates lots of faith for people to pray big prayers for others in the room. One of our disciplines is to pray for those who are sick. One time several of us prayed for a guy with a headache and God healed him instantly. We have prayed for lots of healing and, although we haven't seen as much as we would like, we are still persevering.

Our dream is to continue to raise up leaders, to help equip the saints for holy and powerful living, hence the exploration of spiritual gifts. At the beginning of last fall, we challenged people to be more committed this year. It is true that you only get out of it what you put in.

What Might a Typical Meeting Look Like?

Very simply? It varies.

The quick answer is that there is a mixture of community, mission and training. This is expressed through the lens of UP, IN and OUT. So, at one level, anything that honors Christ and falls within the vision of the MC is legitimate.

Of course that is a little too vague and, in practice, MCs do tend to do certain things pretty regularly, albeit in slightly different ways according to their context. But before we list some examples, we again want to speak grace and creativity to you as you ponder what this should all look like in your missional context. Take these principles and begin to play with them with your community. Your mission context will greatly affect how you do these things.

Here are a few general ideas (not in priority order) to start your thinking process. These are aimed at the Missional Community gathering where people meet to grow closer to God and one another and pray into their missional context. A gathering might include:

- Food, ideally sharing a meal together
- Socializing/laughing/having fun
- Breaking bread/sharing Communion (see further on for some comments on Communion in MCs)
- Story-telling (i.e., testimony), particularly things for which we are thankful to God
- Bringing praise and worship to God
- Offering prayer for healing to anyone who has a particular need
- Studying the Scriptures together, especially from what God has been speaking to the leader (or whoever is leading that portion) about during the past week
- Praying for the wider community that you are seeking to reach, as well as for your witness there
- Planning practicalities for mission activities

We would summarize this as a 1 Corinthians 11-14 model, which seems the fullest unpacking of how a church *oikos* would meet and express its life together. From what Paul writes, it is also clear that such gatherings were led in such a way that people who weren't yet Christians could come in and be welcomed, without it throwing all the plans into confusion.

As well, the MC will do OUT together in specific missional activities, to serve and witness to their place of calling. Such events need to be regular and rhythmic, so that the group sees this as an integral part of its life together, just as eating or praying together would be. For this reason, we would encourage a brand new Missional Community to start doing OUT activities from the get-go, so that they are included from day one. Don't wait until group members get to know each other better. Our experience is that the groups that gel the fastest are the ones whose members share common battle stories and missional escapades (successful and less so).

Ryan on Doing Mission in Partnership with Our City Council:

We were becoming increasingly involved in serving our community when one of our city council members asked us to come and address a council meeting. We turned up en masse—I don't think they'd ever seen so many young people in one of their meetings before! But we had tons of favor with them. We asked them if there was anything that we could do for them and, to our surprise, they said yes, there was. They had been selected as part of a small national trial in providing prescription drug discounts for those without health insurance. The plan was to give out special discount cards to those who could possibly need them, but the program had come about quickly, and the council did not know how to put the discount cards in the hands of those who most needed them; and so they asked if we would help. We said yes—after all, we were being asked by the authorities to go out into our community and give away something valuable that we did not have to pay for or provide, but which would nevertheless open all sorts of doorways!

So we gathered the troops and canvassed our neighborhood with the prescription cards. We went door to door handing them out, as well as asking people if we could pray for them. What we found was that people loved to talk and were far more welcoming than we had thought (or feared). Personally, I prayed for several people. One lady even prayed for us, which was awesome. Our MC got together for a worship time that night and many who hadn't come on the outreach were inspired and encouraged to take part in our next OUT. A few months later, we did a movie night in the park—the whole MC showed up for that; they were way into it. We provided drinks and popcorn free of charge and showed a great family movie on a huge screen made of bed sheets! It was a perfect night. Including our MC (30 people), there were over 100 people out in the park. The MC met new people, with lots of encouraging conversations happening throughout the night. We hope to do another one in the spring. We had several neighbors tell us that they would like to help next time, so we will ask them for that. A great way to build relationships with our neighbors will be to plan and organize something together. We also got the city councilman's approval for doing the movie. This got them on board and they promoted it within their monthly newsletters to the neighborhood. This also helped to land me a position on the planning and zoning commission, and now I am more involved with our neighborhood and meeting lots of other neighbors.

Where Do Missional Communities Meet?

The general rule is anywhere other than the church building!

> **“If the intent of MCs is to expand the reach and influence of the church community, it makes sense to move beyond the existing places that we occupy.”**

The other principle is that the mission context should dictate the location. If your MC is reaching out to the homeless, having an MC that meets in a big posh suburban home may not be the best plan.

So Missional Communities meet in a variety of locations. Probably the most common is in a home, generally the one that has the most space (and most gracious hosts), which seems to follow the pattern of the early church oikos communities. If we are following the principle of the Person of Peace, then it may well be that we allow that person to host the gathering, especially if it is reaching into his/her social network. Just as some groups have a fixed spot, others move around week by week. Some might meet in workplaces as their missional context, although others might not find those conducive to ongoing community life.

Many others find a ‘Third Place’, that is neither home nor work, such as cafés, restaurants (which often have a function room that can be used if people buy drinks or food), community halls, schools, parks, beaches, hospitals... the list is as broad as your creativity allows! The great benefit of using third places is that as people are reached, they are resourced to live the Christian life there, rather than being withdrawn out of their culture of belonging (and now mission) and converted into a Christian sub-culture.

Andrew Williams writes about the variety of meeting places for the Missional Communities that he oversaw. “We had MCs for the youth, for the elderly, for the deaf community, for many different neighborhoods and communities. We had MCs planning to meet in Starbucks, community halls, school halls, Scout huts, in the midst of car boot sales and even in a coffee shop called Café Nero. Given that the Roman Emperor Nero had ruthlessly persecuted Christians, the historical irony of this was curious. Nero’s also agreed to serve the MC coffee at a discount price, which was insufficient recompense for Caesar’s bad attitude but a nice touch nevertheless.”[82]

There will be a few notable exceptions to this principle; for example, someone who is converted out of a highly addictive lifestyle might need to move to a different place in order to remove him/herself from those who enabled the addiction. Overall, though, being out in the wider community is the New Testament pattern; see, for instance, Luke 8:26-39, where Jesus sent the formerly demon-possessed man back to his home town.

Jessica on how God Provided a Place to Meet:

A college MC had gone through a transition of leadership between semesters, but with the graduation of the previous leaders, their meeting place also disappeared. The new leaders kept looking and trying, but could not find a suitable venue. Going to bed one night, one of the leaders asked God to show her as she slept what to do! That night, she had a vivid dream where she saw two students whom she knew, who went to another church. In the dream, she went up to them and asked if her Missional Community could use their apartment, to which they agreed. The dream then ended. The next day, she walked onto campus and straight into the two students from the dream. Wondering if this might be God, she decided to take the plunge and ask them. She wasn't able to even complete her explanation before they said yes! They said that they viewed their apartment as being there for ministry and that they would love to host the group. It turned out that they had a beautiful place, furnished to a far higher standard than a typical college place, and it has proven to be an amazing base right next to the campus.

When Do MCs Meet?

Missional Communities meet whenever they want, both formally and spontaneously. MCs usually need a regular formal meeting pattern during the month, including gatherings that are fully OUT-focused, to provide some intentionality to their core activities. These regular and more recognizably organized meetings are valuable and important. We suggest that an MC meet together as a whole group weekly when it first begins, as this allows the MC to become the primary place of identity (rather than a small group). Over time, this may well shift to perhaps once every two weeks. **To meet less often on a formal basis can only be pulled off if the group is networking and relating very consistently outside of the formal meeting.**

To only gather monthly will make it extremely difficult for substantive bonds of community to be formed. These bonds are what act as the cohesive glue that pull the MC out in well-supported missional endeavors. We have often coached MC leaders who are frustrated that their group members are not very committed to their mission focus, but won't lead the MC to meet together more than monthly. There is a causal link here between time together and mission commitment.

Missional Communities work much better when people within them are gathering throughout the week, in smaller and larger settings. It might be as small as two people meeting for coffee, through a couple of households sharing a meal, to a party for a bunch of people and their friends, to a big gathering in the local park to play flag football or exercise the children on the playground or to enjoy a picnic together. However it takes place, MCs stand or fall on both the number and the strength of the relationships within the community, *and then inviting people to join in on the fun.* This type of community is addictive for people who aren't in it.

It is hard to over-emphasize this: People need time together if they are going to commit together to serve and go. The key missional dynamic is that we are not doing mission individually, but as part of a wider group. As this is such a counter-cultural mindset, we have to do all that we can to give MCs the best chance of success. By creating dynamic community, we have a much stronger platform to call the more reluctant to go out with us—people who, in spite of their hesitancy, might be highly effective once they do eventually go in mission. This is how we expand the circle of mission well beyond the most gifted and pioneering, starting to create a broader church culture that is committed to missional living.

Meeting on Sundays?

In some churches, communities meet OUT in their missional context at least once a month on a Sunday, rather than gathering at the main church. One such church explained it this way, **"The heart of our church really is about being community where we live, rather than spending time in a building every Sunday."**

For many Christians, this is a major cultural shift. And if we are really honest, it is often the clergy and key leaders who find this the hardest, for it means that there will be fewer people in church on Sunday, which means fewer people to listen to us preach, put money into the collection plate and help to run Sunday School.

So why enable MCs to meet on Sundays?

The first thing to say is that Sunday gatherings are wonderful and we are not saying to do away with them. We personally know many people who have come into the main Minster church building on a Sunday morning, whether by themselves or brought by a friend, and that has proven to be a key point in their journey to Christ. At the same time, however, that is not a strategy that is going to reach everyone, let alone a majority of the population. To use a fishing analogy, we need more than one type of bait in the water to catch all the varieties of fish!

As we looked at in the Minster church section, historically as churches developed in Europe, they planted a network of chapels and churches in the surrounding area. Often the language of mother and children was used in relation to the Minster church and the mission centers. In time, this developed into the European parish system of cathedrals and churches. Today, more dynamic metaphors of planets in orbit around the sun might be helpful. The orbital pattern of MCs brings them into the light and warmth of the Sunday gathering at the central Minster, which equips them to launch again into the cold and dark world that they are trying to reach.

As a rule of thumb, most mature Missional Communities will find themselves gathering with the wider church at a Celebration no less than once a month and no more than three times a month.

Clearly, the high accountability of a discipling culture allows for the low control of this kind of strategy and structure. We put the responsibility onto the individual MC leader to determine his/her rhythm and simply hold him/her accountable for being healthy and missionally purposeful. More specifically, we hold MC leaders accountable for making a healthy rhythm that will not simply pull them into a high-demand Christian sub-culture. At the same time, they need to ensure that they engage on a consistent basis with the wider church community, having a regular diet of accountability, mission, community, public worship and challenging teaching. The key is to set the balance between the three sizes of gathering: Weekend Celebration (Public Space), Missional Community (Social Space) and Small Group accountability (Personal Space).

The Spectrum of MCs and Sundays

The spectrum that results (after a number of years, not immediately!) might look something like this.

- Some will prioritize the Sunday celebration except for one Sunday a month, when they go out in mission with their MC into their place of calling, incarnating the Gospel there to the people whom they are trying to reach.
- Some others will have a rhythm where they are always at Sunday celebration, maybe because they are called to serve there, or the people whom they are called to reach might well be the sort of people who are indeed attracted to such a gathering. Sometimes churches have OUT Sundays, when they don't hold any services and send everyone out in mission through MCs, gathering later for stories and to celebrate what God has done through them all.
- Some will feel that they only need to celebrate once a month with the whole church body, so for the rest of the month their energy goes into the mission and the community of their MC. They might not meet on Sunday mornings in their MC, but it is about the overall balance of their schedules (for instance, the time they spend in mission on Saturdays and throughout the week means that Sunday morning needs to be spent cutting the lawn or catching up on work). While the principle of a day of rest is really important, let's not assume that for everyone this will be on Sundays.

All of these are legitimate responses and none is better than the other. But in an increasingly diverse society, we need to graciously allow one another to express our faith and witness in broader ways than a one size fits all mentality. If we take seriously the call of Christ, the witness of Scripture and the experience of the church over 2,000 years, we need to be willing to rethink our expectations of what faithful church membership looks like. We must not shy away from distinguishing our cultural norms and personal preferences from what are genuinely the underlying and lasting principles of church life.

We readily admit that this is not an easy thing for a church to do, since it feels as if we are undervaluing what has gone before. However, our cultural context in the United States and the Western world continues to change dramatically, so we cannot cement into place models and practices that grew up to reach a different time and culture. They may feel safe and comfortable, but those are not the words that best describe the call of Christ. Yes, this is a sacrifice. Yes, it is a challenge. Yes, we will make mistakes along the way in exploring these new—or more accurately, ancient—ways. But we are compelled to do so if we are submitted to the call of Christ to go to the lost, in his name, sharing his words and works as we go.

How Does Worship Work in an MC?

Worship can be a wonderful experience in a Missional Community, often with a deeper sense of intimacy than the large church celebration.

MC worship should remain as lightweight as possible for the people organizing it, so it shouldn't take too long to plan. The aim is to give people the opportunity to engage with God and allow space for the Spirit to move through people at that time. It's not the activity that will bring us into God's presence; it's how we choose to involve ourselves and what we make of it. People shouldn't feel pressured to come up with something amazing—this is not to replace the large-scale weekend Celebration. It's an opportunity to do something different, more intimate, and more personal for your group.

Stephanie on Worship When No One Plays an Instrument:

For years, our Missional Community lacked any serious musical capabilities. For a long time, this meant that praise and worship was confined to the remote for my iPod dock. Fortunately, we serve a creative God and his community is equally innovative. Often our MC enjoyed art worship (cheap canvas, paint, markers, colored pencils), journaling, spoken word and poetry, a cappella singing and even silence in order to focus our hearts. Nothing need stop us from finding meaningful and memorable ways to worship our great God!

The Worship Curve[83]

Here is a tool that might help you to develop the worshipping life of your community. The intention is to encourage and empower your worship leaders to be creative and responsive to their context, while also giving them a clear framework (which we call the worship curve) around which to build.

The worship curve is a simple, biblical framework to help us to explain our typical journey in a time of worship. Many churches design services around it, as it shows how all the different aspects of the service are part of a journey towards God and responding to him. This includes parts of worship that you wouldn't expect, such as the sermon. If you were to follow the worship curve, you should end up with a balanced Missional Community meeting that allows people's hearts to meet with God, be prepared for the discussion and respond to the challenges that it may present.

How to Use the Worship Curve

- Choose things from the stages to help to set the order of the MC meeting. You do not have to do something from every stage. Just try to get the flavor of the journey. The first two stages (exaltation and reflection) could be done in any order as they both shift the focus from us to God, which is a great way to start any gathering. It is, however, useful to pick from them in order beyond this; otherwise you might end up doing something for which people aren't spiritually prepared, e.g. Communion without a time of confession beforehand.
- It's best to create variety. Try to avoid picking lots of things that 'feel' the same, e.g. things that are all paper-based or activities that are all intercession-based.
- Don't feel that you have to rely on sung worship. This is just one aspect of worshipping God.
- Look at the ideas for commission. As long as you remember the options, you could decide this on the day as the Spirit prompts you.
- You can use the festivals to guide your activity choices, e.g. during Lent, you might want to include some quieter, repentance-based activity, or at Easter more celebration and thanksgiving relating to the cross.
- Don't get hung up on it. It's there to help, not hinder or restrict. If you want to try something or change your plans as the Spirit leads on the day, go for it. It's a learning curve too.

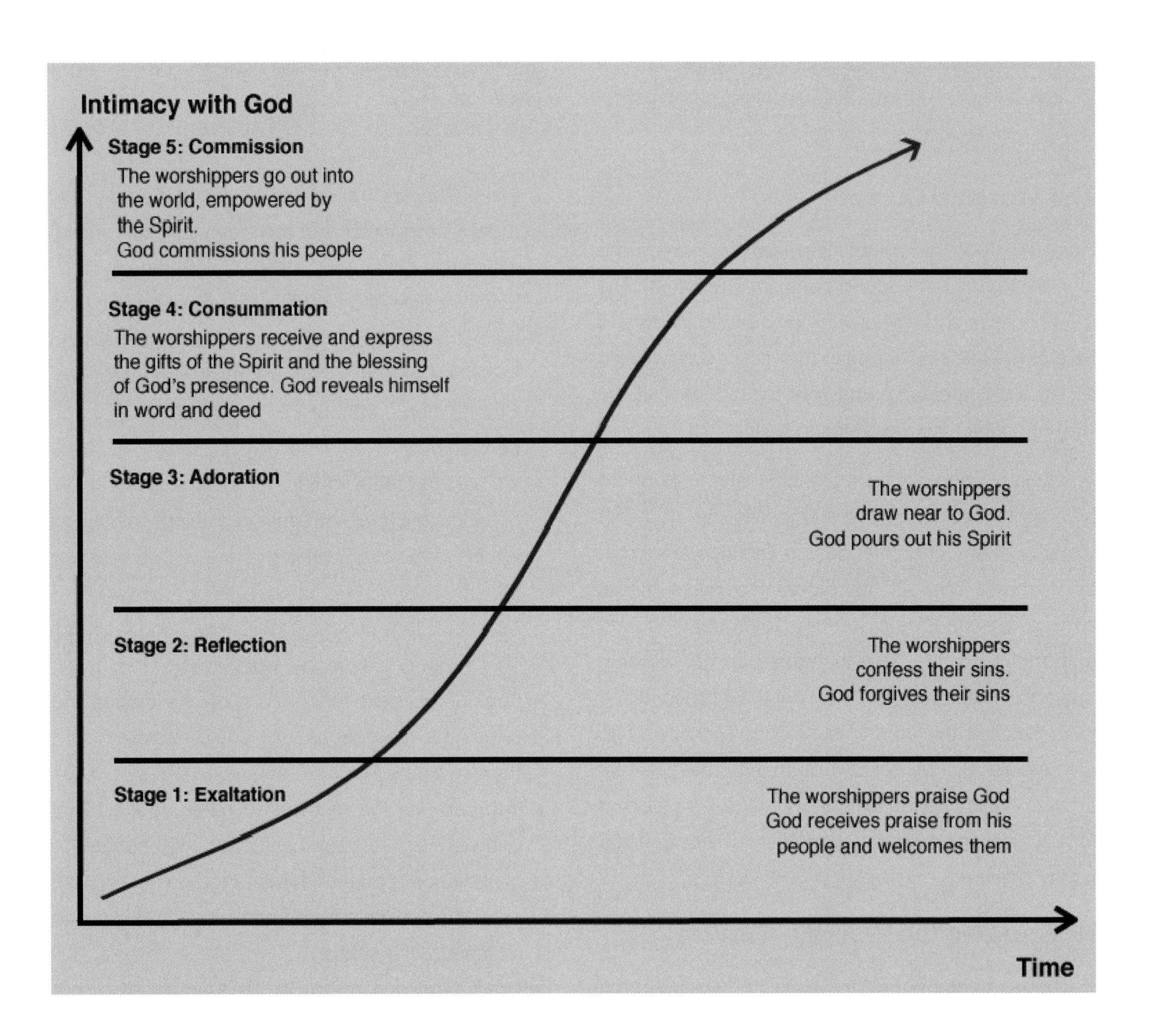
Intimacy with God
Stage 5: Commission
The worshippers go out into the world, empowered by the Spirit.
God commissions his people
Stage 4: Consummation
The worshippers receive and express the gifts of the Spirit and the blessing of God's presence. God reveals himself in word and deed
Stage 3: Adoration
The worshippers draw near to God.
God pours out his Spirit
Stage 2: Reflection
The worshippers confess their sins.
God forgives their sins
Stage 1: Exaltation
The worshippers praise God
God receives praise from his people and welcomes them
Time

Joel on Reaching People Through Worship Leading:

We have decided to run a training session for people in Missional Communities who want to develop their skills in worship leading. Last night, one of our leaders brought along a guy from his MC—a colleague of his from a local university. Anyway, this friend came to the session and in the introductions made it clear that he wasn't a Christian and was just searching spiritually. Nevertheless, it turned out that he's a musician and loves worship, both in Sunday celebrations and at MC. 'But it's just the music that's pulling me in!' He came wanting to learn how to lead and play so that he could contribute to the community. So he's gone back to his MC and we'll see what, or Who, is truly pulling him in.

Worshipping with Children

Having children worship with you is a beautiful part of a Missional Community. Children need to be reminded of the purpose of worship. It can be helpful to interject comments throughout their worship time to help keep the focus.

There are countless ideas for engaging children in worship, and no doubt you will have plenty. We asked some MC leaders for their best ideas to add to yours, and we hope that they add to your experience.

Here are some of their suggestions:

- Children can be given paper and crayons to draw what they are sensing in worship (this is also helpful if the group is just waiting on God with instrumental music). Kids may sense, hear or see something that they can communicate to you in a picture. It may also be helpful to give children small instruments or streamers to use during worship.
- Sometimes MCs worship together as a whole group but with a child leading. This is always really powerful and humbling. Interestingly, groups that have done this have found the children engaged far more readily, no doubt because of the increased ownership and responsibility that they had taken on.
- Let kids pray over the MC and lay hands on the adults
- Ask the kids how we can pray for them—example: how is school going?—then have the adults gather around and pray for them
- Ask simple questions for all to answer
- Amazing God story from the Bible
- Make instruments (paper plates and beans) with the kids, or bring age-appropriate instruments (shaker eggs, tambourines, pots & pans, etc.) and let people worship with them
- Drama
- Encourage kids to dance—and thus adults too!
- Just worship like normal
- Have worship with art; let kids create art while worshipping
- Singing; both celebrating wildly and practicing the discipline of being reflective during more intimate songs
- We taught our kids sign language for the songs
- Communion time
- Memorize Scripture; make it fun!
- Use video clips with music
- Bring tithes and offerings and celebrate that together

STAGE	WHAT IT DOES/HOW IT FEELS	IDEAS FOR US
Exaltation	Remembering what God's done	• Testimony–spoken or written • Create a testimony wall • Reading Psalms/Scriptures that exalt God • Thanksgiving circle–sit in a ring and each person says briefly something for which they're thankful since the last time • Writing our own Psalms based on a repeating theme; i.e., remembering something that God has done followed by 'his love endures forever'
Reflection	Recalling who God is	• Reading Scriptures about God's character • Collective creed • Sung praise about God's character • Thanksgiving prayer • Communion, if focus is on thanksgiving/celebration (which would dictate confession and absolution beforehand in earlier stages) • This could be the context for studying the Bible, if the expected response is moving into adoration etc.
Adoration	Where we begin to tune into God's presence and transition to a closer time with God	• Silence/Listening to God • Operating out of spiritual gifts • Repentance, confession and absolution ideas, e.g., you could include a 'sin shredder', writing confessions down and feeding them into the machine to be shredded • Reading Scriptures about God's relationship with us or forgiveness • Offering • Prayer for different things as prompted by the Holy Spirit, e.g., healing, intercession • Using different physical postures, e.g., kneeling, bowing, standing • Led meditation based around how we feel about God, especially in relation to any shared passages that have been read
Consummation	Intimacy	• Worship songs that are about how we feel about God and how he feels about us • This could be the context for studying the Bible, if the expected response is moving into commission • Communion, if focus is more reflective • Prayer ministry-type stuff that may have been prompted by earlier spiritual gifts or by God speaking to us
Commission	Preparing to go out	• Whole group summarizing discussion with spontaneous highlighting of challenges • One person summing up the main threads that have been discussed and potential responses • Silence/contemplative prayer • Breaking into small groups, discussing application then agreeing to remain accountable midweek • Intercession for upcoming week/events

Annamarie on Involving Children:

To some extent, children don't really mind what they are doing if they are being involved in a productive and relevant way. When we taught about prophecy, we let the children learn and practice hearing words as well. One girl started speaking some really significant prophetic words of life over the adults. She didn't have a grid for this not being acceptable, so she just did it and carried on with life straight afterwards! When we make teaching accessible to children, they too can begin to express the gifts that God has put in them.

How to Pray with Children[84]

- Let them pray first. This helps them to feel ownership since it's their prayer time. If you pray with them, don't dominate the prayer time. Let your prayer be a confirmation of theirs.
- Avoid long, drawn out prayers. Instead, pray short, one- or two-sentence prayers.
- Pray conversationally (one topic at a time). Talk to God without using big words.
- Give the children prayer 'targets' on which to focus. Example: 'Ryan, will you pray for God to bless our governor?' 'Rachel, will you ask God to give him wisdom?' This helps to draw shy children out and encourages everyone to participate.
- Assure them that God is listening. Remind them that God will hear their prayers.
- Pray about whatever they ask. If they get the impression that something is insignificant, we are teaching them that God doesn't really care. If they want to pray for the trees, then with all your heart, pray for the trees.
- Model a prayer for them. Kids learn by example. If you are praying for Sarah to be healed, then say a one-sentence prayer for her to be healed and then ask a child to pray the same thing. Or ask, 'What else can we pray for Sarah?' Give them time to respond and then make suggestions. 'Why don't we pray that she won't miss too much school?' If you pray specific prayers, they will learn to do the same.
- Have the children lay hands on each other and pray for each other. Hopefully this will impart a heart for intercession that they will carry for the rest of their lives. Even if they don't want to pray out loud, ask them to lay hands on the person for whom you are praying as a way of participating in and agreeing with your prayers.
- Play 'Psalm Consequences' (write a line, fold it down so that it can't be seen and pass the paper on to the next person. The end reading is lots of fun!). This can work equally well with all ages together.
- Write a group Psalm—everyone makes up a line in turn around the circle. This is similar to the above, but done knowing what has gone before you.
- Learning to hear God—talk about how God speaks in different ways (thoughts, pictures, feelings etc.). The children can then lie on the floor listening to quiet music, before drawing or writing what they felt God had said to them.
- Use the Huddle questions, adapted for children. This is a way of encouraging them to share their needs. They then write a prayer for the person on their right/left and you can go around the group reading out the prayers.

- Have someone sit on the 'Hot Seat' in the middle of the circle, while the others lay on hands and pray for them.
- Keep a prayer diary of what you have prayed for as a group and the answers that you have received.
- The Lord's Prayer works really well as another tool for learning to pray out loud
- If all else fails and no one wants to pray, be thankful. There is always something for which to be thankful! Make suggestions that remind them that without God we would not be alive. Thank God for the air, trees, flowers, food, soccer balls, little brothers, etc.!
- At the end of the prayer time, always remind them that they can talk to Jesus anytime, anywhere. No matter how they feel, or what's going on around them, Jesus is their very special friend who wants to talk with them too!

A Children's Peer-Led Small Group

Some Missional Communities have developed a peer-led children's small group (for ages 7 upwards). Each child takes it in turns to lead, taking a resource book home (there are many available) and preparing some or all of it, depending upon their age and confidence. Adults will take it in turns to be the 'wise person' present, preparing some of the material if it is a younger leader. As the group develops, the 'wise person's' role will often reduce to very little.

Angie on Including Children in Bible Study:

Being a Missional Community with a lot of young children can be a struggle! We've always felt that Missional Community is just as much for them as it is for the adults, so we're constantly looking for ways to keep the kids included and involved. We've recently begun having the older kids lead the younger kids in Bible stories and crafts. We just give an older kid the basic theme and let them run with it! One week, Roz, one of our older girls, used 'Webkinz' stuffed animals to act out the whole story of Joseph. She kept the younger kids' attention throughout, which I've never seen an adult do. It's great to see our Missional Community become a place where our kids get to discover and use their spiritual gifts and disciple one another.

A Word about Holy Communion

Discussions, debates and even deaths have surrounded different understandings of how the sacraments work and should be administered. Clearly, we wouldn't dream of trying to resolve those issues here.

However, we would encourage you to think through what role MCs play in Communion and Baptism. If your church is one at which they can only be administered by ordained clergy, what does it look like for Missional Community life to be brought into those celebrations? Presumably, the central Minster church will play a larger role there. What parts of those times could be undertaken by MC leaders and members? Even in churches with less strong sacramental traditions, there will be unwritten rules and expectations that need to be unpacked and reapplied for MCs.

Specifically with Communion, is a more informal mode allowed when people are meeting in their homes? Many denominational churches have found an acceptable middle ground to be to ask MCs to not try to mimic Sunday services; for instance, avoiding the use of the official liturgies and maybe even referring to it as a simple breaking of bread. Again, we are not telling you what to do, since this must be decided at the local level, but we want to at least acknowledge the dilemma and to encourage some creative thinking. With the help of the Holy Spirit, it is possible to find paths that both honor our heritage and yet allow for new forms of missional church life to emerge.

Spiritual Warfare

As we have watched and helped many churches embrace Missional Communities, we have observed significant levels of spiritual warfare that occur as a result. This comes in many forms—congregational conflict with a small but vocal and well organized group of opponents to missional living, relational stress on staff teams, marriage pressures, sickness, huge bureaucratic hold-ups with the authorities, doubt and fear leading some to give up, oppression and depression, even physical threat. The enemy clearly hates anything that releases missional life or greater power in the body of the church, so we should not be surprised that this occurs; neither should you be surprised when this happens in your context.

We stand against the evil one, a spiritual being who is the source of all evil and is utterly opposed to the purposes of God. The name satan means 'adversary' or 'one who resists,' and that tells us everything about the battle that we are in. The term devil means 'slanderer,' so he lies, attacks and distorts the truth, especially the truth of our relationship with God. He tries to prevent the Kingdom of God from advancing and people from having a deeper covenant relationship with our heavenly Father, since both of those are things that he fears deeply.

However, he is nothing like God. He is neither omniscient, omnipotent nor omnipresent, which means that his resources are way fewer than our Heavenly Father's. Furthermore, we are on the winning side. So while it can be incredibly hard and challenging in the immediate, we are not without hope, since Jesus is the undisputable victor. Through what Jesus achieved on the cross, the power of satan is broken, and he only has a short time left before that defeat is completely driven home. "But thanks be to God! He gives us the victory through our Lord Jesus Christ" (1 Corinthians 15:57).

So really, whether you like it or not, you are engaged in spiritual warfare. Jesus said in Matthew 11:12,

"From the days of John the Baptist until now, the Kingdom of heaven has been forcefully advancing, and forceful men lay hold of it." Our tendency is to think of spiritual warfare primarily as the enemy attacking us, but it is we who are to be the aggressors. Developing a church with MCs counts as an act of warfare, so do not be surprised if the enemy pushes back hard.

This is why prayer is so important so that the mighty weapon of prayer can be deployed, and you will not be unaware of the enemy's schemes. We remember that our battle is not against flesh and blood, however frustrating those people may be.

We would also strongly encourage you to find other leaders on the same journey, so that you can share notes, swap stories, learn from one another's strategies and generally find a place of support. This is another reason why leaders themselves need to be in a Huddle, where they can let their guard down and interact with others in similar situations.

So, we should be honest about the realities of spiritual warfare that seem to strongly surround MCs. There is a struggle to be faced here that in some situations can prove highly challenging. However, be encouraged and hopeful, for God is on the move and we are a part of the battle and victory of the Kingdom.

Patty on Spiritual Warfare and Mission:

One memorable outreach effort was participating in Fall Festival for a nearby elementary school. Several Missional Communities were involved, with each one responsible for manning different tables and activities. Our contribution was to share a children's gospel presentation with our guests. The presentation was very effective and did a great job of commanding the kids' attention and communicating the gospel clearly. We were scheduled to do four or five performances throughout the evening. The children from our Missional Community had integral parts in the presentation, so consequently had very limited opportunity to enjoy all the fun events around them. We gave them a short break between performances to go and get some candy. Our youngest son took the lead in racing down the hall—and ran head-first at full speed into a huge auditorium door that had suddenly swung open unexpectedly. He ended up bleeding profusely, with a nasty gash on his forehead.

God was good; the closest adult at the scene was a nurse and one of our Missional Community members is a physician and close friend. We were so thankful that he was there to care for him immediately (and the rest of the MC was there to calm and comfort us!) Soon after, we were on our way to the emergency room for stitches. It turned out that only one presentation was cancelled and then the group re-shuffled parts and did a final presentation without us. We walked away from the experience with a strong sense that we had just been through an attack by the enemy to disrupt and derail our witness. The fact that our son bore the brunt of that attack made it a little too personal for our comfort level, to say the least. We had been praying a lot about the event, specifically for impact and fruitfulness, but hadn't really thought about a need to pray for protection. It was a clear reminder of how strongly the enemy resists the proclamation of the gospel, and it impressed upon us the very practical need for effective spiritual warfare.

IN

Children and Families

When God blesses parents with children, they are given the privilege of making disciples and helping them take on the values of the Kingdom, within the context of the wider community of faith. Missional Communities are a great place for 'extended family' to nurture children in walking with God. Jesus valued every child, and so should we.

Educators tell us that rather than giving children information to digest, they best understand and value following Christ when they experience it for themselves and see it modeled in everyday life. Children are very tangible in how they process life, so they want to see it working in practice.

Of course, to intentionally include children does require an investment of energy and effort! One MC leader put it like this, "When we began leading our Missional Community, we discovered that 'low-maintenance kids work' is a contradiction in terms. However, by trial and error we discovered some things that worked really well and by the end of three years, the kids' work was considerably more 'low-maintenance' than leading the adults! Moreover, we saw the greatest growth in faith and risk taking place amongst the children."

Families of Mixed Faith

Families and households in which one parent follows Christ and the other does not can be places of extraordinary tension. The couple, who perhaps fell in love with one set of shared values, now finds that there

is a wedge being driven between them. If the Christian parent has the overzealousness of the new convert, or perhaps a lack of emotional and spiritual maturity, then this can cause major conflict. Any children the couple may have will, of course, be highly sensitive towards this. Maybe they like going to church with Mommy, but then wonder why Daddy stays at home if it is as important as Mommy says it is.

Missional Communities are not a magic bullet for this and similar pastoral issues. However, due to their more relaxed nature and strong community elements, we have observed that the non-Christian partner often feels far more able to join in there rather than at regular Sunday services. For instance, he/she may well be happy to join in with service projects in which the MC is engaged. As with anyone who is floating around the edges of an MC, it is vital that s/he is not treated as a project, but simply interacted with in a relational way. Missional Communities do create space for this to occur more naturally and can be less threatening for the variety of households that we encounter in our culture today. We are called to simply be good news, and MCs are a great context for living and modeling that.

Children and Community Life

Clearly children are a valuable and wonderful gift to any MC. However, they do bring with them a whole set of questions and issues, often related to how much involvement they should have in the MC. The tension is that adults want to see children discipled and grow—they are, after all, just as much part of the church of today as we are—yet, simultaneously, neither do they want all their experiences of Missional Community to be 'Disneyfied'!

The answer to this question will vary among different groups. For a community of young adults, the arrival of the first baby makes very little difference, other than being a fun community plaything (in fact, our experience (Alex) was that we checked our first baby in at the start of the evening and rarely touched him again until the end!). But as the number of babies increases, and they stop sitting and cooing and instead start running and yelling, things usually have to change.

Missional Communities with many families can find that stressed parents are desperate to have an hour or two without their children, so they make free use of the DVD player in the other room. We have seen a group at this stage solve this issue by jointly paying for child care to take place in an entirely separate (nearby) house, with a syllabus for the kids to work through, freeing parents up for their own adult time. We recognize that some will think this genius and others will be horrified!

Other MCs are led by people determined to include their children in almost everything, which makes for lively and noisy gatherings, where people need to be willing to go with the flow and set expectations for conversation appropriately. It probably is advisable to make clear the style of gathering to people who are thinking of trying out the community, since it could be a shock to some.

Still, other communities opt for some sort of hybrid solution, the children being with the adults for some of the time, before the two groups separate. For the time that the adults are with the children, it is really important for the adults to engage with them fully and enthusiastically, so that they feel valued and welcomed as members of the community.

One of the things that we have found to be important is what happens at the small group size of gathering. Missional Communities that intentionally involve and include children seem to be healthier and more balanced where there is space for adults to meet just with adults, particularly in 'personal space'. In social and public space, this pressure is lower, since people are not expecting to be processing their private thoughts and feelings. However, in personal space, it is natural—indeed right—for adults to be able to share about the realities of their lives and walk with God without having to put everything through an age-appropriate filter first.

As one MC leader who is very committed to including children as much as possible put it, "Let's face it—it's hard to share a heartfelt prayer request or receive prayer ministry when you have a three year old jumping on your lap yelling 'hi-ho silver!'" So, however you choose to involve children, make sure that you are equally deliberate in carving out personal space in the rhythm of the MC.

Alongside this, look to start a small group for your children. From experience we have found that somewhere around the age of seven is a good time to start this, as they are old enough to benefit from it and contribute helpfully. They enjoy all the spiritual food and information that they can get, especially as they explore their increasing knowledge of, and relationship with, God. The leader should go beyond teaching, into discussing biblical truths and how they are applied to life. The children can also learn how to pray for one other and how to reach out to other children who do not know Jesus. Don't forget to make it lots of fun—games, competitions and snacks are an important part of the time!

The fairly obvious point to make is that flexibility is important, since group dynamics will change quickly as children age, new babies are born and new families—in all their different shapes and types—are added into the MC.

> **“We are not prescribing only one way to disciple children in Missional Communities; this is something that each MC (and whole church) needs to work out for itself. “**

Remember that no one manages to do this perfectly, so make sure that parents and leaders are not sucked into a trap of feeling guilty half the time for not doing a 'good enough job' with the children. The encouraging news is that as your whole church grows in experience in family community life, you will gain a reservoir of stories and knowledge that will be immeasurably helpful and encouraging to groups and leaders alike.

In the UP section on Worship, we list a number of practical suggestions for MCs with children that we hope will help you to think through the practicalities. Whatever structural way in which you choose to handle things, Missional Community is an excellent place for children to be trained in the things of God. It is a relational context where things are caught as much as taught, where children can see them being lived out in real life. Of course, the downside is that they are watching to see if it really is true in the lives of the adults; children will be very quick to spot (and comment on!) inconsistencies.

Child Welfare Issues

As they rarely meet in church-owned buildings, are small enough to know one another and are built around relationships, Missional Communities inevitably have a less formalized approach to the issues around child welfare. If you are gathering in a private home, then clearly you don't expect the same level of provision and structure as you would do in a Sunday service, whether it's back-lit fire exit signs, a first aid comfort box or children having to be signed out of the gathering by a named parent. However, this is never an excuse to compromise on core issues to do with child protection and welfare.

One church faced this problem when a family-oriented Missional Community was joined by a man who, over a decade previously, had spent time in jail on charges related to child abuse. On the one hand, the man had demonstrated considerable change and accountability in the intervening years and had submitted to all the boundaries that the church leaders had rightly put around him for Sunday services. Now as the church embraced MCs, he naturally wanted to be in one, and the desire to demonstrate grace and acknowledge his changed life was a strong pull for the group leaders.

However, our strong advice was that it would be deeply inappropriate for this man to be part of a Missional Community at which children were present. Inevitably, relationships with families and children would be formed, since that is usually a very healthy dynamic within MC life. People connect and start to share their lives during the week, including visiting one another's homes.

Whilst there was no indication that any ulterior motives were at work, the leaders of the Missional Community have a clear responsibility towards the children in their community. If one of our values is that we prioritize and sacrifice for the next generation, we can never knowingly put them in a position where grave harm could even be the merest possibility. This is not about removing all risk from life—children in MCs should experience adventure and challenge—but child welfare is an entirely different matter.

It may be hard, even harsh, for the man concerned, especially after so much time has elapsed, but the risk is simply not worth taking. The priority has to be towards the most vulnerable and thus the man cannot be in a Missional Community in which children are part of the life together. If there are no MCs without children then, unfortunately, he cannot be in one until an adult-only group is formed.

Pros and Cons of Different Models with Children in MCs

These positives and negatives have come from Missional Community leaders with experience of leading and being in MCs with children. You will be able to think up other reflections to go alongside the ones recorded here.

WHEN ADULTS AND CHILDREN ARE TOGETHER	
POSITIVES	NEGATIVES
Other adults 'love on' your children	Chaotic, messy, noisy
Children learn to love adults	Hard to focus
Children keep adults young	Moms are distracted
Laughter	Limited depth in sharing
Adults learn from children	
Children learn from adults	
Children see tears and joy	
Children experience community	
Children can see the fullness of church life	

WHEN ADULTS AND CHILDREN ARE SEPARATE (WITH CHILDREN BEING ENTERTAINED)	
POSITIVES	NEGATIVES
Adults can connect	Children don't witness community
Sanity	At what age do you start and stop this?
More depth	Adults might not stay if children aren't being taught
It can be good to have a break from your children, especially if you've been together all day!	Lose a person from the group for childcare, or cost of babysitting
	Burdensome to childcare person
	Lack of space

WHEN ADULTS AND CHILDREN ARE SEPARATE (WITH CHILDREN BEING EQUIPPED/TAUGHT)	
POSITIVES	NEGATIVES
All have training (meat and milk)	Separates Children from us
Parents have a break	Children don't witness how the Holy Spirit is working with adults
Adults can engage more easily	Children feel devalued
People without children enjoy it more	Adults don't hear children's hearts
Deeper level of discussion	Have to find childcare
Children learn more	Have to equip (and pay) childcare leaders
	Need space to put two groups
	A variety of ages can be hard to train
	For young children, how much 'spiritual training' really takes place?
	Do children need to be taught for the whole time? Can't they just have fun?

Helpful Hints on Dealing with Children

These practical things will help you to keep the peace on the inside and the outside when you work with children.

- **Energy** - You will keep a child's attention if YOU are interested in what you are saying. No matter what your personality, read stories with enthusiasm! It's fine to act how you might not necessarily act in a room full of adults!
- **Eye Contact** - Use your eyes and face to connect with children. Your face will tell the story before your lips ever utter a sound! Look directly into the children's eyes. They will feel loved when you do.
- **Realistic Expectations** - Children are squirmy and no matter how enthusiastic you are, they need time to get the wiggles out! Put on a CD and have them

sing and dance with hand gestures, clap their hands or play simple games like musical chairs (if you don't have space for chairs, you can use paper that they hop on when the music stops). Also think through the entire length of your meeting for the sake of the children. Children's sleep schedules may encourage a group to meet during the day or on a Sunday afternoon.

- **Exposure to Prayer** - Children love to pray when they are given the opportunity to try it. They have amazing faith and often have faith in God for big things!

House Guidelines – Setting Boundaries in MCs for Naughty Children!

Generally, children can be expected to follow these two guidelines:

- I will treat others (and their things) with kindness.
- I will follow directions.

If there are other guidelines that you want the children and their parents to follow, give that instruction at the beginning of your meeting.

If a child does not follow the guidelines:

- Tell the child of inappropriate behavior and guide them towards appropriate behavior.
- If the inappropriate behavior continues, the child should be taken back to the parent with an explanation of the situation. All discipline will be the responsibility of the parents, unless the parents have given other instructions.

One Church's Regulations for Working with Children in Missional Communities

This is how one church formalized its rules for people working with children in Missional Communities. We include this not to lay down the law, but to give you an example to process in your context:

Because of our love and concern for the well-being of children in our Missional Communities, the following regulations have been set in place. All volunteers wishing to work with children in an MC or small group must agree to uphold all of the following guidelines and procedures.

- No adult is to be left alone with another person's child at any time. Always have at least one other person present with you.
- A volunteer may never take a child to the bathroom alone; they must have another adult or another child of the same sex with them. Allow children as much privacy as possible. Assist younger children only when absolutely necessary, leaving the door ajar as an extra precaution. Children over three years old may be sent to the bathroom alone, but workers should monitor this situation closely.
- Volunteers working with children are required to have considered us their church home for at least three months and be a regular member of their MC.
- Children must have appropriate supervision at all times. If you go to the bathroom, always make sure that there is another worker who can supervise the children while you are gone.
- Children should not wander around the house during the meeting.
- Children are to be released only to their parents or the guardian who brought them.
- All volunteers should have the full trust of all core parents and the community's leadership team.
- Any injuries or accidents should be reported promptly to the parents and treated under their supervision.
- Be careful in your use of touch. Although we encourage hugging, avoid any contact or situation

that could be considered questionable. God's children are of extreme importance to Him. Steer clear of anything that could create even the slightest appearance of evil. Any questionable volunteer behavior should be reported to the MC leader and parents when it occurs.

- Above all, love every child as a currently active and viable member of the Kingdom of God.

Bob on Children Growing Up in MC:

Children have been part of the DNA of our group since we started. There were children in the group out of which we multiplied, and we've always had children with us since then. Our reason for having our children there was to have them grow up with a love for genuine community. We wanted them to feel so comfortable in MCs that they would naturally seek them out when they got older and were on their own. Our children became so accustomed to being involved in the group that one time when we were getting ready to go to a leaders-only function, our children were disappointed that they weren't invited. We explained to our son Andrew that our Missional Community had children present most of the time and that only once in a while would we have a meeting without them. We told him that there were some Missional Communities that had most of their meetings without children and only had children attend on special occasions. He very solemnly shook his head from side to side and said, 'No children at Missional Community? That's a bad law!' We laughed at that, but we were glad that he had caught the vision about small groups.

We recently had the opportunity to celebrate a new Missional Community. It was meeting at a local university, and we realized that five of our MC's children were there, all meeting together and beginning their own group. We realized that this was an answer to our prayers and a confirmation of our Missional Community vision to pass a legacy of faith on to our children (our group's name is Legacy).

Children have been a part of our outreach efforts as well. A new member recently shared that one of the teenage girls in our group made a huge impact on her daughter. The mom said that when they had left after their first visit, the daughter informed her mother that, 'They had found their Missional Community home!' One of the regular teens, Suzie, had made our visitor so welcome that she wanted to belong. Several months later, that same woman was asking a friend of hers about how her friend's daughter was acclimating to moving up to the junior high school youth group. Her friend shared that there was a girl in the junior high group who had really welcomed her daughter and made her feel welcomed and connected. It was Suzie again! She had been the glue that had helped two families to connect into the life of the church.

Youth

Missional Communities give great opportunities for teens who are longing for community, to gather, to identify with a group and feel at home. Different churches do it in different ways, and obviously local issues will influence how you run your youth groups, such as how scattered the church body is geographically, what alternative events (such as Young Life) gather teenagers, how many youth you already have in your church body, and whether you have youth leaders available who can do a great job in leading teen groups.

Some include teens in their family groups at the MC level, which has the advantage of teens being discipled by a variety of ages and learning to serve within that context as well. They often make excellent leaders within children's small groups (although you might need to rethink if they have a younger sibling there!) Another alternative is MCs specifically for the teen-aged group. Teens will naturally desire to gain some independence from their parents and other authority figures and they need to begin to practice the Christian life with their peers, while also having places where they connect with (benefitting and serving) the wider body. An advantage of teen-only MCs is that the particular issues that teenagers face in the journey through adolescence and towards adulthood can be talked about in a more overt way.

CASE STUDY:
'Target' Youth MissionalCommunities

We talked to our friend Rich Atkinson, Director of Youth Ministries at St. Thomas Church Philadelphia, Sheffield. Over the last three years, Rich and his team of mainly volunteers have planted over 40 Missional Communities in one of the toughest urban environments in the UK (less than 2% of teenagers in church) and now has over 800 high school students (ages 10-19), mostly unchurched, meeting weekly and being part of a community.

They call their youth MCs 'Targets' and they all run on the same underlying principles of UP, IN and OUT, with a clear vision of reaching young people with the good news and making disciples. Although the MCs all look very different, they all have the same four stages of **Contact, Community, Connection and Commission**. We asked Rich how they got started, and he kindly gave us some extracts from his book, *Hitting the Target*.[85]

This generation of young people is desperate for someone, somewhere, to share with them the good news of Jesus in a place in which they have community to process it safely. A Target is all about reaching and discipling young people. We all believe that seeing young people's lives changed and transformed by God is the most exciting thing in the world! An effective Target keeps momentum in meeting young people, building community, making disciples and being able to multiply. It's surprisingly simple if you follow some simple steps and allow God to do the hard work!

1. Contact

There are young people everywhere in this world attempting to go on a journey without a guide. This leads to them drawing all of the wrong conclusions about what they find. Instead of discovering Jesus, they have a barrage of false guides driving them away from finding the Truth. Remember, this is not a battle against flesh and blood! Young people are all searching and seeking. They are all on a journey, during which they will make decisions about their understanding of the world that they will often keep for the rest of their lives. On the road to Emmaus, Jesus encounters some guys who are so similar to the young people we meet. The Emmaus road guys have no one to lead them, and therefore as they are searching for the meaning held within the world they are drawing the wrong conclusions. Jesus simply makes contact with these guys and begins to walk along the journey with them.

Jesus gives us a great picture for how youth work can work well—with passionate, on fire people who can help to explain the searching and seeking through which young people are always going. Young people are not generally looking to the church for answers to their questions about life. This means that it is no good putting on flashy things in the church and simply hoping that they will come and start asking questions. We as leaders have to go out and make contact with young people. We have to make the first step and the first step is listening and engaging with their conversations. Young people turning up to something that you're putting on, is not the same as making contact.

So how do we make contact with a generation which has largely lost contact with the church?

This is where it gets tempting to move into the world of prescriptive models of communities or methods that we have found to work. But our Targets (or Missional Communities, whatever you choose to call them) are incredibly diverse and do not conform to a specific copy of something that has already been done. We need to get creative, to find out about their lives, to simply start really listening to their conversations—just like Jesus did on the road to Emmaus. So much of the conversation between youth leaders and their young people are based around prescriptive discussions that the leaders have set up for one-word answers that the young people know the youth leader will want to hear! What are your young people really talking about? What sport, music, TV, fashion? Then come up with a strategy along with the young people you know for how you can start to make contact with their non-Christian friends. If you have several different distinct groups of young people then this will need to be a multiple community approach rather than one single target. For some crazy reason, most youth workers (including myself for several years) thought that they knew what young people wanted and tried very hard to 'put it on'. The only snag with this approach is that it seems to take a seriously large amount of effort with seriously poor results!

Here are a few other things that we've learned:

1. ***Find teenagers to drive the vision for the Target.*** The best groups are always driven by teenagers. These can even be driven by young people who don't yet know Jesus but get to know leaders (sometimes through detached work). The leaders discuss with the young people how to create a vision for an activity-based gathering. The reason this is vital is that the teenagers need to be the people who invite the non-Christians.

2. ***Don't do 'one size fits all'.*** Big is never better for Target contact work. Indeed, having a larger number of small and specifically focused groups based around a specific activity is the most productive way of making contact with many young people.
3. ***Be prepared for mess.*** You need to release control that everything will be really neat and tidy! As you invite teenagers to come up with the ideas and start to drive targets alongside you, you'll find that it can often be confusing and messy.
4. ***Don't make it too heavy.*** These groups don't need to be the most flashy groups in the world as the activity is not going to be the basis for the group in the long term—you're aiming to build Community. Don't set up an activity that is going to be too hard to keep running in the long term. Ideally, you'll want to get young people to do a significant amount of the organization, and to facilitate this, you'll need to make it lightweight.

2. Community

Initial contact with young people must then lead to a place in which a community of people can go on a journey of faith discovery together. If you don't build successful community, the enemy finds it too easy to pick off the seeds which God sows in the young people because there is no community within which they can process them.

Targets begin as being defined by common interest (whatever they've decided that is), but they become a real community when they share common characteristics and critically perceive themselves as distinct. The young people who are part of it actually feel a sense of ownership over that group of people beyond just showing up for the activity on offer. This is crucial because it takes the relationship between the leaders and the young people beyond the provider-client to a relationship where the leader can begin to speak into the conversations that are happening, to challenge the status quo and engage with them as disciples. We see in Jesus' relationship with the guys on the Emmaus road how initially he simply listens into the exploration of life in which they are engaging with each other, and then he proactively seeks to develop depth between himself and the disciples on their journey.

What is it that you have in common? This can be anything from an activity, an area, a type of music, a program, a belief, debating, eating etc. It really can be anything! Usually, youth groups and youth leaders struggle to create a community because they do not allow a commonality. Most youth programs try and do so much in one evening that it's almost impossible for there to be one thing to which all the young people can sign up and say...'yes that's what we do!' You as a leader need to work out with your young people what the commonality—the main thing—of your Target is going to be. You don't need to be over spiritual about this and come up with a scripture attached to your church's vision statement! Remember, in order that non-Christians can be part of this community the commonality needs to be something to which everyone can sign up. The whole community is still based around Jesus...He is at the center of everything that we do, but in order for non-Christians to feel like they can be part of the community, they need to feel part of the commonality.

We all know that young people are longing for community. They are looking for places in which they are loved, accepted, led, part of something, and free to explore the world. At all stages of a Target, we try to balance our three relationships:

UP – Embracing God - the leaders and Christian young people in your Target can begin to share your story. Building deeper relationships comes from you being vulnerable and sharing what God is doing in your life. You can do this either by having a structured time when you share what God has done in your life, or you can get all of your leaders to be proactive in their chats with the young people during the activities in sharing their story. Remember to keep it short (get to the point and share what God has done), keep it personal (only tell your own story), and keep it recent (God is constantly working in us and speaking to us, and so we should always have something to share!)

IN – Embracing One Another - look for anything that will build relationships. Look for your young People of Peace. As you notice these key young people, you'll want to make extra time for them, arrange to meet them separately for coffee or breakfast, develop deep relationships with these 'gatekeepers' to the rest of the young people.

Also, you'll need to make sure that you spend a significant amount of time with your own team praying and eating together so that you are operating in community as a team.

OUT – Embracing the Lost - You will need to be really praying as a team for the young people. Write down their names, and start praying for them every week by name. I always think that it's really exciting to do this as the young people might never have been mentioned by any saints before the Father until now...you might be the first! Time to battle for these young people! Encourage them to bring new people, and at this point, the community that you've already built becomes your powerhouse of discipleship to process what God is doing in the lives of these young people.

3. Connection

The spiritual atmosphere of the whole Target will need to increase, bringing the event of salvation to the whole community in some way. This is often best done by sharing testimony in the Target of what God has done. Ideally, get the young people to share; but if they're not ready, then you can do it. Often we've started small groups attached to the Target when people have the opportunity to meet Jesus, which we've usually done just before the main Target gathering so that it all remains connected. This will sometimes need multiple small groups for young people at different stages. Run through the basics of faith, and discuss what things they want to investigate. If the Target is small and most have come to faith, then it's tempting to turn the whole community into a small group; but it's still best to do an extra time before or after the main Target because the principle of keeping the commonality of the community still applies. Resist totally changing the structure of what you've been doing up until now, but make space for people to share the testimony of what God has done and give thanks for it. Keeping the community will help as you move forward to multiplication.

There are so many youth groups out there trying desperately to 'protect' their young people from the big bad world. While I totally understand the heart behind this idea, I have seen it create masses of young people living double lives. One of these lives is their lovely Christian persona where they know all the right answers. The other one usually comes out with their non-Christian friends, and the two can look completely different. I get asked by lots of youth workers...how do you break this double life? The answer is simple...**Commission** them!

4. **Commission**

You will never be able to 'teach' your young people into breaking the cycle of living a double life. The only way through it is to make the two worlds collide. To do this, the young people need to be in Targets with their non-Christian friends. I firmly believe that there is no better time to do this than as soon as they make a connection with Jesus.

As you get a Target which has seen lots of young people become Christians, then it's time to ponder how you commission them. How can they lead their friends on the same process that they've been on? One of the main options for this is multiplication of your Target. Encourage the young people to consider if they have a vision for a method of creating contact with other young people.

You have to trust me when I say that commissioning young people for mission is THE BEST discipleship tool I've ever found. I'm convinced that running Youth Missional Communities is the most effective way of reaching young people and creating disciples. You'll have an incredible time as you lead a bunch of young people on a journey you'll never forget and nor will they!

College Missional Communities

Missional Communities are tremendously effective when reaching young adults, including those in college. That age group naturally operates in communities, with networks and neighborhoods of friends gathering informally throughout the week, at all sorts of strange hours! It is also a stage of life at which people are very open to discussing the deeper things of life, as beliefs and opinions are shaped and formed in the 'ideas environment' of a college campus.

The most effective missionaries to reach such an open environment are other college students, and MCs are an excellent way to facilitate such outreach. We see the Person of Peace principle working well, as a group of friends identifies others—for instance, in the same dormitory floor, sports team, fraternity or class—and naturally and organically builds relationships and sees where the Lord is at work in hearts.

At the same time, young adults are often very keen to make a difference and serve in a meaningful way. Again with the emphasis on service, an MC that gives time and energy to transforming some aspect of society will be highly attractive, as well as enhancing their wider credibility. There will be many avenues of opportunity for service, not just at the university but also within the surrounding city and further afield (for instance, summer trips to developing nations).

In most areas, churches do not need to treat college MCs in any way different to other adult groups. Indeed, young adults would much prefer to be treated as adults rather than 'kids'. However, there are some particular things to bear in mind:

- Do treat them like adult groups, but realize that they have less leadership and life experience. Situations that older groups would take in their stride might be huge for a leader who is only twenty years old, since he/she may well have never been caught up in that dilemma before (after all, experience has to be gained from somewhere!).
- Their lifestyle is very different from everyone else in the church (e.g., staying up past midnight is the norm, not the exception), so don't be surprised at the ways in which they live and operate.
- They tend to have intense seasons within the year when they are very visible in the church community, followed by college vacations where

you can go for months without seeing or hearing from them. This will affect when you do key training and activities for MC leaders.

- This is a very passionate age group, where life is lived with great intensity. Perhaps more than any demographic, young adults want an authentic cause to which to devote themselves. This means that you encourage and support MC visions that are audacious and challenging, since this age loves to be stretched. When it comes to the wider church, they will want to be part of celebrations and whole church activities that work in the same way. For instance, a prayer meeting at 8pm might not be well attended, but ask them to do the 3am shift on a night of prayer and they'll be all over it!
- This means that whoever is tasked with leading the college groups will need to do so with energy and enthusiasm, mixed with great wisdom and patience.
- Young adults long to have spiritual fathers and mothers. They love to be mentored and shaped by older and wiser heads, to feel that they are not just a group of young people by themselves. This opens the way for some older people, even grandparent age, to partner with Missional Communities and their leaders. They don't need to be at everything, but they are there in the background, encouraging, supporting and offering wisdom in the issues of life with which young adults wrestle (especially around faith, relationships and careers). This is a wonderful way to have the different generations grow together and build the wider body of Christ.
- If your church is reaching a number of different colleges and campuses, then great value can be had by bringing leaders together from those different places to learn from one another, develop best practice and be a mutual encouragement.
- You will need to always be looking for who the next generation of leaders will be. While this is true anywhere, it is especially true here, since the turnover is so fast as people move towards graduation and look to hand the MC on. This can be tricky as often there won't be mature or experienced new leaders at hand, hence the need to work out how emerging leaders can be recruited and trained ahead of time.
- Sometimes a college Missional Community will have a bumper year, when they have a lot of members, followed by a much thinner year. While generally you will be expecting to persevere through the lean times, there may be occasions when you need to let a group come to an end, trusting that God will give you fresh vision and leaders for future seasons. Hanging onto the tail end of an ineffective group is not usually the wise thing to do.

Stephanie on Campus Mission:

Our MC had incredible difficulties establishing a missional focus. We struggled with attendance for our outreach events and an overall passion for one particular thing. As college students, the possibilities were endless; coming up with a missional focus proved more divisive and offensive than beneficial to the Kingdom. So, our community settled on a broad missional focus for Missional Community as a whole, utilizing our small groups for pointed ministries that each was really passionate about. One group visited the battered women's shelter, another ministered in the dorms, yet another group focused on evangelistic prayer for healing. As a whole, we prayer walked the campus and our surrounding neighborhoods.

Missional Communities for Seniors and Empty-Nesters

Although we have talked a lot about reaching young adults and families, MCs are a powerful way to reach the more mature generations. Our culture is increasingly an aging one, with people living longer and healthier lives. For example, in 1900 average life expectancy was 47 years, while today it is almost 80 and continuing to rise.

With an ageing population comes an unprecedented harvest field amongst the older generations, many of whom will be increasingly aware of their mortality and the questions of eternity. There is much witnessing to be done here. Regarding service, there are many empty nesters and seniors with lots of life, energy and experience that can be put to great use for the Father. There is no such thing as retirement in the Kingdom of God.

Often one of the underlying issues for older generations is coming to terms with the gradual transition from being at the center of activity, decision-making and power. Their children will have grown up and left home (hence empty-nesters). Careers will be coming to an end or moving into a different phase, whereby the reins are being handed on to the next generation. Bodies are becoming older and less responsive, while all the young bucks seem to be sprinting past.

> **“Even at church, change feels like it is increasingly imposed on, rather than being initiated by, them and their peers. .”**

It is, therefore, not surprising that the shift towards a discipling culture and MCs can feel like part of this same pattern. This can lead people to resist these things, whether directly (seeking to use political means to prevent the church changing direction) or indirectly (refusing to take part in MCs, instead retreating to the models that they know and feel work for them). The sensitive leader will be aware of this bigger picture and find ways to work with key members of this generation, in order to demonstrate that MCs are actually a wonderful opportunity for them and their peers.

Our suggestion is that the primary approach to this age group is concentrating on vision and what is positive, rather than what will be lost or changed. Talk about how MCs will be a structure that can enhance our witnessing and service in our city. In fact, an MC's decentralized and low control flavor can be highly appealing, since there is lots of scope for people to discover the freedom to initiate, lead and shape a community.

Rather than creating conflict by saying ‘no’ to what they currently do, whether that is golf, socializing, Bible studies or whatever, try to help them to see how those things can become the basis for significant mission. It is about taking what they love to do and putting it through UP, IN and OUT. What does intentionally evangelistic golf look like? What would it be to seek the Person of Peace in their social network and deliberately find ways to bring Jesus and His Kingdom into that relationship? How can their Bible studies become truly missional?

Some church leaders decide to hold a special meeting for the older members of the church (or address them at a regular meeting for seniors). This gives room for them to hear the vision afresh and to respond, including raising any particular concerns that they might have. Try to encourage those in that age group who like the idea of Missional Communities to speak up, as that will add greater credibility. Part of the reassurance is that, while it is a Kingdom thing to sacrifice for the next generation, they do have a massively important role to play in the life of the church right now. They can be mentors to those younger leaders and groups, where so many people are under-parented.

Chris Saxton, Teaching Pastor at Church of the Good Shepherd in Torrance CA, illustrates this principle:

Some of the older ladies in our previous church held a baby shower for a couple of our Bhutanese refugees. They wanted a way to get to know the women, since Bhutanese cultural norms meant that it was hard to find contexts for relationship building if men would be present. So these ladies from the church made the effort to arrange a time with them, to explain through various means (language and cultural barrier) what a baby shower is and their desire to organize it for them as a Christian blessing for their newborns. I think the older women did what they knew they were good at—loving on little children and new mums—and incorporated that into a mission idea in a community context.

RITES OF PASSAGE

Baptism and Baby Dedications

Whatever your theology of Baptism, you will probably be baptizing adults and either baptizing or dedicating infants. As a wider church, you will need to decide which things can be done at Missional Community level and which things are to be celebrated by the whole church.

If you are delegating much of this to MC gatherings (baptizing people in baths, lakes and swimming pools), it will be extremely helpful to MC leaders to provide them with a default pattern for such occasions. They are highly significant events for the people concerned, so some thought needs to go into them in advance. Even if you value being laidback and spontaneous, don't assume that every MC leader can operate in such a way.

As an example, we have learned to give those baptizing others the specific words to say, as otherwise they end up saying far too much or far too little, resulting in either nearly hypothermic baptismal candidates or non-Trinitarian Baptisms! Planning is also important to create a sense of occasion that serves as a marker both for the individual, his/her friends and family, as well as for the group, and thus something on which to build as you present the Gospel.

If you prefer to do these things in celebrations, maybe with a clergy person or senior leader conducting the actual rite, there are still many ways to include and value the MC at that time. This is the place to which the person being baptized or dedicated belongs; it is right to honor that and involve members from the group, perhaps in praying for the candidate, introducing the ceremony or preaching. Don't forget that if he/she brings unsaved friends and family to watch, it is the MC that will follow them up and seek to build relationship with them.

Marriage

Missional Communities are wonderfully placed to help couples to prepare for marriage, have a beautiful wedding and, most importantly, build a strong and healthy marriage. They are also great places for couples to start dating—in fact, some of our young adult MCs appear to be marriage machines.

The best marriage preparation takes place when an older couple is in relationship with the engaged couple. They are able to share the ups and downs of marriage and help the new couple to think through their expectations of how marriage will work for them. If this can occur within an MC, then there is a natural and ongoing context for such conversations, with the whole community supporting and encouraging the couple as they prepare for their wedding and marriage.

The community will then often want to be highly involved in the actual wedding, both by serving the couple and also in the actual ceremony itself. Increasingly, we see MC leaders being asked to conduct or take part in the ceremony, especially when the group is well established. After all, for group members, their closest leader is the MC leader, so this is an entirely natural and healthy progression (albeit a challenging one for some church leaders). Obviously, you may have local or denominational practices that put some restrictions in place, but there are a variety of options available with a little flexibility and creative thinking.

Death, Bereavement and Funerals

Inevitably, MC members will suffer bereavements, whether of close or more distant relatives and friends. The Missional Community is the first line of support, since that is the place where someone is known, loved and can be practically cared for.

Clearly, some deaths have more impact than others, so the death of a spouse or child is different to that of a great-aunt, however sad that may be. In the more traumatic times, it might be that the MC leader has to clear the official MC schedule and, with the group, work to serve and support the bereaved person or family.

Often people feel ill-equipped to deal with such traumas, but actually, it is the little practical things that make all the difference. Putting together a sign-up sheet to provide evening meals, cleaning their house, going with someone to the funeral directors and lawyers, helping them to walk through some of the practical decision-making that they will face at such a time, offering to organize and run the hospitality for mourners—all those things will make a massive impact (not just to the group member, but to his/her friends and family as well).

Aside from the practical support, the most important skill that a leader needs is to be fully present for the bereaved person. This means offering a sensitive, compassionate listening ear, allowing him/her to talk and process as he/she wish, without the leader feeling the need to offer answers or solutions. Again, this does not need to be overwhelming, and it may well be that someone else in the MC is the best placed (and skilled) person to offer the bulk of such care.

This is a time when MC leaders can greatly benefit from the support of the whole church staff and leaders. They may well want to know anyway, but they can also provide the leader with other resources and support. This is especially true in the most traumatic of times, such as with a suicide or the death of a child.

Well handled, a time of bereavement can prove to be a powerful and significant time for building the Missional Community's sense of life together. It can prove to be hard work and challenging; yet, underneath it is an opportunity for the community to live out the hope we have in Christ, so that even death is not to be feared. We start to sense what Paul wrote: "Where, O death, is your victory? Where, O death, is your sting?" (1 Corinthians 15:55).

Sickness and Pastoral Needs

Missional Communities should be the primary place of support, both spiritual and practical, when people and households are dealing with sickness. It may sound obvious, but the bedside visits to homes and hospitals will come mostly, even solely, from within the MC. Sometimes the wider church staff may be part of this, either through seriousness of circumstance or personal relationship, but increasingly the aim is to wean Christians off expecting a clergy visit as a mark of the church demonstrating care. This is a vital process, as it allows the church to grow without there being a bottleneck caused by the availability of the paid staff/clergy/elders. Whichever form of church government you have, some church members will still tend towards having the senior people pray for them, even if with their lips they loudly proclaim their belief in body ministry!([86]

We have found that pastoral care can 'kill' communities as they often begin to deal with people who do have very serious needs. It is important to have a strategy for pastoral care to help both the people with the needs as well as the people in the MC. One church we know has equipped leaders with a simple, introductory course that lasts for something like three weeks: 'Introduction to Pastoral Care.' It helps MC leaders to deal with things like manipulative behavior, co-dependency and needs that should be addressed by professionals.

When to Refer People Outside of the Group

As much as we empower our MC communities, it is at the same time important to help them to set boundaries to their care and support. In MC life, there will be people whose needs are such that they require help and support beyond what can be offered in that community. Examples might include an adult who opens up to having been abused as a child, someone with mental health problems, a couple on the verge of divorce, someone with a strong addiction, or a person with huge financial problems. In such circumstances, what is needed is highly competent and trained support and guidance in processing that problem, which best creates the emotional, practical and spiritual space for the Lord to start to bring healing.

Missional leaders are not trained counselors, and thus they are not required to be experts in marriage, finances, relationships or addictions. *We need to teach them to know their limit, and not to go wading in where they are out of their depth.*

While many situations of life can be best processed in MC, there are some that are best dealt with elsewhere. The church centrally should have resources and contacts in hand to give to MC leaders as they need them. The group can then simply focus on loving, caring and praying for the individuals concerned, but without their situation dominating the agenda of the community, or the leader feeling the need to come up with all the answers. Sometimes the most loving response is to outsource the provision of care elsewhere.

SMALL GROUPS

What Is the Difference Between a Small Group and a Huddle?

This is quite simple. A Huddle is an intentional discipling group for leaders, and a small group is a microcosm of the church. Small groups, like mid-sized groups and large groups, should have an UP, IN and OUT lifestyle representing the life of Jesus. As such, a Huddle may not have as fully rounded a three-dimensional lifestyle as a small group, because its focus is on personal discipleship.

> **“Huddles are about discipling and developing leaders who can be deployed to lead small groups, Missional Communities, even churches.”**

Of course, a Huddle leader may want to disciple the members of his/her Huddle in missional activities, and this will require the OUT dimension; but again, it is for the express purpose of leadership development.

How Do Small Groups Work in Missional Communities?

To determine this, go back to the core values for each size of gathering (see Four Spaces section in *Key Concepts*). For us, the words were invitation, challenge and closeness, but yours may be a little different. Whichever ones you have chosen, however, will define what the specific structures look like. The aim is to create a model that is lightweight, flexible and low maintenance; it is rarely life-giving to be putting tons of energy into simply ‘keeping the show on the road’. Thus your energy should go into selling the values, not the structures or forcing people to turn up to meetings!

When we evaluate a gathering that is in the small group space, we ask whether it is characterized by invitation, challenge and closeness. This is informed by the material on the four spaces; to be specific, is it facilitating the sharing of private thoughts and feelings for the sake of accountability and encouragement?

There are many ways that this can be worked out in practice, from a mixed group of around nine or ten, perhaps four or five people of the same sex, a couple of couples, or a tight-knit prayer triplet or even an accountability partner. They are varied in expression, but each could do invitation, challenge and closeness.

As an aside, we are increasingly convinced that this size of gathering works best when it is at the smaller end of that size range. Of course, some people love the bigger small group, which of course is totally fine. The problem, though, is that they tend to require a lot more organization and, if you are not careful, can easily start to overlap with the function of the Missional Community, particularly if it is a smaller one.

The reason that many churches have had large small groups is that they have had no other expression of church, except Sundays. With the rediscovery of the *oikos* size gathering, many of those pressures are taken off small groups; so, to some extent, they start to become redundant in their larger expressions. Instead, the small group shifts to a small gathering of around two to five people who are committed to genuine openness and candor with one another. To go back to Edward Hall’s ‘Four Spaces’, this is located at the intimate end of personal space (i.e., people really do share and speak into one another’s private thoughts, feelings and actions).

Starting Small Groups

The priority is to start and establish the Missional Community, then small groups flow out of that life and identity. This is by far the easier way to do things, since it is much easier to sub-divide something than it is to multiply it. For instance, it is fairly simple to have a regular point in an MC gathering where people break into regular groups of three or four to share what’s going on in their life. Trying to turn a bunch of separate small groups into one Missional Community is much harder, since there is a primary and thus stronger affinity to the small group than to the MC. This means that in any conflict over resources, time or priority, the MC will always lose. That is a quick way to diminish both community and mission!

When starting small groups, as well as Missional Communities, social engineering (telling people which group to be in) is often used. While this is well-intentioned, generally it is not a highly effective strategy. Instead, far stronger ties of loyalty and commitment are born when people can choose where they belong (as happens in the rest of life!). So with MCs, the choice is centered on mission focus (more practical tips on that later). For small groups, the choice is who people really want to be with, or feel called to be with. Basically, they are choosing to commit to a few others and share their burdens with one another. Generally, everyone is able to be drawn into a group this way.

Occasionally you find someone who is poorly connected with others, either because he/she is new in or is not easy to be with socially. Nevertheless, we have seen those people drawn into small groups, often by people who have the grace and capacity to make that happen. It might require a little nudge from a leader, although ultimately we cannot force someone to partner up with someone with whom they really don't want to be.

Remember, though, that we should never allow ourselves to become co-dependent with these difficult people; so, if they are genuinely highly vexing person, then they might not be able to be in a small group until they face up to that as a major issue. At that point, it could fall to one of the leaders of the Missional Community to draw such a person aside and intentionally disciple them for a season, until such a point that God has broken down some of their less attractive personality traits and they can be a healthy contributor to a small group environment.

Once small groups have been in existence for a while, it can be hard to work out where new additions to the MC can fit in, since the other groups are already well-established. This is particularly an issue when a community is growing quickly or with a sudden influx of people. There are four options for them:

1. Join an existing group (especially where they have some personal relationship). This does require a generosity of spirit from the existing members—but don't be coy about asking for this!
2. If you have several new people, have them form a small group together. If they don't know any other option, they'll probably just assume that's normal!
3. Ask a more mature Christian to start a new small group specifically for some new people (especially if they aren't yet Christians or they aren't mature in their faith). The mature Christian may or may not choose to stop going to his/her previous small group.
4. Simply share with them the values for small groups (e.g., support, challenge and closeness) but leave them to work out for themselves with whom to do this. This sink or swim approach isn't necessarily as uncaring as it might sound, as some types of people will be fine with that and will rise to the challenge. Of course, this is also an expression of the value that we don't do provider-client relationships, and thus we are not responsible for meeting all their spiritual needs.

Another scenario is that a member of a Missional Community is in a small group with people who are not part of that particular MC. For us that is fine since the underlying values are being met. When their MC has small group time, that person makes him/herself available for new people, facilitating a small group experience for those who are guests or not yet in a small group.

Church Finances

- As you increasingly prioritize Missional Communities and release power away from the center, this will have implications for how you spend money out of central funds. Each church will need to think this through according to its ongoing commitments (e.g., staff, mortgage, fixed costs etc.) and context; but how much say will MC leaders have on how money is being prioritized and spent?

- You may choose to organize things differently, but we strongly favor having one central fund, rather than each Missional Community having its own bank account, etc. This flows partly from our lightweight low-maintenance approach (having to deal with banks, do accounts, provide proper accountability, etc. is not lightweight), and it is partly because we believe in there being a common purse. This means that wealthier groups contribute more, but all groups have equal access. For existing churches, this route also has the advantage of not causing chaos with your existing system for collecting tithes and offerings, so you don't have to force people to choose between giving to Sunday church and Missional Communities. After all, who wants to pay for the gas bill on the church building? But a common purse stops these things becoming issues and keeps everything simple for everyone.

- Although we value UP, IN and OUT, we tend to only allow MCs to spend money on mission. This is for several reasons, notably that most church spending tends to already be on IN and UP items, so the emphasis needs to be on more finance going into mission, which MCs are best placed to do. We have been asked for money for groups to do a big social meal, or to pay for their week-by-week childcare (by an MC that hires babysitters rather than bring children into its main meetings), or to buy Bible study material. Our tendency is to turn each of those down for resourcing from central funds, partly because they feel non-missional and partly because if you do that for one group, you have to do it for all. We think that people would not be happy about their tithe being spent on free meals every week for church members.

  You may have a different view, which is fine, but you need to make clear and understandable rules. We came up with the money is for mission only approach after discussing the different options with leaders at an MC leaders' meeting. We have regularly mentioned it, including stating that we are open to a different approach if that's what the majority of MC leaders would prefer. That is a genuine offer, since we do want leaders to have both authority and responsibility. We also happen to think that most people in the church will agree with our position, hence our eagerness to be open and candid about money.

- One good option is to encourage MCs to put in for a budget if they have significant expenditure on the horizon for the year ahead. This then goes into the wider budget-setting process for the church. For instance, one group working with international students put in for a budget to rent a building and run an international student café, which was a big success. The church paid their fixed costs as well as subsidizing the drinks, as we wanted to support this initiative by a segment of the church that didn't have much spare money for spending.

- Within your budget, plan for some funds to be there for small-scale or unexpected expenditure by MCs.

- For MC leaders who are poorer (for instance, economically poor households, college students and those we know to have very tight budgets), we will quietly make known to them that we are happy to reimburse them for their costs involved in leading the group, driving to leaders' events, etc. Many people won't take us up on the offer, but they are really grateful to be thought of and, of course, we're totally happy to do it if they do put in a claim. We don't ever want money to be an inhibitor to otherwise excellent leaders playing their role within the church body.
- As groups develop and are either around less often on Sundays, or in a more decentralized church set-up, practical provision needs to be made for collecting tithes and gifts via Missional Communities. We always have all monies paid into the church's central accounts, for the sake of accountability, legal compliance (e.g., for tax returns), and also because it stops leaders with a tendency towards less accountability from setting up their own private slush fund for spending. All should contribute on the basis of how God has blessed them, and then all have equal access to the common purse as their missional needs arise.
- Having said that we try to restrict spending from central funds to mission, we do recognize that individuals and households will, from time to time, need some extra pastoral support, including a gift from the church. Traditionally, this has gone through church staff, but we try to decentralize this to Missional Community leaders. A good way to do this is to authorize them to make gifts up to a certain limit (e.g., $250) that does not need prior staff approval. We have yet to encounter a situation where this is abused, but obviously whoever writes the checks just needs to be generally aware of what is going on and speak with you if they are concerned by any unusual patterns. If the situation requires larger scale intervention, the leader just needs to speak to the staff member/treasurer and together they can agree to an appropriate plan.

How Do You Measure Church Growth Now?

As a church body, you will use certain metrics to measure your church (even if all you do is count the offering). Many churches carefully count Sunday attendance and make that their main measure of health. As MCs become more established, how will that change what you count? How will you feel if numbers attending MCs each month outstrip numbers attending the Sunday services (as we have experienced)? Do you just count how many attend a large celebration at the central resourcing church, or how many are involved in MCs?

> **“What you record and report to the church sends all sorts of signals to people about your priorities.”**

We know of one church that began to include each week in the Sunday bulletin sheet the number of people who had registered interest in a Missional Community. This gave encouragement to everyone who had already joined a group, as well as helping the late adopters to realize that this change was worth joining.

It is harder to objectively assess quality of relationship and depth of discipleship, but there are creative tools to help you on the way; you could look at Reggie

McNeal's lists of how to measure important aspects of church life, such as prayer, discipleship and mission. Try taking his examples and work out how to translate them into your particular context.[87]

More Ideas for the IN-ward Dimension of Your MC

- Hang out together in general
- Time to use words of encouragement
- Family dinners/eating together
- Play together – board games, basketball, outdoor games, etc. Hold game nights
- Discussion time – expect all ages to answer (and ask) questions
- Ice breakers for all, e.g., tossing a ball to someone and saying a positive or encouraging thing about them
- Have paper with someone's name on top, and write something positive about each person
- Involve children in meal preparation
- When you eat together, have older children help adults with childcare
- Give kids responsibilities so that they feel valued and needed
- Work through a book on a certain topic that interests children as well as adults
- Provide for each other's needs
- Children are people too! There is no true community without them
- Park night
- Play games like hide and seek at MC—just for fun!
- Arts and crafts, whether just to try something or to illustrate something you are learning, or in preparation for a mission activity
- Puppets for teaching
- Field trips
- Take dinners to families e.g., with newborns
- Go bowling/paint-balling/swimming/night hiking/bike riding etc.

Stephanie on Being Transformed by Scripture and Openness:

The most impacting encounter I have had with the core value of IN was during a season our whole church was studying the Sermon on the Mount. After each Sunday sermon, our MC would dialogue about the talk and respond to the passage during our community gathering.

One girl in our community felt led to read Matthew 5:4. She said that she felt like God wanted us to camp out on Jesus' words for a while and so she asked, 'What is each of you mourning today?'. Immediately, it was as if our collective community had the weight of expectation and self-composure lifted. Each person shared the heaviness of their heart. One shared the recent loss of a loved one. Another felt as though the dreams and ambition he once knew had been stolen by his circumstance. Together, we wept. Our community had an enormous breakthrough as we genuinely and openly shared our lives together that night. More importantly, as we gathered for prayer, the Great Comforter met us, individually and corporately, in a living room.

OUT

Communities on Mission together

How to Gather People Around a Specific Mission Focus

An obvious question is how do you divide people from an existing church body into Missional Communities? Should they be assigned, or can it really happen just by relationship?

We have tried all sorts of different ways over the years and our conclusion is that you want to aim as far as possible for the organic, relational approach.

When social engineering takes place (in other words, the leaders of the church assign people to different groups), they almost always end up as infertile groups. They may have lots of fun together and do some worthwhile mission, but the problem is that people have not necessarily bought into the distinct mission vision that the leader is casting. Thus they are lumped with a vision that they don't share or particularly wish to support, while the leader is lumped with a group whose members are at best half-hearted about the people whom they are called to reach.

This goes back to one of the core values: low control, high accountability. To pre-assign people to particular groups is a high control approach, however well-intentioned it may be. Instead, we need to free things up to allow people to make their own choices and decisions about where they are to belong. Again, you cannot force people to belong somewhere. They need to freely enter into that network, or *oikos*, of relationships.

Having said all that, you do need to create some simplified options so that people know where they should choose to go, in a way that does not pander merely to our 'me and my needs' culture. It is about calling them to a greater vision beyond themselves, where they can both belong and meaningfully serve their King.

When talking about this publicly and rallying involvement in Missional Communities, we tell people that we find that in any MC three types of people follow the mission vision:

a. Those who hear the vision and genuinely share it, even if they hadn't known that was their heart before they heard it and/or they didn't have language to express it.

b. Those who want to serve that vision. It might not be their personal call, but they are very happy to serve to make this vision come about, because they can see it as a worthy and compelling cause.

c. Those who want to serve the MC leaders as people. They're not all that bothered about what they do, as they are more interested in supporting the leaders, learning from and building community with them.

We thus ask people to be attentive to what the Holy Spirit is saying to them and to recognize that God's nudge may come in any of those three ways.

If you follow the logic of this approach through, it also means that as new MCs emerge, some people currently in a group will want to be blessed and released to go to other groups, where they more closely share that vision or have significant relationship with those leaders. It is important for MC leaders to see this as healthy and normal and nothing to feel bad about—and, of course, they can be reminded that such a free market in MCs will work the other way too.

Leaders can take it personally when someone visits their Missional Community and never comes back, so this is a principle to remind them about, as well as reaffirming that this is not a comment on their value. However, if they are never seeing anyone stick, there might be a more systemic problem, which will need addressing, whether in a Huddle or privately.

There may also be people in a group who need to be released to start a new Missional Community, with a mission vision that they carry. The role of MC leaders (assuming the emerging leader meets your leadership criteria) is to work with you to encourage and bless them as they follow the Lord's leading into the battle.

Andy on How Habitat for Humanity Built Its Mission Vision:

Over the past couple of years, we've been connected to a 'Habitat for Humanity' neighbor-hood near to where we live. We began by supporting one of our Missional Community members, Kelsey, as she began the year-long application process to have a home built by Habitat. In an answer to our prayers, she was approved and we were then able to help her to complete volunteer hours towards her own home, which also included working on Habitat sites all over the city. Move-in day was a great day, as our whole Missional Community helped her to move out of her old apartment and into her brand new house! Now that she is settled in her new home and is part of this unique community, which is mainly comprised of single-mother households, we were able to put on a 'VBS' program in the neighbor-hood park this past summer. We were able to connect with many families in the neighborhood and look forward to doing more outreach. It's been exciting to see how our simple prayers for God to provide a nice home for Kelsey opened up a whole mission field to our Missional Community!

Neighborhood Mission Ideas

Do you all live in a specific neighborhood? How about neighborhood clean-up days, mowing peoples' lawns for free, prayer walks, distributing light bulbs, or monthly block parties to have community with your neighbors? How about organizing evenings that are purely social? One pioneering couple started men's poker nights to compliment the neighborhood women's bunko evenings.

Do you have kids that all go to the same school? Or is there an elementary school near your area? Adopt it, and volunteer to help with cleanup and repairs. Sow into the lives of the staff there.

What local facilities are there that you like to use? This could be businesses, shops, services, parks, public transport, the school bus, etc. Be intentional about being fully present when you are there, seeing if the Lord brings People of Peace across your path. If someone identifies a Person of Peace, as a group you can work together to build relationship and reinforce that initial relationship.

Do you all frequent a local restaurant? Have MC meetings there, and build friendships with the owner and the staff. Invest in their lives. Tip well!

Jason on His First Attempt at OUT:

Our first OUT was to organize a trash pick-up around where we live, and we invited our Neighborhood Association to join us. When the day came around, only five people showed up, including my wife and me plus one other leader from our group. Needless to say, we were a little discouraged by the turnout, but our neighbors were happy with our desire to invest in the locality, and the next week one of them showed up at our house with a thank you note and homemade bread! It also caught the attention of the major landlord in the area, leading us to have had tons of favor since then. The Neighborhood Association has begun to outsource a lot of neighborhood projects to our Missional Community. As they have shown more trust in us, it has encouraged our MC members to be more dedicated to doing OUT. For us as a Missional Community, it went to show how faith the size of a mustard seed can be used by God to accomplish more than we can often imagine.

Network Mission Ideas

What about social or business networks? Do several of you work in the same field? Start a businesspersons' breakfast and invite your other co-workers or people with whom you do business. Don't whack them with the Bible, but rather have excellent speakers who will genuinely equip them with skills or motivation for the workplace (and life in general). Add value to their lives, in the name of Christ, and see who responds.

Are you a stay-at-home mom? Organize a moms' play day, inviting others whom you and your friends know. Often young moms are some of the loneliest and most isolated (and tired!) people, so it is very simple to think of things that will draw people and build community. Perhaps you could occasionally have a moms' evening out together and do something more glamorous that is NOT child-focused!! Don't forget that increasingly there are stay-at-home dads; how might they be included as well?

Maybe you have a heart for a specific people group, like the inner city poor or local refugees. Join with an existing organization and volunteer there. See what relationships start to form. Alternatively, if you can see a clear unmet need, recruit a team to start to make a tangible difference.

Do you have a particular hobby or interest? Start being properly involved and build relationships. Maybe you like playing soccer or softball. If so, grab a couple of friends, who in turn invite their friends and colleagues, and form a team. Make sure that your team selection policy and attitude (and language!) on the field of play represents Christ well. Be intentional about hanging out with people before and after games and practices. Look for the People of Peace on your team. Alternatively, your interest may not be a team sport, but the same principles apply—it is a highly biblical model to seek to disciple others through everyday activities.

Mission and Sports

A well-worn path is to turn playing sports into missional opportunity. This can work with a huge variety of recreational activities in which people will gather to take part. For instance, if you enjoy playing soccer, then gather some friends to play in a park, invite them to bring their friends and colleagues, and over time you'll soon have a good group of people. If you want, look to join a local recreational league, and have lots of fun playing—or, as some of our friends did, even start your own league.

The key thing is act as Christ would in that context. That may sound obvious, but it is easier said than done for the highly competitive amongst you. But as we all know, your attitude on and off the pitch is infectious. From the first ever time you play, pray together at the end of the team talk before a game begins (pray about attitude, fun, safety, performing to the best of your abilities, etc., rather than that you would win). If someone is injured, treat him/her medically, and pray for him/her then and there. Work hard to make sure that you don't disrespect the officials. Watch your language! After the game or practice, have a regular time when you can hang out socially, so that you can build relationships even more deeply. In all this, you are looking for the People of Peace, who are interested not only in the sport, but also in you and the message you bring.

We have seen a number of friends come to Christ this way; and when they are baptized, make sure the whole team is invited. The key is to take what you love to do, pray and ask Jesus how to bring his Kingdom in that context. Sow the seed of the Gospel generously as you build relationships around that activity, then watch for the People of Peace where Jesus is about to come, and be highly present.

Ideas for the OUT-ward Dimension

(All of which come from MC leaders)

- Have a dinner with people from your MC and have each couple bring People of Peace
- Have a backyard baseball/softball game that's family-friendly and have your children invite their friends and family to fill the rosters
- Parents with children in strollers have perfect cover for prayer walking!
- Identify a Person of Peace from school and have the MC pray for that person
- Play games with people who don't know Jesus
- Have children bring friends to MC
- Picnic at the park and invite other families
- Kids help make a meal for a neighbor and deliver it
- Pray for friends at school
- Operation Christmas Child (run by Samaritan's Purse) or similar 'hands-on' service and giving
- Homeless packs and sack lunches to put in car and give away when passing by homeless at street corners
- Adopt-a-family
- Ask the children what sort of mission is on their heart and help them to complete it
- Have a globe, atlas or book of flags—pick one out (in a fun way!) and pray for that country
- Children have faith! Let them pray, especially for healing!
- Get the kids involved in raising money for missionaries, organizations, charities, etc.
- Ask everyone, 'What would Jesus want you to do tomorrow to share his love?'
- Neighborhood service activities like washing windows, raking leaves, painting porches, gathering trash, etc.
- Prayer walking your neighborhood
- Involve children in your service (one idea: visit a retirement home, the children will be the stars!). Model and encourage compassion and empathy
- Tell a short story about your neighborhood or network so that children can see where they live and how they can pray
- Ask the Holy Spirit to lead and then follow
- Give out popsicles in the summer
- Go to the emergency room and pass out snacks and prayer to those in the waiting room.
- Take children on mission trips
- Sponsor a child as an MC (e.g., through Compassion or World Vision) and write to them

Pam on an MC serving a Disadvantaged Single Mom:

When our church moved to its present building, we had a God-given vision to impact our local area zip code, which is known for high crime, drugs and gangs. We want to help break this cycle and the many strongholds. Our Missional Community is heavily involved in this through Whiz Kids, a faith-based literacy program that allows us to connect with families of elementary-aged children and take the light of Jesus into their homes.

This past summer, a young couple in our MC felt God challenge them to give their car away. They contacted me and I suggested giving it to one of the single mothers with whom we have regular relationship through Whiz Kids. She had two daughters in Whiz Kids and two sons in prison. She worked hard at her job, but needed dependable transportation. The resource staff at church helped to manage the process of transfer of title and I had the privilege of taking her to get her insurance started. After procuring the license tag, I picked her up at work, brought her to church and watched a great big smile appear on her face. You would've thought that we were giving her the biggest and best BMW! As we pulled out of the parking lot, she pulled up beside me, looking like a teenager who just got her first car! With a BIG wave and huge smile, she was off, all the time knowing that Jesus had sent a big blessing her way!

Mission Does Not Need to Be Sophisticated

The leader of an MC had a close non-Christian friend who was clearly a Person of Peace, but she hadn't yet found a natural way to connect her with the members of her Missional Community. Her dog's 13th birthday proved to be the solution.

The friend, who had a Jewish background, suggested that the appropriate thing to do would be to throw a party to celebrate a doggy coming of age—and that it should be called a Barkmitzphah!

So the MC leader started inviting lots of friends from work and from the Missional Community. Everyone had a great evening, and there were lots of relationships formed between two groups of people who wouldn't normally mix, but once they did, found that they had lots in common. This paved the way for lots of ongoing connectivity in the months that followed.

Missional OUT in Highly Urbanized Cities

Some church communities choose to define their missional focus purely by geography. So MCs meet in a particular area, gathering those from the church who live nearest to them. Their commitment is to represent Christ into that neighborhood. This approach seems to be most common in highly urbanized large cities, where it is not easy to travel quickly by car or public transport.

In such a context, people generally have had their fill of commuting once they return from work, so a strongly geographic connection makes a lot more sense there. One leader in a highly urban context commented that the longer someone lives in the city, the more he/she wants to be able to walk to his/her commitments of choice. Again, this is about knowing the culture to which you are called, and reworking the principles so that you can maximize your effectiveness wherever you find yourself.

Andrea on a Missional Community for Nepalese College Students:

Each season in a Missional Community brings different blessings and challenges. In the beginnings of our Missional Community, we were one group with one heart. We were all involved in the same avenues of ministry, sharing life and outreach together. It was a beautiful time. In particular, we were blessed to be adopted by a large group of Nepali students and through this divine connection, we created a diverse community where we simply loved them and shared Jesus with them. The relationships grew so strong that our Nepali friends forcibly elected me, a white American girl, onto the committee of the University Nepal Society! The connections established then still exist today, even though many of them have moved on to other states now, or back to Nepal. Those guys knew that we loved them and knew that we served Jesus.

Children and Mission

One of the benefits of Missional Communities for parents is that it is a really healthy context for building church life that values family culture. This is not an exclusive thing either; in fact, singles love being part of a wider extended household of faith, since it enables them to interact with ages in a way that often won't otherwise consistently happen.

In terms of involvement, we have generally found that the more groups with children actively include them, the better. Very occasionally, there will be a particular OUT activity to which it is not appropriate to bring children along (for instance, we have friends working to reach and rescue women caught up in human trafficking and prostitution), but generally 'no-go for kids' times are far fewer than many would imagine.

On regular occasions, we (Alex and my wife) have taken our elementary age sons into an inner city context to serve the poor and work at improving the neighborhood with our friends who live there. As we stop and chat with the homeless and poor, the children will listen in and learn. We have had so many opportunities later on to answer their questions, including being able to point out the terrible consequences of drug addiction. They have seen low-level drug pushers try to sell their product to us, watching as we've responded to them with love and mercy (and a clear "no thank you!").

Obviously, every parent needs to make the call based on the uniqueness of his/her son or daughter, but our experience is that, if given room to talk and process, children are more than able to have faith for the power of Christ to transform such broken lives. We have worked on involving our boys in praying for the homeless people whom we meet and the poor families whom we've served, and although they are kids (and thirty seconds after praying they can be fighting their brother), they will connect with what they have seen and come out with some amazingly thoughtful insights. Their future is in the Lord's hands, but we hope that they will emerge as adults who always have a compassion and generosity towards the poor and marginalized, whatever their primary call ends up being.

Families who live missionally have the benefit of raising their children in a home culture and community in which the children grow up not knowing any other way to live life. Generally, young children are willing to do whatever the parents are excited about, so parents in MCs often find that their children follow through on the logic and quickly end up pushing them further and faster into mission!

This is such an asset to parents trying to raise their children to be devoted disciples of Jesus. It is so much easier to model this from the beginning, instead of having to go back and teach children much later on that Christians are meant to be looking beyond themselves and their church. We want our children to understand for themselves that being missional is a way of life, not just an activity. While specific activities make everything tangible, we hope that they learn to think and act missionally throughout their lives, not just at an occasional time for doing religious works. So we try to help them to think about how they can take what they have learned and apply it at school, or in prayer for their friends, or as they play sport, etc.

From the infant to the teen, there is something for everyone in missional outreach. One of things that we have repeatedly seen is that children are amazing at opening doors to people who may not have otherwise spoken to an adult. A homeless lady may find the presence of God more by holding a child than by listening to our words. Younger children love to intercede for a mission focus by drawing out God's heart with crayons and paint before the event or meeting, which engages them even if they don't physically go. Teens can learn how to strategize and plan by joining with the adults in making preparations. All ages can help serve by cooking, cleaning, praying, picking up trash, sweeping, welcoming, offering drinks, shaking hands, etc. Don't exclude your children—they can do so much!

Andrea on Allowing God to Direct the Group as It Develops:

Our group went through a season of diversity, where we were all feeling our hearts pulled in different missional directions and having difficulty finding a missional common ground. In some ways, we are still there and trying to work through what mission means for us as a group. It's been a challenge, but we have stuck together through it and this has made our relationships stronger. Also, changing leaders provides quite the challenge, but the Lord is always faithful to provide.

A Missional Community can be a place of significant growth for each individual if he/she fully invests him/herself in it. It truly becomes a family where everyone is known beyond just the generics of what they do, especially when they are known and loved in their ugliest times. Really all anyone wants and needs is to be known to the core through the messy, ugly, beautiful times of our lives. And it doesn't have to be complicated. Some of the sweetest times in our group have been Sunday afternoon lunches and small worship sessions with an acoustic guitar. One of the most important aspects of a Missional Community is spending time in prayer for both each other and the people to whom you are ministering.

Missional Communities in the Workplace

In his wonderful book *The Culture Code*, Clotaire Rapaille[88] notes that Americans are defined by their work more than any other Western nation. Work is very much at the center of our lives (as he points out, hard work is seen as the pathway to achieving the American dream). Thus, the first question you are asked upon meeting someone new is, 'What do you do?' Many people are in the workplace for over 50 hours a week and are expected to give 110% to the cause.

We think that an important question for churches to consider is whether their members are expected to come home and just focus on family and church life, or are they called to represent Christ in the workplace?

We live such compartmentalized lives, and part of the church's redemptive role in society is to break that down. For instance, someone who is an elementary school teacher in a rough, urban context needs to be encouraged and supported to see his/her colleagues, students and parents as a Kingdom ministry. What does it mean for him/her to be ministering in the education system?

Although it includes evangelism, does it also include playing his/her part in bringing more of the Father's heart to bear upon both individuals and the structures? What does this look like as he/she wrestles with inadequate resources, unsupportive parents and children with endless needs?

Taken to the non-profit sector, how would a highly profitable, Kingdom-oriented multinational business operate? Could devoted followers of Christ climb to the top of the corporate ladder in a way that is totally holistic with their life at church and with their family? How can they be held accountable in an environment where money, sex and power are often greatly idolized?

We have seen MCs operate with great effectiveness in such contexts. Obviously, the principles set out elsewhere in this book apply, so our point here is mostly to open eyes to this as possibility and to encourage people to pioneer into this context, if that is the place of mission to which they are called.

One of the keys for (any) successful MC is learning how to model a different worldview. For instance, when a direct report shares a need or concern, Kingdom wisdom and prayer is a response that helps to make space for a Person of Peace to be identified. When your boss is sick and struggling through the workday, is prayer for healing such a natural response that you earn thanks rather than a rebuke? When it comes to ethics, do you operate at work based off what the Father says, or what a boss or board set as your below-par standard?

> **" From a Kingdom perspective, people need to truly believe that they can simultaneously work for their company and be an effective representative of the Father, with whom we are in covenant. "**

The two are not in conflict. People of integrity will ultimately win in most corporate cultures. Missional Communities that are workplace-oriented are about who you are and how you live your life 24/7. Whether in the back yard or skyscraper, integrity will shine.

When Missional Communities Multiply

As you develop increasing numbers of Missional Communities, and they begin to grow and eventually birth new groups out of themselves, you will begin to realize that you are no longer managing an organization, but you are instead facilitating a movement. There seems to be a tipping point that churches reach whereby MC life becomes so strong that it is an unstoppable force in your wider environment.

People who experience this level of community mixed with such effective mission will not be willing to go back to the way things used to be in church culture. They will be willing to give, serve and sacrifice to see more of this life spread further, wider and deeper into your city and beyond. You will increasingly be aware that you are not in control of very much of what is going on, and you certainly know only a small fraction of what God is up to. When this occurs, you have begun to experience the power of a Kingdom movement.

Exactly when that tipping point occurs will, of course, be unique to each individual church. If you are starting a pioneering work, then the whole culture will be infused with missional DNA from the outset, so the real issue will be demonstrating that MCs can grow, multiply and expand the Kingdom in your context. Probably once you have done that a couple of times, the debate will, to all intents, be over, and MC life will be totally ingrained.

Then it's off to the races.

When you are transitioning a church, there are so many more variables to bear in mind.

How united are the church leaders (both office holders and the real opinion formers) behind this approach?

How well communicated has it been to the church body?

Has the process of change management been properly done?

What is the overall health of the church (for instance, as in nature, a sick body takes longer to adapt and change)?

If your church places a high value on Sunday service(s), how open are people to MCs not being there every single week?

The answer to these questions rests on the process that you use to draw together vision and values around the principle of a missional church with a strong discipling culture. If there is major resistance to that in key areas of the church, then almost certainly one day there will be a time of conflict when those opposed to the changes will seek to reassert control. However, if you do have an agreed mind amongst the key players in the church community, and they, in turn, are positively influencing others, then, given a healthy process of change, the tipping point is definitely reachable. It's hard to say exactly what percentage of the church needs to become part of a Missional Community. As a guess, probably once you move on past the one-third mark, you will be begin to see significant shifts in the overall culture of your church.

A practical fruit of growth will be the birthing of new celebrations. This will occur when a Missional Community multiplies into two (or more) groups that still wish to meet all together on occasion. If they are located in a distinct neighborhood, especially if it is geographically or culturally distant from where the church building is located, this is an entirely appropriate thing to do, if we are committed to seeing the Kingdom advance.

Bob on Leaving a Large MC to Start a New One:

It was intimidating to come from a large Missional Community and begin our own. We started with only three people, and God showed us a scripture to encourage us, "Do not despise the day of small beginnings, for the Lord rejoices to see the work begin" (Zechariah 4:8). This made it easier to just be obedient and not worry about how big we were supposed to be. As time has gone by, we have grown into a full-sized MC, which has been truly faith-building to watch happen around us.

One of the things that Missional Communities enable you to do is to pioneer new Kingdom works in previously unreached (or under-reached) contexts. This is because it is an incredibly lightweight and flexible way to plant a church community. Financially, it is so much less expensive than traditional planting models, which means the balance on the cost/benefit axis tilts massively towards the benefit end.

When such pioneer mission contexts start to take and then grow, it is important for the rest of the wider church body not to measure success by whether the people being reached come along to the main Sunday services in the existing church building. There needs to be a release for the leaders in pioneer MCs not to even have that as an expectation. Their priority is to incarnate the gospel into that culture, thereby enabling people who come to Christ to stay where they are and start to reach their friends, family and neighbors.

The temptation for the main church is to (in effect) demand that if people are being converted, then they need to travel to the mother church, crossing whatever cultural boundaries that are there, in order to prove that the church is united/people really are being reached (i.e., make themselves feel good about their church doing mission).

We think a far more generous (and we would argue, a more gospel-honoring) approach is to release those growing MCs that are reaching into pioneer contexts (by either geography or culture). They should be free to start to create celebration gatherings in their context, so that the people who are coming to Christ can worship him in ways that make sense to them and their friends, rather than in ways that make sense to us and our friends.

Clearly, this is not going to be the case every time an MC multiplies; indeed, it won't be the reality in the majority of multiplications. Sometimes, though, it will be what is best, and our job as church leaders is to train the church body to give away and be generous without expecting anything back in return, including more people sitting in our pews.

Again, this is why we talk about building a movement rather than an institution. We are playing our part in growing a Kingdom movement that transforms our city, rather than trying to build our own church's private empire.

Multi-Site Churches

Recently in the United States, we have seen an increasing movement towards multi-site churches. These are churches which are committed to reaching the lost by releasing multiple expressions of celebration size gatherings in different locations. The best analysis of this development has been done by Geoff Surratt, Greg Ligon and Warren Bird, who state that at least 1,500 US churches were multi-site in

2006.[89] Although mega-churches have been the most notable drivers of this move, Surratt notes that churches of all sizes have been experimenting with this way of releasing growth.

From the perspective of Missional Communities, there is definitely much to be learned from multi-site churches. As MCs grow and multiply, thereby often (although not necessarily) forming new celebrations as those MCs re-gather to celebrate all that the Lord is doing in their mission contexts, a framework is needed to build unity in the midst of the diversity. It could well be that a hybrid model emerges, that draws from the experience of multi-site churches (even if they don't use Missional Communities) to enhance what God is doing with Missional Communities.

CASE STUDY: LifeChurch.tv

One of the most notable adopters of the multi-site approach has been Life Church, known as LifeChurch.tv[90], which, in 2009, was the United States' second largest church[91]. Initially based in Edmond, Oklahoma, Life Church has used the multi-site approach to plant campuses not only across metro OKC (which in geographic area is second only to metro Los Angeles), but also across the state of Oklahoma and into four other states. They currently gather people to thirteen sites, including an online campus.[92]

Clearly, there is much to learn. Kevin Penry is one of the five-person senior leadership team. In discussing this book with Kevin, he was immensely humble, gracious and encouraging towards leaders who are seeking to build Missional Communities from the ground up as a way of reaching the lost. Listening to him, a deep passion shone out to bring people to Christ as their Savior and Lord, through as many avenues as God opens up.

Five particular areas of conversation stood out as we reflected on how churches building with Missional Communities could interact with and learn from the experiences of multi-site churches.

1. The balance between centralizing and decentralizing is a difficult one for every size of church. The danger of being overly flexible is that we can morph too far to fit the culture, so that we end up not reaching our desired destination (the wider society being transformed by Christ). Alternatively, we can become overly controlling with those whom we lead, which eventually creates a void of creativity and inspiration. People in such cultures will stop thinking and just follow procedures (think back to when you last encountered a bored, rule-bound bureaucrat).

What is apparent is that the balancing point between centralizing and decentralizing for an organization is not a static one. Different phases of the journey require a particular place of equilibrium. Often the earlier stages will require a more controlled feel, as the vision is cast, and the first generation starts to implement it. This will be especially true when what you are doing has not been seen before, and there is no existing model to which people can aspire. Kevin recalled when Life Church first started, the role of a Campus Pastor—there was no real template for that.

Because of that, at the outset they had to be very

strict on defining the role. As the years have gone by, they have been able to loosen up the boundaries of the role to allow creativity; but they can do so knowing that they are not resorting to a lowest common denominator approach where anything goes.

2. It is important neither to impose our culture upon those we are trying to reach, nor to release people to go and pioneer who are clearly not ready. People may have the best of intentions, but they can end up hurting others and even causing more damage than good. A good example of this is when we dash in from the suburbs to 'do something for the poor', but end up devaluing the individuals concerned as we thrust things at them that we think they need without taking the time to build a relationship first and listen to their story and context.

   One way to counteract this is to be intentional in recording and thus drawing from our experiences as a church. This will create a community knowledge base, as we learn together from our leaders and practitioners in the field. This can then be used to balance out and train even the most extreme entrepreneurial leaders, who can have a tendency to impose their plans without stopping to observe, reflect and learn first (we say that as natural entrepreneurs ourselves).

3. At LifeChurch, as multiple sites developed (Kevin said that the third location was the tipping point), they very deliberately changed the staff structure. Their aim was to make all locations feel equal, rather than having satellites held in orbit by the sheer mass of the big body around which they were circling. So, rather than having one mother church that sucks in most of the resources, they enable future campuses to exceed it (in size, influence, etc.). This was achieved by an organizational structure that brought parity to all locations and shared resources fairly across the sites. Around 50% of the staff are on the central resource team, with the rest allocated to campus-specific roles (such as Campus Pastor).

   The application for Missional Community churches from Life Church's experience comes at two levels.

   First, at the Missional Community scale, we see all MCs as equal, supporting them fairly from the central resources of the whole church. This means that we use a matrix very similar to that of LifeChurch. Imagine a grid, or trellis, of intersecting vertical and horizontal lines. The vertical lines represent the different MCs (campuses in the case of Life Church), and the horizontal lines are the ministries of the whole church that exist to serve the MCs. The horizontal lines (ministries, etc.) are there to serve the vertical lines (MCs), but no vertical line is more important than any other.

   Second, as multiple celebrations develop (i.e., multiple centralized worship locations), the test will be whether we choose to resource them well and see them as equal in importance to the original celebrations (or mother church). If we truly want to see this as a church-planting movement, this latter decision will be a critical one for churches to talk through and put into action. If we fail to do this, the emerging celebrations could wither on the vine as people suffocate in the air of feeling like under-resourced second-class citizens.

4. How to grow from sixty to two hundred (i.e., the transition from social space to public space) is an interesting journey. When LifeChurch has planted new sites outside of Oklahoma City, they have

tended to do a soft launch once they have around sixty people. However, they have found that until the group is around two hundred in size, people don't properly experience LifeChurch as it is intended to be; for instance, a large band and sound system needs a certain size congregation to not feel completely overwhelming.

That would be inappropriate for the size of the group, violating one of our 'Four spaces' rules.

In growing from around sixty to two hundred people, Kevin noted two key attributes in the leaders who made that transition successfully.

First, they have strong relational skills. People want to know that the leader cares for them: he/she learns their names, is there for them, builds relationships with them and invests in their lives.

Second, the most effective leaders cast vision for what they are doing and express it with great enthusiasm and energy. They model expectancy that God is going to move and bring lost people into his Kingdom through the efforts of their group.

Obviously, these insights will apply to leaders whose MCs are multiplying like rabbits and grouping together into new celebration locations. n addition, there is application for leaders whose MCs are new and in the teens in size and thus need to properly shift from private to social space. Taking a community through any such change requires both relational and visionary skills, albeit to a greater degree when it is from social to public space. It is relatively unusual to find someone who is highly competent in both areas, hence the need to encourage those we lead to be growing in each one.

5. One of the characteristics of most mega-churches is that they are not afraid to measure and review results. To some readers, we suspect that this may feel hollow or make you a bit cynical.

   However, think about it this way: You measure what you value. It's not whether we should measure, it's whether we are measuring the right things.

   So, if we value making disciples, we need to be able to measure how we are doing at making disciples.

   If being missional, both individually and communally, is something we value, we need a metric for measuring our effectiveness.

   If teaching people to pray in such a way that things actually happen is important to your community, how do you know if you are succeeding at teaching people to do this?

   We need to be able to determine what is working and what is not working well. It is up to you not only to choose your metrics wisely, but to honestly observe them and review candidly when you are not measuring up to them.

Finishing Well - When a Missional Community Comes to an End

Like everything else in creation, MCs have a natural lifespan to them. In fact, in most cases, a community that remains static and unchanging over a number of years is in all likelihood not doing the mission about which it claims to be.

As a Missional Community develops, it will see people join, commit more deeply and, over time, some of those will emerge into leadership in their own right. This will result in new groups being birthed out of the MC, even to the extent that on occasion, so many new groups are born that the original group effectively comes to an end. Other times, the leaders of the group themselves receive a completely fresh assignment from God—perhaps to form a different MC, or to serve him in some other way—and no one else in the group wants to step into leadership. Sometimes the leaders are forced to step back, such as when a new job in a different city forces a move, or when a life change happens, and a season of resting from active leadership is where God is leading. Whatever the causes and circumstances, it is important for the group to finish well.

Practical Tips on Finishing a Group Well

- The members need open, clear and timely communication. If a leader is planning to end, a two to three month warning is appropriate, so that people have time to adjust and think about where they might go next.
- If there is a possibility of others having the opportunity to step into leadership, then there needs to be a clear process set out, including time for due consideration to take place.
- The group should be encouraged to go out with a bang; maybe a concluding missional activity and certainly a party for the group members to thank God and celebrate all that has happened in their midst. This is important because a group coming to an end should not be characterized as a failure.
- At your celebration-size gathering, you might want to find away to acknowledge what this MC has done. This will honor the leaders and value the group members, as well as being a powerful witness to the wider church body about how you process change and transition.
- Find a way to tangibly thank leaders of groups. A note and a small gift of thanks (such as you might do for Christmas appreciation) will go down really well. You want ex-leaders in your church to be talking about how well you helped them transition out and saying that they left leadership feeling valued and loved.
- Group members need to be helped with practical suggestions for where they might wish to go next. Some will scatter in different directions, others will want to stay together as knots, or larger groups, of friends. This may need processing with the leader of the new MC that they are joining, so that transition can go as smoothly as possible. Often this can be facilitated by central staff/leaders who oversee MCs.
- Leaders of MCs should be given some sort of exit interview, whether face-to-face or in writing. This is an invaluable opportunity to learn what is going well, and not so well, in terms of leader support. Often times no particular issues (or issues with which you could reasonably be expected to deal!) come to light, but sometimes they do. This is a

chance for your church to grow in how you train and support leaders. Questions to ask include how they have found support, training, Huddles, resourcing and the task of leadership. This can be a little uncomfortable, but if you can process the responses fairly (yes, sometimes leaders step down in a bad way, and that will be reflected in their answers), you can glean valuable ideas and information from people who have nothing to hide from you.

- If you have had to compel a leader to step down from leadership, this process will be far more complex. Such situations require delicate handling and need to be given high priority by church staff/key leaders. The above points are all valid, but people will need greater support and wise guidance in setting up the strategy for ending the group, including creating room to grieve if necessary. We can't give you a specific strategy as each situation will be unique, but we would encourage you to work extra hard on clear communication, moving promptly to draw out any pain and hurt before the enemy can turn it septic (which can happen surprisingly quickly).
- In the case of multiplying, and it may often be helpful for ending, have the group pray for the leaders and send them out to their next endeavor. This helps all concerned to find a sense of completion on what went before, as well as release for what will come.

MY NOTES

MY NOTES

CASE STUDIES
TALES OF VICTORY

War stories and reflections from people who have pioneered MCs in the United States.

CASE STUDY 1: NORMAN COMMUNITY CHURCH

The Four-Year MC Plan at Norman Community Church[93], Norman, Oklahoma, by Senior Pastor Ken Primrose

(Missional Communities are known as house churches, and small groups are called D-groups. To keep the local flavor, we've left those terms in place.)

Our Main Steps during the First Four Years

It took four years to fully launch and establish Norman Community Church (NCC). For each year, we can look back and see the major developments for each of the three sizes of gathering (house church, celebration, and D-group). I have also included my major goals for each of those phases.

Year 1

House Churches

- Began casting the vision for a network of mid-sized Missional Communities.
- Concentrated on developing a vision and understanding of 'doing church' for this mid-sized group. Gained courage that it really is an acceptable form of church.
- Aware of the frustration some people felt at losing their 'consumer' relationship with church.
- Started with three house churches, organized by stage of life rather than vision; it was necessary, but we were already telling our community that these would eventually give way to a missional driver.

Celebrations

- Started with three celebrations a month and one house church Sunday morning per month.

D-Groups

- People met in groups of ten to fifteen, with the primary function of fellowship.

My goals as a leader during the first six months included the following:

- Having at least one mid-sized community off the ground during this time. Since this expression of church was new to me, I knew I would need to lead it. I needed this experience to coach my other leaders down the road.
- Starting a house church with a couple or a leader as an apprentice, who would lead the next house church when we multiplied. I talked about multiplication from the outset, to set expectations.
- Taking 1 Corinthians 14:26 as a workable model for the foundational expression of church life. I began to talk about this model with others and to model this type of meeting in house church.
- Writing down my reasons for why we were doing

church like this. I needed clarity about this, and creating a several paragraph vision statement was helpful. I gave it to our leaders and allowed them to chew on it and give me feedback. I worked on articulating my vision in a thirty-second statement to give before every house church meeting.

- Teaching about the biblical value of the New Testament model for church life (i.e., mid-sized Missional Communities) in our worship services and had others on our teaching team do so as well. I wanted to lay a biblical framework for what we were doing. People didn't have to understand all of it, but they needed to know that I did and that my thinking was coming from the Bible and not some church growth book or a cool conference!
- If this was Paul's model for the primary expression of church life, I asked our leaders, "What are the implications for us?" I made this an ongoing conversation with our emerging leaders. We created an atmosphere of adventurous learning about house churches.
- Beginning to steward the paradigm shift from a receiving mode of church life to a 'giving' mode. I asked myself, "What values and practices must be challenged and changed to reflect this new paradigm in our community?" I began to put those values into practice.

My goals as a leader during the second six months included the following:

- Growing an awareness of how I (and my group) could develop and function within a mid-sized community. I tried to take notes about what I was learning and talk about it with my emerging leaders. I felt as if I still needed to be leading a house church because soon I knew I would be overseeing other house church leaders, and I needed this hands-on experience to help problem-solve with them later. By the sixth-month mark, I began to diligently pray for an apprentice who would be the next leader of the house church when we multiplied (I handed off leadership of this first house church after three years, but I multiplied all of our existing house churches out of it). I began to include my apprentice in more visible leadership. After an initial season of consolidating the leaders' leadership within a new house church, I encouraged our house church leaders to attempt to lead from behind the scenes as much as possible. I told them (and still do), "If you, as the leader, are doing anything other than a minimal amount of facilitating the transitions of the meeting, you need to stop." That means they shouldn't lead worship, do all the teaching, or host the house church at their house, or bring the food, or do the announcements, or schedule any administrative stuff, etc. My willingness to delegate becomes the first step toward becoming a church that comes to give, as opposed to one that merely comes to receive.
- Encouraging the idea of house church to become normal in our community. The terminology of 'house church' began to pop up in the vocabulary of the whole community. House church still may have felt unusual and difficult to articulate, but house churches should be able to point to a certain life-giving experience that permeates the community.
- Teaching and using the Triangle as a tool to help give our whole community a simple yet comprehensive picture of a balanced Christian life. By the end of this year, our community understood the Triangle and the vocabulary that developed around it (UP, IN and OUT).

- Encouraging our emerging leaders to share in communicating the vision whenever possible. I needed to find ways to gather our leaders regularly for equipping and encouraging. At this stage of church life, our leaders' gatherings were heavy on the vision side and practical equipping.

Year 2

House Churches

- Began casting the vision for mid-sized communities to function as Missional Communities. Started to put practical steps in place, including inviting specific people to start praying and thinking about leading this kind of Missional Community.
- Soaked the ground with the vision for Missional Communities for about a year.

Celebrations

- Dropped a celebration over the summer, thus meeting twice a month in house churches on Sunday mornings and twice a month in celebration.

D-Groups

- No change—the small group size was ten to fifteen people, meeting for fellowship.
- Changed the name to discipleship groups and began casting a vision for a more focused expression of discipleship values and activities.

My goals as a leader during the second year included the following:

- Helping others catch the vision properly, by experiencing it. By the second year, I had a clear picture of what house churches were and how they would function in our context. I articulated that pretty well. I found, however, that until someone was in a house church for a while the vision alone only (at best) intrigued people. No one got it just by having me explain it to them (and I thought I was pretty compelling!).

  Some were still waiting for us to quit this crazy experiment called house churches. People still frequently complained, "I don't like this having to bring something out of my life to house church stuff" or "Let's just get back to the way we have always done it." In some quarters, the complaints actually intensified during the second year.
- Aligning our structure to our stated value of house churches. If house churches were going to be our primary expression of church life, then our structures needed to reflect that. So we very deliberately began to meet in house churches more often than in celebration. This stretched those who'd been in churches for many years, since this was a completely different model. However, by God's good grace, none of those people left, and, in fact, many became D-group leaders and energetic advocates of our model of church and way of life together.
- Articulating that house churches would be our primary expression of church life. I was careful not to denigrate the celebration or make our small groups irrelevant, but I strongly felt that house churches had to be seen by our community as the focal context for church life.

Year 3

House Churches

- People began talking about missional house churches with enthusiasm, and new house church ideas begin to emerge (not all were viable).

- Launched the first house church with a clear missional focus (to Greek students at University of Oklahoma).

Celebrations

- Dropped another celebration over the summer and thus had three open Sundays per month (most, but not all, house churches still met on Sundays) and one celebration per month.
- Began to wonder what celebrations were for—did we even need them? Up to this point, we had done them as an anchor point, so that we would have a normal piece of church life while we tinkered with everything else, but that no longer felt a good enough reason for continuing celebrations. Our conclusion, however, was that instead of dropping celebrations we needed to create a clearly defined vision for them, which we did.

D-Groups

- We created clear steps to guide the whole community through the transition from small groups to discipleship groups. The core aim was to support house churches and strengthen our focus on being and making disciples.
- These D-groups became gender-specific groups of about three to five people, who met weekly or bi-weekly to help facilitate the process of listening and responding to Jesus in their lives.

My goals as a leader during the third year included the following:

- Turning over house church leadership to others and moving to a more dedicated coaching role for the six house churches we had.
- Spending more time with my house church leaders and less time with any random issue or person who came up. I began to expect pastoral issues to reach me only after they had been addressed at the D-group and house church level first. I began asking people who wanted to meet with me whether they had shared this with their cell group and house church leader first, asking them to do that before we met. Most of the time, we never needed to meet. This was an important stage for people to move from seeing me as their functional pastor to their house church leaders being their functional pastors.
- Moving to the original vision of only one celebration and three house churches per month. This left no doubt about what we were going to consider our primary expression of church life. We were really putting all our eggs in the house church basket. A crucial point for many people was when they experienced two celebrations a month alongside two house churches. That so shattered the traditional pattern of church that moving to one celebration a month felt expected and normal.

Year 4

House Churches

- One house church ended over the summer, and two new ones, defined by mission, began. This gave us five in total, all of which now had a clear missional focus.

  Mercy House Church: We are building a community that brings the heart of Jesus to the poor and needy of Norman.

  Neighborhood House Church: We exist to equip spiritual mothers and fathers for mission.

  Greek House Church: We exist to reach those who

do not know Jesus in the Greek System, equip those who do, and send out disciples.

International House Church: We are building a community with international students, glorifying God by loving the lost into the fold of Christ and discipling them to do the same.

Campus House Church: We invite college students into deeper friendship with God through community and equip them in hearing and responding to the voice of Jesus.

Celebrations

- Began redesigning celebration to fit our slightly different goal for this large group time. Our focus included building community-wide vision, teaching, growing an awareness of being a part of something bigger, giving a sense about what is happening with other house churches, and enabling corporate prayer.

D-Groups

- Discipleship groups were a big hit. The synergy of D-groups and house churches formed a very powerful expectation of growth, and nearly everyone involved could point to specific areas of growth in their lives over the year.

Some more general reflections

- *Being the leader means modeling change first*
  We all know we can't expect anyone to do anything we are not willing to do ourselves. This definitely applies to living the life of a disciple of Jesus. If you're the leader, then you go first. You show that you are walking the talk and living the life. That, if you think about it, may be the very definition of leadership.

- *The wet cement principle*

I found a common pattern happening with our leaders, which was the tendency to wait a while before introducing any difficult or uncomfortable ideas or practices into the groups. Things like evangelism, multiplication, and accountability were put off, while the leader attempted to develop a sense of community first. Almost without fail, however, once the group's expectations were set and certain grooves began to develop for what was normal, the leader was unable to implement the ideas he or she had avoided initially.

I began talking to our leaders about the wet cement principle. When a group first starts, the expectations are like wet cement. You can put in just about whatever you want during the starting phase of a group, but expectations quickly dry and harden. Once the wet cement of the group's expectations solidifies, the only way to change them is with a jackhammer! This jolting and rattling process will bust up the foundations of the group. Often a group can't survive a jackhammer approach.

- *Make evangelism a do-or-die issue*
  The temptation is to settle for just giving the already converted a new spot to hang out. I read about a church in Ohio where the percentage of their congregation who were either non-Christians or new believers was around 80% (of 5,000 members)! I was blown away. I took two of our core leaders, and we went for a visit. One of the staff we met with told us how they had noticed a drop in the numbers (they kept statistical data on everything) for non-Christians being invited to their home groups, and thus new professions of faith and baptisms had dropped. Their senior leadership team began to confess this dropping energy for evangelism as sin

and cancelled classes at their training center for a season to make evangelism a foundational obedience issue again. The pastor stood in front of the whole church, told the church how terrible this was and personally repented for his participation in the lack of commitment to the unsaved. The church responded, and scores of people began coming to Christ again. The lesson our leaders and I took away was that evangelism is a do-or-die issue. It really isn't that much of a stretch to ask ourselves, "If people are not coming to Jesus in our community, what are we really doing?"

- *Try to use just one funnel*
  I look at the structure of church as a funnel that we then pour the life of the community through. The structure acts just as a funnel in that it steers the direction of the life within the community. So when we use the three-tiered structure for church life, celebration is the big meeting where the whole tribe comes together. House churches are the mid-sized group where we build a community that goes in mission, while D-groups are the cell level of church life that focus very purposefully on discipleship. To allow healthy growth, we need to create room for a wide variety of God-given dreams to grow to full maturity, while being very clear that we have one main route, or funnel, that we express this through. Thus, when one of our energetic young people who attended our celebration wanted to do a "house church that wasn't really a house church," by just having people over to his house and "hanging out a lot and worshipping if we feel like," I asked him to bring that back and pour it back through our simple structure for community life that we already had in place.

  The other way this impacts leadership decisions is my attempt to keep good but potentially distracting programs from cropping up all over the place. If there is a cry for more teaching, for instance, I try to reduce that to its most basic issue and pour that through the present structure, without starting a series of evening classes or weekend seminars. So far, the only additional classes I have felt we really needed were for equipping our leaders through our retreats and new house church leaders training classes.

Today

Norman Community Church has more than 450 people involved in the community and twelve Missional Communities/house churches.

CASE STUDY 2: EIKON COMMUNITY CHURCH

Planting a Church Using MCs at Eikon Community Church, Richmond, Virginia

Planted in Richmond, Virginia, in 2008, Eikon[94] describes itself in the following way:

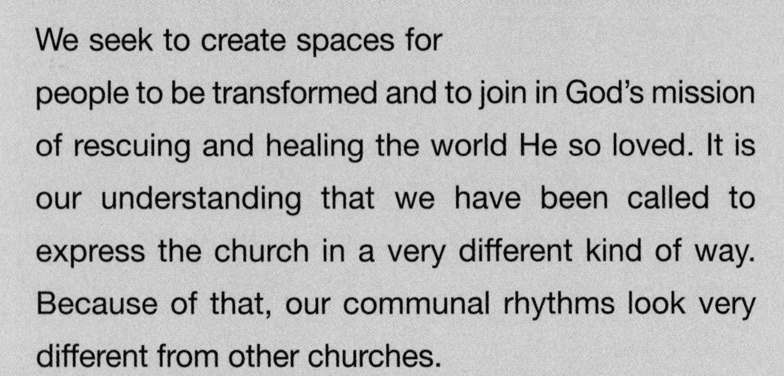

We seek to create spaces for people to be transformed and to join in God's mission of rescuing and healing the world He so loved. It is our understanding that we have been called to express the church in a very different kind of way. Because of that, our communal rhythms look very different from other churches.

We have one worship service a month: We always meet on the second Sunday of the month at 5:30 p.m.

The other weekends of the month, we have groups of people (anywhere from twenty to fifty) meeting in Missional Communities at various points during the weekend, depending on the group. These groups have different flavors, appeal to different kinds of people, and are 'being the church' in very different ways.

Doug Paul, the Directional Pastor for Eikon, explained that, for the first eleven months of the church's existence, members met in Missional Communities once a month, with weekly small group meetings and a service every Sunday. The members realized that this led to Missional Community being always seen as something optional and on the periphery, whereas they had wanted it to be the place of identity and belonging. However, after interacting with Mike Breen and seeing how MCs could actually work in practice, the church members were able to transition the church to a greater focus on them.

The resulting pattern of gathering was a once-a-month service, MCs on the other three (or four) weeks, and Huddles every two weeks. The church members have decided not to have small groups but rather use the Huddle model as a structure for rapid and intentional development of missional leaders.

Doug pointed out that this transition was not without its cost: around 40% of their original group left, mainly because they said that they missed his teaching each week. As much as they were missed, within three months the church had gained more new people than the church had lost, and the new pattern was embedded well.

More broadly, Doug's top advice to planters was to start a Huddle as soon as possible. He said that the critical thing is to disciple people and, in particular, train them to hear the voice of God for themselves. As they start to do so, they can then dream and discern what God is calling them to do mission-wise, and thus new Missional Communities will be birthed. He has concluded that strong Huddles will produce multiplying MCs within six to twelve months.

Doug's other pointer for planters is that planting and leading a church to the tipping point (of being a healthy, growing, multiplying, self-funding, group of life-giving communities who impact their wider context) take time. Momentum will build, traction will come, but generally it doesn't appear as one giant surge. Rather, planting is a gradual thing that takes a few years to come about.

The temptation to go the full-on attractional route will probably be constantly on the backburner. The idea of short-cutting the process never really goes away. The only way to survive and see the process unfold has to be an unflinching belief that the tipping point of exponential growth while keeping deep, substantive disciples is worth the extra time. From our experience, it definitely is.

We would definitely concur with this point about allowing time for a Missional Community–based plant to become properly rooted and established. It takes time to build an authentic witness into a neighborhood or network, since everything stands or falls on relationships—which don't come overnight! David Putnam and Shawn Lovejoy commented on this in a recent article: "If you haven't planted a church, you can count on three things: it's going to take longer, require more money and be harder than you imagined! As church planters, we are often guilty of getting 'drunk on vision.' We're so 'intoxicated' with the desire to plant that it clouds our good judgment. When we're intoxicated, we fail to listen to others, think clearly, and make wise decisions. Jesus tells us to count the cost. It always pays to listen to him."[95]

As the church's Missional Communities have multiplied and leadership has become more decentralized, Eikon has added a second worship gathering each month so that people get the support they need when hitting the missional frontier and are on the frontlines. Doug added, "More than likely, we will end up with services every week a few years down the road, though the expectation will never be that people attend every week. We strongly value the worship gathering but want to make sure we are gathering for the right reasons. Are we gathering because that's what we are supposed to do and hoping we can avoid mission by having a service? Or are we gathering because we have been missional, have something to celebrate before our God, want to be part of the bigger story he is weaving together and come to his Throne to worship together?"

The following is a mapped-out version of Eikon's first two years:

Months 0–6

Public worship service: Weekly

Missional Communities: Once a month for a total of two MCs

Small Groups: Four SGs that met weekly

***Thoughts on the first six months:** Our first six months, we really had no idea what we were doing. We experimented quite a bit with different missional expressions and different communal rhythms, but nothing really worked. We tried a hybrid between an attractional and missional model, and it pretty much fell on its face. We continued to meet weekly in our small groups and worship service because we didn't know what else to do, and at least this had a measure of stability to it. Our service grew quickly, reaching close to one hundred people in only a few months, but it wasn't really reaching people who didn't know Jesus. By all church planting metrics, we were doing quite well, but in our guts we knew it wasn't what God was calling us to. We weren't being terribly missional, and as much as we put a heavy emphasis on discipleship, there was very little spiritual movement. We just couldn't figure out the way forward.

Months 7–12

Public worship service: Weekly

Missional Communities: Zero (at least in how we would currently describe a MC)

Huddles/Small Groups: One Huddle that met every other week and four SGs that met weekly

***Thoughts on months 7–12:** During this time, we met Mike Breen and joined a 3DM Learning Community. For us, this was the big game-changer. Being in a community with other churches, both transitioning churches and church plants, all going for the same goals—it was unbelievable. I honestly don't think we could have done it apart from the Learning Community, even if I had this book three years ago, before it all began. In this period of time and since then, Huddles proved to be the Silver Bullet. We were seeing transformation in people's lives that we had never seen before. People grew more in that six-month period than they had the entirety of their Christian lives. Amazing. It also gave us the glimmer of light we needed to make some significant changes in the months to come. We decided to put all of our eggs in the discipleship basket, and that decision paid off.

Months 13–18

Public worship service: Once a month

Missional Communities: Each MC officially met three times a month for a total of two MCs

Huddles/Small Groups: Two Huddles that met every other week and zero SGs

***Thoughts on months 13–18:** This was probably the most difficult time in our church plant but, oddly, also one of the most invigorating. We were seeing spiritual breakthrough the likes none of us had ever seen because of our Huddles (by this time, we had successfully killed all of our small groups). The robust numbers we had seen early on had dwindled as people started to see we were serious about being a missional, discipleship-driven community. I suppose you could say we lost our trendy sex appeal. We lost a little more than 40% of our original core group when we went from having a weekly worship gathering to having one once a month. We have talked and reflected on this decision quite a bit in the aftermath, and in the end, we believe we made the right decision. As we have evaluated it, looking at the people who left, while it was personally heartbreaking for me, I'm pretty confident they were people who would have left further down the road if we had gone with a longer, more drawn-out transition. The exciting thing, though, was the continued growth as we discipled people, saw new people coming into the community, and the statistic that of the people we lost, only one person left who was in a Huddle. Huddles were proving to be quite sticky.

Months 19–24

Public worship service: Once a month (getting ready to add a second, though)

Missional Communities: Each MC officially meets three to four times a month for a total of five MCs

Huddles: One Leader Huddle and four Discipleship Huddles

***Thoughts on months 19–24:** Our first wave of multiplication swept our community. We multiplied all of our Huddles, finally allowing me to Huddle all of our leaders in one group, while my leaders Huddled our second generation of Huddles (a collection of future leaders that we call Discipleship Huddles). One of our Missional Communities, a homeless MC, didn't make it, which is the nature of this kind of thing, but the members regrouped and came out swinging with a new group. This one was focused on artists. Our other MC multiplied four times over, giving us a total of five Missional Communities (hello exponential growth). With this many people on the missional frontier, we are about to add a second worship gathering, that features music, many stories of how God is moving, communion, strong teaching, and lots of laughter. One of the things we are most excited about is a retreat weekend for our MC leaders that will happen every six months, which will be a leisurely weekend of reflection, fun, prayer, teaching, and planning. We sense this will propel our community to the next level.

CASE STUDY 3: THRESHOLD CHURCH

Planting MCs at Threshold Church, Toledo, Ohio

Planted in April 2009 by ELCA pastor Tom Schaeffer, Threshold Church is built around Missional Communities (which it terms Call-Out Ministries) and celebrates on Sunday mornings in a bar. The church's local newspaper profiled them in a lengthy article,[96] from which the following extract is taken. (In itself, the article provides an interesting insight into how the wider culture views MCs; for instance, note the number of terms in the section quoted below that are put inside quotation marks!).

One of the key components of Threshold is its 'call-out' ministries. These groups of twenty to forty people are led by lay members and serve a missional function, providing a service or mission to the community.

Josh Humberger, 38, of Oregon, is the head of Threshold's "Pay It Forward Call-Out." He said group members had set a goal of feeding 5,000 people in its first year—a number inspired by the biblical accounts of Jesus' miraculous feedings.

The call-out members began by giving meals (and blankets) to homeless people on downtown streets, passing out free hotdogs during tailgate parties, and feeding the University of Toledo football team after a practice.

They set up a grill on Bancroft Street and waved a 'free hotdogs' sign for passing motorists and pedestrians. One minister pulled in, asked what was going on, and offered to make a donation, but Mr. Humberger said the call-out members would not accept any money.

Toledo police also stopped by; he said to make sure there wasn't any funny business going on.

The call-out group met its goal of feeding 5,000 in only five months, so the new target is "to feed as many people in the Toledo area as we can," Mr. Humberger said.

The call-out group also holds '11-7' meetings—gathering at local pizza places on the eleventh day of the month at 7 p.m. The group members pray, often partake in Communion, and perform a random act of kindness at every 11-7 meeting by picking up the bill for an individual, group, or family at a nearby table—no sermons or strings attached. "Their first reaction is usually shock," Mr. Humberger said. "Everyone's on guard these days, and they think there's a catch."

Aside from telling the beneficiary that the tab was picked up by members of Threshold Church, the only catch is "spreading God's love in a heartfelt way," Mr. Humberger said.

Threshold's other call-out ministry, called 'Artfelt' (like heartfelt, Mr. Schaeffer explained), is on a mission to minister to Toledo's arts community.

Mr. Schaeffer said church members create the call-outs' mission and lead the groups, adding that his goal as pastor is low control, high accountability. He meets with nine church lay leaders for a weekly Huddle in which participants talk openly and honestly about their relationships from an UP, IN, and OUT perspective. UP is their relationship with Jesus Christ, IN is with the church, and OUT is with the world. If the church leaders have healthy UP, IN, and OUT relationships, Mr. Schaeffer said, then he does not have to micro-manage their ministries.

CASE STUDY 4: ST. PHILIP'S CHURCH

Transitioning an Existing Church into MCs - Interview with the Pastor of St. Philip's, Pittsburgh

In the previous case studies, we looked at pioneering situations, where someone is either starting a new church plant or a significant new area of ministry. We learned from some church planters and reflected a little on some of the unique aspects of the journey that occur in such a context. Now we want to spend a few pages reflecting on the process of transition for a team leading an existing church that wants to start using Missional Communities. However, even if you are in a pioneering context, the content here will still be useful to you, since Christians who join your emerging community will more than likely come with some of the baggage that this chapter starts to address.

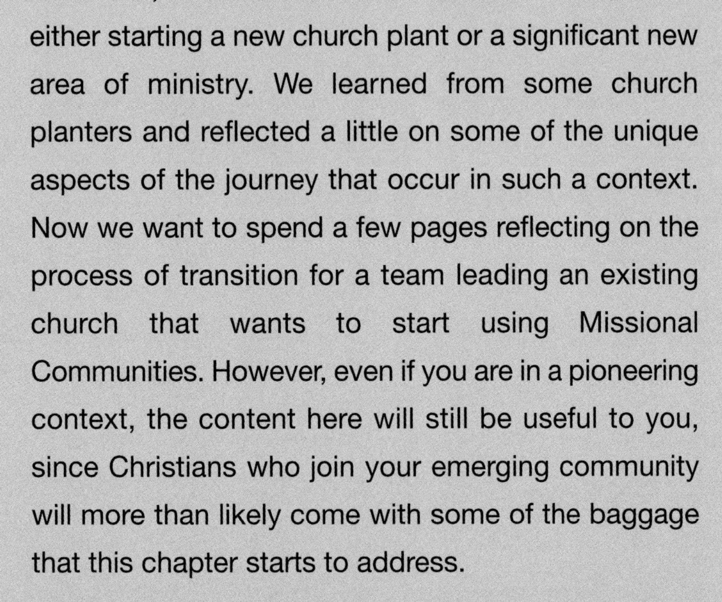

We turned to our friend Eric Taylor, who leads St. Philip's Church, Moon Township, a suburb of Pittsburgh, in Pennsylvania.[97] Eric has led the church for more than fifteen years and has been gradually implementing a more mission-oriented approach, including MCs and Huddles, for almost five years. This has given him a wealth of wisdom about the journey of transition and how to avoid many of the pitfalls that lie on that pathway.

Here are some of our better questions and Eric's responses to them.

- ***Why should existing churches make all the effort to implement Missional Communities and the mindset they represent?***

Eric: I've thought a great deal about this, and I'm increasingly convinced that, as pastors of churches, we are producing what I call 'two-thirds' disciples. This is taken from the Triangle (UP, IN, OUT) that models the three directions of relationships we are called to develop and sustain. Most churches train people in UP and some IN, but don't train them to do OUT at the local level. Generally, church leaders have never modeled this, and this creates a major problem. They are creating disciples who don't know how to do OUT, or perhaps if they think about it, then they can bring a friend to a guest event or a program. If those we disciple in this way become the next generation of leaders, then two-thirds disciples become two-thirds leaders who create two-thirds communities. Seminaries generally only reinforce this, by teaching people how to run celebrations and offer personal pastoral care, with almost no practical equipping in how to lead a church OUT.

Practically, people generally like to experience something before they are asked to lead out in it. Missional Communities create a context to address the two-thirds disciple, although the process does not happen overnight. We are taking someone who doesn't know much about doing OUT in the wider world and rebooting the whole model of what is means to be a disciple. However, MCs are the perfect size to do that and help people experience a different way of being a disciple and thus a leader.

- ***Talk us through some of the stages of transitioning a church.***

1. People need to see, feel, and experience this missional way of operating, of what a truly discipling culture looks like.
2. To help the senior leaders set this new template, I strongly recommend that they are part of a *Learning Community* with 3DM, as this will equip them practically as they walk this out.
3. Huddles are vital, and leaders need to start doing this as early as possible with their key people.
4. Don't be too cautious. Sometimes you simply have to start throwing things at the walls to see what sticks in your context!
5. Realize that first-generation Missional Communities create a context for people to 'see it,' even if the MCs won't be effective missionally until the second generation. However, that journey is important, as the first-generation MCs give people a chance to live this out and make some of their best mistakes, and generally you all gain some shared experience. As long as you reflect upon what has gone on, you will be surprisingly well equipped to birth Missional Communities that genuinely can grow and multiply as the lost are reached.

- ***Why was learning to listen to the Holy Spirit so important in the process?***

Part of the shift of culture is from expecting the senior pastor to be the one who hears everything from God to everyone expecting to be listening to the voice of God and hearing his guidance, including for mission. This doesn't mean everyone has to become a full-on charismatic, but they do need to become comfortable with listening to God and being aware of his direction, in the community and the missional aspects of church life.

- ***How can leaders win their church board to back this transition?***

The board (or whatever structure you have) will need time and energy investing in them so that they have this major change in culture clearly communicated to them. This includes them being able to count the cost in advance—in terms of numbers in the pews, giving, how Sunday services will transition, etc. Part of the role of a board is to ask, "Show me the bottom line," and so board members deserve open and honest preparation for the journey. Moving from a primarily attractional to a primarily discipling approach means that you will lose people, because you are raising the bar on discipleship and inevitably that is threatening, especially to those with much invested in the inherited mode of doing church. The best way to keep the support of your board is to help board members understand that this will be a costly change in the short and medium run, so that they go in with their eyes wide open.

- ***How long do you think this journey takes?***

Obviously that depends on your context, but to me, there are two major transitions here. One is learning to listen to God—if that has not been part of your regular culture, then that will take time to form. The other shift, whereby you start to build Missional Communities, is structurally a very visible change for people. To do one by itself is tricky, so to do both simultaneously is a major task.

Part of the difficulty is that you will think you and the church have got it, but then something will happen, and you will realize that you haven't. For some churches, this will not just be about introducing Missional Communities and Huddles, but it will be about bringing a complete change of culture. This will take time. I am reminded that when a new vine is planted you don't harvest any fruit for at least three years, and if you want to turn that into good wine, then you need several more years.

One of the things that can be a creative help is to allow the strengths of both Pioneers and Developers to come to the fore. What Pioneers do best is to challenge and innovate, but when that is going on, what people most need is encouragement. Developers are excellent at listening, loving, and encouraging, but a culture that is stuck in that place most needs challenge and innovation. So a healthy mix of the two ends of the spectrum is really important in a major transition like this.

MY NOTES

MY NOTES

Appendices

APPENDIX 1 | EXPECTATIONS OF AN MC LEADERSHIP TEAM

One couple aiming to reach an inner-city high school (which we'll call JFK High School) wanted to set out the commitment they expected from their wider leadership team. As they looked at the MC as a whole, they recognized that they basically had two levels of involvement. They described the two types of people in the following way:

Tier 1 involves practical service to JFK HS. Anyone can do it—new believers, non-believers, kids, anybody. All are encouraged to participate, but no time commitment is asked for or expected. We don't really keep track of who is doing what. This keeps everyone involved and lets everybody play, without putting people in situations that are too much or too early, overwhelming, or inappropriate. This also allows everyone to experience all the communal elements of Missional Community.

Tier 2 people are actively building discipling relationships with kids at the school. We call these people our Missional Community Leaders. If you want to do this, you have to commit to a list of things, but you then get extra investment. Personally, we spend most of our time focused on investing in and raising up our leaders (roots and fruits). We do leaders' meetings twice a month. We put together a leaders' commitment and our commitment to them (we basically stole Young Life's leaders' commitment and just changed a few things!). We did it like this because making disciples in a mentoring capacity in a tough high school isn't something that anybody can or should be doing. We wanted to make sure that the people we were putting in relationships with kids really honored the Father and loved kids well.

The Tier 2 people are asked to make the following commitment:

Ministry Theme Verse

We loved you so much that we were delighted to share with you not only the gospel of God but our lives as well, because you had become so dear to us. (1 Thessalonians 2:8)

As a leader in our Missional Community, I commit to these things through the remainder of this school year:

- Spend personal time with Jesus via prayer and Bible study at least five days a week
- Pursue kids at JFK HS this school year with the goal of building at least one meaningful relationship
- Show up in the kids' lives once a week (go to their game, grab food, help lead every-other-Saturday small groups, etc.)
- Text, Facebook, call, etc. throughout the week
- Pray for my kids regularly
- Work with, support, and pray for my JFK ministry teammate
- Aspire to live a life inwardly and outwardly that reflects the character of Christ
- Stay vulnerable, accountable, and consistent in a small group
- Attend Missional Community Friday night gatherings as consistently as possible. Every other Friday @ 7 PM (Missional Community meal and prayer for JFK)

- Attend leaders' Huddles as consistently as possible—every other Friday @ 6 PM (before the MC gathering)
- Married couples: keep the relationship with my spouse of first importance in time, prayer, and affection

Our commitment to you:

As we honestly looked at the best way we could serve the kids at JFK, we realized that it was by serving and investing in you the leaders. For this reason, we have decided not to have a group of dudes at JFK (which absolutely kills us!), and instead focus our time with each of you (we're super stoked about you guys, we just wish we could do both!). You will be receiving training, encouragement, and equipping from us throughout the year. Our desire is that each of you takes steps this year toward being "mature and full grown in the Lord, measuring up to the full stature of Christ" (Ephesians 4:13). We will be doing this twice a month at leaders' Huddles and personally throughout the month as much as we can. If you commit to being a leader in reaching JFK, we commit extra time to you.

MY NOTES

APPENDIX 2 | SUGGESTED PLANS FOR PILOT MC MEETINGS

Our Suggested Pattern of Meetings for Your Pilot

This planner for your Pilot MC is designed to prepare your leaders for a mid-January launch of Missional Communities in the wider church body. We are not saying you have to launch then, but our aim is to give you a specific example to study. Obviously, there are plenty of ways that you could tweak and adjust what is here!

MONTH	WEEK	TYPE OF MEETING	DETAIL
MAIN FOCUS: UP – Vision			
September	1	Gathering 1	Introducing the Group and the Pilot MC
	2	Mission 1	Prayer Walk
	3	Huddle 1	Processing What God Is Saying about the Vision
	4	–	Free Week
MAIN FOCUS: IN – Community			
October	1	Gathering 2	How to Build Your Group
	2	Huddle 2	Processing Group-building Skills
	3	–	Free Week
MAIN FOCUS: OUT – Mission			
October	4	Gathering 3	How to Grow Your Group
November	1	–	Free Week
	2	Mission 2	Saturday Mission Day
	3	Huddle 3	Processing Mission + Person of Peace
	4	–	Free Week
MAIN FOCUS: COMMISSIONING – Public Launch			
December	1	Gathering 4	Party + Holy Spirit Commissioning + Having a Healthy Rhythm
	2	Huddle 4	Planning for the First Six Months
	3 + 4	–	Free Weeks
January	early	Huddle 5	The Realities of Leadership
	mid-Jan	Launch Sunday - Public Release of New MCs	
	soon after...	Huddle 6	The Skills Deficit

Gathering 1 – Introducing the Group and the Pilot MC

Wherever possible, host the Pilot Gathering in the home of the senior pastor. It's important that people are encouraged to be punctual, so start at the agreed time. Two hours is an ideal time for an MC Gathering.

Connecting Activity: Have name badges, fun introductory activities, or questions to ask as people meet and mingle, perhaps with prizes, etc.

(E.g., print out a list of sixteen various achievements or skills and have people solicit signatures of the people in the room who fulfill the criteria.)

Enjoy a Simple Meal Together: As at all extended family gatherings, we suggest that everyone brings a contribution to the meal or refreshments. It is important that catering for the potential MC leaders feels lightweight and low maintenance. We often use paper cups, plates, glasses, and plastic silverware so that cleaning up follows up that key MC axiom of lightweight and low maintenance. The leadership team of the Pilot MC needs to model the cleanup as well at the end of the night.

UP: Move seamlessly into a 1 Corinthians 11-14 style meeting by, for example, reading some of that Scripture and then inviting testimonies or thanksgivings from those present.

As the leader, you need to be directive and start the ball rolling in sharing a testimony or thanksgiving. Share in the way you want others to imitate. Don't set the bar for participation too high by talking for a long time or describing how your shadow healed three people on the way home. If your church policy allows, you can break bread together, sing a song of praise, and pray for anyone who is sick. Just bear in mind that your primary task is to model MC leadership that others can imitate and repeat after Launch Sunday.

IN: On a flip chart, share with the group a quick overview of the Triangle (UP, IN, and OUT). Explain that the terms of this is a new concept. Have the group break into smaller groups of three or four and score themselves out of 10 (1=very weak, 10=very strong, 5 is banned for being on the fence!) for where they are in each of the three directions, before they very briefly share their scores with their small group. Then have the group members repeat the exercise as a group, but this time scoring your church as a whole. When they have agreed on numbers, have the members come and write their scores for the church on a large sheet at the front. Reconvene as one group to discuss which area is felt overall to be your strongest and which is seen as the weakest.

You'll notice that we mention a few shapes (the Triangle, Square etc.) in these teaching times, which are pulled from Building a Discipling Culture by Mike Breen and Steve Cockram, which explains in a simple structured way how to build and establish a discipling culture.

Equipping: Recast the vision for Missional Communities and what you see as their potential in your church context for addressing your areas of weakness and strength. Include space for discussion, but remember that not everything needs to be answered this evening as you have four months. Then set out the plan for the Pilot, explaining the main elements of what the next four months will entail. Have a short Q&A on those practicalities. Cover any specifics necessary to prepare for Mission 1 and Huddle 1.

OUT: Pray for your city and your church's impact upon the city. Wait on the Holy Spirit, asking him to birth in you, both individually and as leaders in God's church, a fresh compassion for the lost, the last, and the least in your city.

Mission 1 – Prayer Walk

Meet at an agreed time and location. Explain that this is the territory where future missional OUTs will take place and emphasize the importance of spiritual preparation.

Prepare a simple guide for prayer walking that people can take with them. Cover the practicalities of prayer walking (e.g., walk in small numbers, don't act weird, be nice to people you meet because they could be People of Peace, etc.) and some specific prayer needs for that context. Divide people into small teams and send them out with a map and a time and place to end, perhaps about an hour later.

At the end, re-gather for feedback, sharing, and encouragement.

Huddle 1 – Processing What God Is Saying about the Vision

Focus: UP—your character as a leader

Processing Tools: The Triangle, the Learning Circle

Kairos: "Leaders define culture, and you can't lead people beyond where the Lord has led you."

Question: As you think about Missional Communities and the vision that has been shared, what is God saying to you?

Use the Triangle to provoke a personal Kairos by asking individuals where they are strongest and weakest as missional leaders. Encourage them to think more in terms of their character rather than skills (e.g., personal spiritual disciplines, motivations, capacity to build relationships, care for those who are lost).

Use the Circle to process the Kairos for a couple of specific individuals in the group. Not everyone has to share, as it is safe to assume that the Kairos will be similar, and modeling the discipling process is important in helping individuals process what the Lord is revealing to them.

Gathering 2 – How to Build Your Group

Connecting Activity: We recommend you use name badges throughout the Pilot MC. Get everyone to think of two Highs and one Low that have happened since the MC last met. They can share these with three separate people before food is served.

Food: Food is a common denominator at each MC Gathering. Make sure the food continues to model the lightweight and low maintenance principle for the host. Again, the cleanup is very important—make sure it's not the same three people doing it every time!

UP: Have some creative worship that does not involve live music. Remember that 70% of the population is sensory, and being able to touch, taste, see, hear, or smell things may connect more readily with people than singing words. You may not be that creative, but there will be people in your community who are!

IN: Model how to share from your daily devotional reading what God is saying to you personally at the moment (i.e., simple, short but very fresh bread). Others should watch and think, "That impacted me, and yet I could do the same thing." Invite sharing and discussion in response to the word you have just shared.

OUT: Break into the same groups that prayer walked together. Pray for the streets, people, and context where the groups walked. If there are specific needs within the group for healing, then have the groups pray for each other.

Equipping: Teach an overview of the Leadership Square[51] and allow time for Q&A. Your aim is to explain how groups grow and develop, from initial vision casting through to multiplication, and that the task of leadership develops along the way.

Huddle 2 – Processing Group-building Skills

Focus: IN—community life

Processing Tools: Leadership Square, Learning Circle

Kairos: MC life is about building a strong community that goes OUT together in mission, inviting those you connect with into that same community. As the leader of the MC, you will have the biggest impact on that community life!

Question: As you look at the different leadership styles Jesus used to take his team around the Leadership Square, where are you personally strongest and weakest? How will you grow in your weak areas?

Use the Circle to process the *Kairos* for a couple of specific individuals in the group. Not everyone has to share (although do pick people who didn't have much focus in the last Huddle!)—you are modeling the discipling process as much as helping individuals process what the Lord is saying to them.

It would be good to spend time on teaching L1/D1 of the Square and coaching leaders on how to invite others to follow vision.

Gathering 3 – How to Grow Your Group

Connecting Activity and Food: See notes above. By now, you should have an idea what works well for your group.

UP: In twos and threes, have people look for Bible verses that illustrate the missional nature of God. What does the Bible say about God's heart for humanity? How is the Father revealed as a God who sends us? How is Jesus revealed as the God who goes? How is the Holy Spirit revealed as the God who anoints and equips us as we go to extend the Kingdom?

After five minutes, pray and invite the whole group to simply call out verses they have found. If you have a musician, have him or her play some music in the background and then lead the group in a song of praise and thanksgiving. If you don't have a musician, just use a CD or iPod.

IN: A short Bible study and training on the idea of Person of Peace (use Luke 9 and 10). Invite people to share stories of how they have seen this principle operate in their own lives.

Equipping: Train your leaders in how to develop a mission vision for their MC. Begin by looking at what it means to start to share God's heart for your city. Encourage them to take time in the days ahead to seek God, for your city/community in general, and for their particular mission focus in this next season. Emphasize what a crucial step it is for them as MC leaders to clearly define their future group's mission vision.

OUT: Have people take some time in twos and threes to name who they think are their People of Peace right now. Talk about what contexts seem to be most favorable to them in terms of open doors for mission. In twos and threes, people should then move into a time of praying for the People of Peace who have been named and for more to be identified. In addition, encourage people to lay hands on one another and pray for the Spirit's filling, as they look to boldly step out in mission and call people to follow into that mission field. Share with one another any Scriptures or prophetic words of encouragement.

Mission 2 – Saturday Mission Day

Whether you make it a whole day or simply a long morning, this is the chance for people to experience mission as a good-sized group who are in relationship with one another. Make sure you begin the day with a time of worship and prayer, as well as a briefing. Likewise, keep time at the end for a time of feedback and thanksgiving. But don't make either session very long—the point is to spend your time out on the streets!

Huddle 3 – Processing Mission and Person of Peace

Focus: OUT—going in mission

Processing Tools: Person of Peace, Triangle

Kairos: The importance of People of Peace in establishing MCs

Question: Go around the Huddle, and ask for a one-minute snapshot, or 'blink,' response to the mission activity. What most struck them (whether encouraging or challenging)?

Go round the group again and have people identify who and where their main People of Peace are located. How might that translate into a mission vision for a MC? Encourage people to be as specific as possible, as they think about what their MC could put its energy into.

Is it a vision others will follow? If it is clear enough, then it will enable you to easily know what opportunities to say yes or no to. Use the Triangle to help people think about maintaining balance in their MC among UP, IN, and OUT.

In all these conversations, encourage other group members to give feedback, speaking challenge and encouragement.

Homework: Encourage your future MC leaders to prayerfully reflect more on what the missional OUT of their MC might be. Locating their People of Peace is often a significant clue as to where the Lord has already gone before them.

Gathering 4 – Party + Holy Spirit Commissioning + Having a Healthy Rhythm

Food: Go the extra mile on this occasion, so that it feels like a real celebration and party. The Pilot is coming to an end, and people are being released into forming Missional Communities—that is well worth celebrating!

UP: Invite a few people to share briefly what God has done in them through the lifespan of the Pilot. Make sure you share what you sense the Father has been up to!

IN/Equipping: Talk about the importance of starting future MCs with a healthy rhythm of meetings and life. This should balance building momentum and life together and help to recognize that we are designed for seasons and that Jesus does not want us to burn out through poor time stewardship.

Give a quick overview of the Semicircle[51] and explain how important it is for them as leaders to model a healthy rhythm of life. There will be temptations to over-work and burn out!

OUT: Have an extended time of laying on of hands and commissioning all those who will be launching the first

MCs. You might have to divide into two groups, with one half praying and prophesying first and then swapping over and themselves receiving prayer.

Huddle 4 – Planning for the First Six Months

Focus: Making your MC sustainable

Processing Tools: Semicircle and Leadership Square

Kairos: It is important to build a community that has impact (on those you gather as well as those you reach) and yet is sustainable over the long run. This means creating a balance over the month and the year. It also entails recognizing the different stages of the Leadership Square and how that impacts rhythm. For instance, in the early days of an MC, you need to have enough activities (events) that can build identity and a sense of momentum, thereby resulting in people committing deeply (process). Your new MC leaders will need help in establishing sustainable rhythms as the leaders adjust to their new responsibilities. There will inevitably be a temptation to strive, and, in their own strength, make things happen.

Question: What will the pattern be for your MC for the first six months? What changes will this mean to your own lifestyle and that of your family/household?

Huddle 5 – The Realities of Leadership

Focus: Inviting people to follow

Processing Tools: Leadership Square, Person of Peace

Kairos: Helping your MC leaders process their internal reactions when people either sign up to follow them or refuse the offer

Question: What sorts of results are you seeing as you talk about and invite people into your MC vision? What's going well, and what are you struggling with? How are you dealing with the different personality types (the bossy ones with a million ideas, the slow adopters who take forever to commit, the overly needy who want you to become co-dependent with them, etc)?

The most important question is: What is Jesus saying to you personally as you put the invitation out there? (Keep taking them back to their foundational identity as a dearly loved child of the King. We will never be able to do anything that will make him love us more!)

Huddle 6 – The Skills Deficit

Focus: What skill needs are most pressing for you?

Processing Tools: The Learning Circle

Kairos: MC leaders realize that they don't have all the skills they need to lead the group

Question: As the group forms and starts to meet and go in mission, you will be only too aware of your own limitations as a leader. What has been the biggest kairos moment for you? What has Jesus been saying to you about that? What are you going to do in response?

MY NOTES

MY NOTES

Footnotes

1. See Mark 8:14-21, when Jesus warns them about the yeast of the Pharisees and they think it's a rebuke for not bringing a picnic with them!
2. For instance, Pisidian Antioch (Acts 13), Iconium (14:1-7), Lystra (14:8-20), Philippi (ch. 16), Thessalonica (17:1-9), and Berea (17:10-15)
3. Reggie McNeal, Missional Renaissance (Jossey-Bass, 2009) , p. 10 (emphasis ours)
4. David J. Bosch, Transforming Mission (Orbis Books, 1991), p. 390
5. "Our mission means our committed participation as God's people, at God's invitation and command, in God's own mission within the history of God's world for the redemption of God's creation." Christopher Wright, The Mission of God (IVP, 2006), p. 23. Much material has been written on the nature of mission, which is not within the scope of this book to rehearse. However, Wright gives a wonderful study into the theology of mission through the Scriptures.
6. Mark Driscoll, Vintage Church (Crossway, 2008), p. 218
7. Ed Stetzer and David Putman, Breaking the Missional Code (B&H Books, 2006), p. 2
8. Eddie Gibbs and Ian Coffey, Church Next (IVP, 2000)
9. Neil Cole, Organic Church (Jossey-Bass, 2005)
10. Stetzer and Putnam, op. cit., p. 48
11. Reggie McNeal, op. cit., p. xvi (he uses these three shifts as the structure of the whole book)
12. Alan Hirsch, The Forgotten Ways (Brazos, 2007)

12a. NT Wright, Surprised by Hope: Rethinking Heaven, the Resurrection, and the Mission of the Church (HarperOne, 2008)

13. Robert Lupton, Compassion, Justice and the Christian Life (Regal, 2007), p. 86-88
14. Dallas Willard, The Divine Conspiracy (Fount, 1998)
15. Laurence Singlehurst, Sowing Reaping Keeping (Crossway, 1995), p. 18. This is a reference to the Engel Scale, which represents the person with the most negative view of God as being -10, coming to faith as 0, and a mature disciple from +5 upwards. This illustrates the notion of discipleship as a series of events or encounters that make sense only as part of an ongoing process or journey.
16. Eddie Gibbs, Ecclesia National Gathering (Washington, DC, 2009)
17. Wolfgang Simson is author of the influential book Houses That Change the World (Authentic, 2001). "In a world where the Church is being ignored, it is time to bring the Church to the people, and not the people to the Church."
18. This information is from Joel News International 710, December 2, 2009, www.joelnews.org.
19. There are a few exceptions (e.g., Stephen in ch. 7, Philip in ch. 8), but those seem to be exceptions (generally created by sudden persecution or angelic intervention). See Acts 3-4 (Peter and John), Acts 10 (Peter and his companions, v. 23), 13:1-4 (Barnabas and Saul), and almost everything thereafter, other than sudden escape from imminent attacks.
20. For instance, 1 Corinthians 16:5-21, 2 Timothy 4:9-21, or Titus 3:12-15.
21. Abraham's call is to be the father of a nation and to be a blessing to all peoples on earth, marking this as part of the identity of that nation when it emerged out of Egypt. Psalm 72:17, Isaiah 42:6, etc., although clearly prophesying about Jesus, also need to be seen as markers of Israel's self-awareness at the time of their writing.
22. Robert D. Putnam, Bowling Alone: The Collapse and Revival of American Community (Simon & Schuster, 2000), p. 19
23. http://www.norc.org/projects/General+Social+Survey.htm
24. John Piper, When I Don't Desire God (Crossway, 2004), p. 229

25. Christian Smith, Souls in Transition – The Religious and Spiritual Lives of Emerging Adults (Oxford University Press, 2009), p. 152
26. Ed Stetzer, Lost and Found: The Younger Unchurched and the Churches that Reach Them (B&H Books, 2009)
27. Christian Smith, op. cit., p. 152
28. David Kinnaman and Gabe Lyons, unChristian: What a New Generation Really Thinks about Christianity... and Why It Matters (Baker, 2007), p. 74
29. Peter Block, Community: The Structure of Belonging (Berrett-Koehler, 2008), p. xii
30. http://www.cbsnews.com/stories/2006/04/21/60minutes/main1532246.shtml
31. Quoted by Mark Batterson in a blog essay on creating a third place for the lost - http://www.qideas.org/essays/postmodern-wells-creating-a-third-place.aspx
32. J.W.C. Wand, A History of the Early Church (Methuen, 1937), p. 91
33. Rodney Stark, The Rise of Christianity (Harper Collins, 1997)
34. Jonathan Hill, History of Christianity (Zondervan, 2006), p. 41
35. Ibid, p.56
36. James Dunn, Romans 9-16 (Word, 1988), p. 891
37. Michael Green, Evangelism in the Early Church (Hodder & Stoughton, 1970)
38. Adweek online, December 15, 2008
39. Neil Cole, op. cit.
40. Edward T. Hall, The Hidden Dimension (Anchor Books/Doubleday, 1966, 1982)
41. Joseph R. Myers, The Search to Belong (Zondervan, 2003), p. 36.
    Myer's book is an excellent read and a truly important resource in thinking through how we gather and help people to belong in Christian community.
42. Stephen Covey, Principle-Centered Leadership (Free Press, 1992)
43. Lesslie Newbigin, Signs Amid the Rubble: The Purposes of God in Human History (Eerdmans, 2003), p. 103
44. If you want to read up on this, we recommend John Finney, Recovering the Past (Darton, Longman & Todd, 1996)
45. Hugh Halter and Matt Smay, AND: The Scattered and Gathered Church (Zondervan, 2010), p. 124
46. Conversation at the Ecclesia National Gathering, February 2009
47. A.D. Amar, Carsten Hentrich, and Vlatka Hlupic, To Be a Better Leader Give Up Authority (Harvard Business Review, December 2009), http://hbr.org/2009/12/to-be-a-better-leader-give-up-authority/ar/pr
48. Bill Hybels, Axiom (Zondervan, 2008), p. 75
49. Rick Warren, The Purpose Driven Church (Zondervan, 1995)
50. David Putman and Shawn Lovejoy, Most Common Mistakes Church Planters Make, in Rick Warren's Ministry Toolbox, January 14, 2010, http://www.pastors.com/blogs/ministrytoolbox/archive/2010/01/14/most-common-mistakes-church-planters-make.aspx
51. Read Mike Breen and Steve Cockram, Building a Discipling Culture (weare3DM.com, 2010)
52. For more on our understanding of the Fivefold Ministry in Ephesians 4, see Building a Discipling Culture, op. cit.
53. Paul Maconochie is the Senior Leader of St. Thomas' Church Philadelphia, Sheffield, UK (www.stthomaschurch.org.uk)
54. This really helpful centripetal/centrifugal force language is found in Eddie Gibbs and Ryan K. Bolger, Emerging Churches (Baker, 2005), p. 50
55. For those who like this sort of thing, the math is: your Huddle of 8 (1x8=8 MC leaders) + their Huddles of 6 (8x6=48 disciples of MC leaders) + their Huddles of 4 (48x4=192 disciples of disciples), so 192+48+8=248. See, it is a real number!

56. www.weare3DM.com/store/Departments/Clusters-and-Huddles.aspx
57. John Maxwell, Developing the Leader Within You (Thomas Nelson, 1993), p. 58
58. Bill Hybels, Axiom (Zondervan, 2008), p. 150
59. We are going to refer to "your city" throughout this book, as shorthand, but we recognize some of you are in towns, villages, and rural communities. So please read this as applying to your context, which will allow the text to flow and not be cluttered up with a long list of other possibilities (campus, ski resort, commune, desert island...)!
60. Bob Biehl, 30 Days to Confident Leadership (Broadman and Holman, 1998)
61. We recognize that there are a wide variety of types of church government (boards, council, vestry, elders, deacons, congregation meeting, etc.), but to maintain readability, we use the term "board" simply as a catch-all label.
62. Luke 22:25-26
63. For excellent insight on this topic, give your key prayer supporters copies of C. Peter Wagner, Prayer Shield – How to intercede for Pastors, Christian Leaders and Others on the Spiritual Frontline (Regal Books, 1992)
64. http://en.wikipedia.org/wiki/Missional_Communities
65. http://www.weare3DM.com/store/Departments/Clusters-and-Huddles.aspx
66. www.lcgs.net
67. www.lcgs.net/ministries/spiritualgrowth
68. www.stphilipsonline.org/our-community/mission-shaped-communities
69. http://lovecanton.com/villages2
70. http://trinitygracechurch.com/community/missional-communities
71. http://www.generationaxis.com
72. http://www.eikoncommunity.org/page/Eikon-7c-Community-Life.aspx
73. http://normcom.com/housechurches
74. Jon Tyson, Renewing Cities Through Missional Tribes (2009) http://www.qideas.org/essays/renewing-cities-through-missional-tribes.aspx
75. Laurence Singlehurst, Sowing, Reaping, Keeping (Crossway, 1995)
76. Hugh Halter and Matt Smay, The Tangible Kingdom (Jossey-Bass, 2008)
77. Missional Communities seminar for the Baptist General Association of Virginia (January 30, 2010)
78. Mick Woodhead is the Vicar of St. Thomas' Crookes, Sheffield, UK.
79. Mark Stibbe and Andrew Williams, Breakout (Authentic, 2008), p. 52
80. Michael Frost and Alan Hirsch, The Shaping of Things to Come (Hendrickson, 2003), p. 30
81. See the work by Stephen J. Drotter and Ram Charan, Building Leaders at Every Level: A Leadership Pipeline (Ivey Business Journal, 2001)—a downloadable 8-page pdf available for free at http://www.iveybusinessjournal.com/article.asp?intArticle_ID=287. The full book is The Leadership Pipeline: How to Build the Leadership Powered Company (Jossey-Bass, 2000).
82. Mark Stibbe and Andrew Williams, op. cit., p. 88
83. Mike Breen, Growing the Smaller Church (Marshall Pickering, 1992)
84. With thanks to Annamarie Slater for much of this excellent material on working with children
85. Rich Atkinson, Hitting the Target (available from www.forgeyouth.com)

86 Provocative ecclesiological thought: you may well have people who quote James 5:14 to you ("Is any one of you sick? He should call the elders of the church to pray over him"), to insist that they must be prayed with by the elders every time they are sick. This, of course, neglects the over-arching New Testament witness that shows Jesus giving authority to heal the sick to all the disciples, not just the leaders. Nevertheless, this is still a relevant verse for praying for the sick, but there is a strong case to be made for saying that the elders in the NT were the leaders of the individual *oikos*. Thus, to translate into today's terminology, this particular anointing for leaders when they pray for the sick could be said to fall upon the leaders of Missional Communities. An interesting thought!

87. Reggie McNeal, op. cit., e.g., p. 74ff on metrics for prayer, p. 117 for discipleship, p. 160 for mission

88. Clotaire Rapaille, The Culture Code (Broadway Books, 2006)

89. Geoff Surratt, Greg Ligon, and Warren Bird, The Multi-Site Church Revolution (Zondervan, 2006)

90. www.lifechurch.tv

91. According to the annual research by Outreach Magazine, which averaged attendance from February and March 2009, showing Life Church had an average attendance of 26,766. This link also shows how quickly Life Church has grown in the last four years from 2006 when attendance was 16,071. http://churchrelevance.com/100-largest-churches-in-america-for-2009

92. http://internet.lifechurch.tv

93. http://normcom.com/home

94. www.eikoncommunity.org

95. Putnam and Lovejoy, op. cit.

96. http://www.toledoblade.com/apps/pbcs.dll/article?AID=/20100109/NEWS10/100109705

97. http://www.stphilipsonline.org